Quine's Philosophy

Also available from Bloomsbury

Knowledge, Number and Reality, edited by Nils Kürbis,
Bahram Assadian, and Jonathan Nassim
Quine's Normative Epistemology, by Michael Shepanski
The Problem of Plurality of Logics, by Pavel Arazim

Quine's Philosophy

An Introduction

Gary Kemp

BLOOMSBURY ACADEMIC
LONDON · NEW YORK · OXFORD · NEW DELHI · SYDNEY

BLOOMSBURY ACADEMIC
Bloomsbury Publishing Plc
50 Bedford Square, London, WC1B 3DP, UK
1385 Broadway, New York, NY 10018, USA
29 Earlsfort Terrace, Dublin 2, Ireland

BLOOMSBURY, BLOOMSBURY ACADEMIC and the Diana logo
are trademarks of Bloomsbury Publishing Plc

First published in Great Britain 2023

Cover design by Louise Dugdale
Cover photograph by Anton Gorlin

A catalogue record for this book is available from the British Library.

A catalog record for this book is available from the Library of Congress.

ISBN: HB: 978-1-3503-4203-3
         PB: 978-1-3503-4202-6
       ePDF: 978-1-3503-4204-0
      eBook: 978-1-3503-4205-7

Typeset by Integra Software Services Pvt. Ltd.
Printed and bound in Great Britain

To find out more about our authors and books visit www.bloomsbury.com
and sign up for our newsletters.

Contents

Preface

Frege and Russell were analytic philosophy's great pioneers. And it was Wittgenstein who inspired something like devotion, and whose name crops up most outside academic philosophy. But within the hardnosed professional practice of analytic philosophy over the past seventy years, the most thoroughly influential has been Willard Van Orman Quine (1908–2000). He formulated the most incisive criticisms of logical positivism in the 1930s and 1940s, inaugurated many of the signature analytic topics of the 1950s and 1960s, elaborated challenging new paradigms in ontology and epistemology in the 1960s, 1970s, and 1980s, and published some of his most lucid philosophical writing as late as the 1990s. Along the way, he not only contributed to the rise of mathematical logic, but, along with Russell and Carnap, did as much as anyone to give it the central role it has come to play in philosophical analysis. Since the Second World War Quine has shaped the philosophical landscape in which we live.

Nevertheless, much of what is most powerful and deeply interesting in Quine is not widely understood, and many of his specific claims have provoked more antagonism than admiration. Indeed a certain caricature of Quine is easy to draw, and widely subscribed to: the naysayer, who is said to be "skeptical" of this or that philosophical idea, to "reject" this one or "deem unintelligible" that one. An imperious party-pooper. The caricature is unjustified, but to explain why is not simple. Quine was above all a systematic philosopher, and the force of his particular claims cannot always be appreciated without understanding the larger framework or perspective from which they emerge. Analytic philosophy often looks as if it has no such framework or perspective, as if it were really only the piece-meal application of a *method*, not the imposition of any particular doctrines. But of course in philosophy as in life we often make more assumptions than we realize. To the extent that one is unaware of them, or that Quine does not share them, it is no wonder that some of what Quine says—often in his inimitably sure-footed way—will sound merely dogmatic, or will seem as if it ignores what one takes to be the real philosophical question. So the main task of this book, in addition to explaining Quine's ideas about particular topics, is to show how those ideas are interconnected, and to try to articulate the more general philosophical perspective from which they issue.

This book is nevertheless an introduction to Quine, suitable for undergraduates and amateurs as well as people higher up the philosophical food chain. In general I have not tried to *evaluate* Quine's philosophy but to *explain* it, true as it is that this means conveying why he or anyone would subscribe to it. This involves sketching in some of the relevant context, both historical and conceptual. That is to say, much about philosophy, logic, and mathematics and their history is needed for understanding Quine, but I have tried to presuppose as little about them as possible; hence not only Hume and Kant but even Plato and Socrates make their appearance. With certain notable exceptions, I have not gone into any depth into contemporary or near contemporary figures for reactions or comparison, as it would lengthen the book considerably as well as blur the focus to do so. I like to think that readers will come away well-equipped to make those comparisons themselves.

Nor have I assumed significant familiarity with Quine's work, though I hope the reader will investigate further. If for nothing else, no student of philosophy should miss one of the finest, and funniest, prose stylists that twentieth-century philosophy has produced. Quite an achievement for such a dry subject-matter. To begin I would suggest the first two chapters of his late book *From Stimulus to Science* and the essay "Things and Their Place in Theories" from *Theories and Things*. Then the essays in the classic and relatively early *From a Logical Point of View*, especially "On What There Is" and "Two Dogmas of Empiricism"; then the biggie *Word and Object*, and the essays in *Ontological Relativity and Other Essays*; then the book *Pursuit of Truth*. The rest of *Theories and Things*, and the collections *Ways of Paradox* and *Confessions of a Confirmed Extensionalist* can be mined according to the reader's interests. Enthusiasts will want to check out the *Roots of Reference* and *Philosophy of Logic*. For more casual visits, Quine's "intermittently philosophical dictionary" *Quiddities* is a treasure with some surprises; it goes on the coffee or bedside table, not the office or library shelf.

For an earlier incarnation in 2006 I thank again Christopher Belshaw, Hans-Johann Glock, Patricia Kemp, David Lumsden, and Jaroslav Peregrin. I set apart my teacher Peter Hylton for more ample gratitude, who introduced me to Quine in a graduate course at the University of California at Santa Barbara, and whose own work has remained an inspiration and model. (His much more detailed book *Quine* came out in 2007, a year after the earlier incarnation of this one.)

For conversation or written comments for this incarnation, I thank Rosa Bell, John Collins, Gary Ebbs, again Peter Hylton, Ayala King, Nathan Kirkwood, Andrew Lugg, Gabriele Mras, Douglas Quine, Sander Verhaegh, Rogério Severo, and Robert Sinclair. For invitations to speak I single out Piotr Stalmaszczyk for the chance as a plenary speaker at Philang 2013, Lodz, Poland, and Jaroslav Peregrin and Vladimir Svoboda, for the chance in 2019, Institute of Philosophy, Czech Academy of Sciences, Prague. For teaching a graduate course on Quine, I thank Peregrin and Koreň Ladislav as well as the students for the chance at Hradec Králové University, Spring 2018. Finally I thank the excellent reader for Bloomsbury, whose efforts saved me from some egg on face.

Gary Kemp September 2022

Glasgow

Abbreviations

Quine's writings are noted in the text according to the following scheme of abbreviation.

CCE   *Confessions of a Confirmed Extensionalist*

FLPV   *From a Logical Point of View*

FSS   *From Stimulus to Science*

ML   *Mathematical Logic*

NEN   "Notes on Existence and Necessity"

OR   *Ontological Relativity and Other Essays*

PL   *Philosophy of Logic*

PT   *Pursuit of Truth*

Q   *Quiddities*

QQ   "Quine on Quine" (sentences by Quine, arranged by Burton Dreben)

RR   *The Roots of Reference*

SLP   *Selected Logic Papers*

TT   *Theories and Things*

WB   *The Web of Belief*

WO   *Word and Object*

WP   *The Ways of Paradox*

WPO?   "Whither Physical Objects?"

Philosophy as Quine Found It

Quine as Philosopher and Anti-philosopher

Epistemology is the theory of knowledge: What is knowledge? What is involved in getting it? *Metaphysics* is the theory of what reality is: What is real? What ultimately, fundamentally, or necessarily exists? These interpenetrate. What features does reality possess "in itself," and what are features only of how we perceive, think, or talk about it?

Along with Ethics, such have been the broadest and most persistent concerns of philosophers in the so-called Western tradition at least since the time of Plato. Although sometimes reformulated in significant ways, they have certainly been the central concerns of the subject of this book, Willard Van Orman Quine. However, it is possible to read Quine without it quite registering that this is so. Quine's answers to the Big Questions of Metaphysics and Epistemology, his ways of arguing for those answers, and his ideas on the proper role and character of philosophy differ markedly not only from those of his predecessors, but from those of many of his contemporaries and immediate successors. So one may come away from a session with one of Quine's articles or books feeling that Quine has not quite addressed the philosophical question, the one that had driven philosophical inquiry into the matter in the first place.

The main reason for this is that, despite his interest in the standard Big Questions, Quine does in many ways find fault with the philosophical tradition. In asking its questions and advancing its arguments and answers, philosophy tends to employ a certain distinctive vocabulary, and often, implicitly or explicitly, makes certain characteristic philosophical assumptions or presuppositions. In ways that partially though by no means completely align him with another big name in the philosophy of the twentieth century, Ludwig Wittgenstein, and with a certain inter-war movement known as logical positivism or logical empiricism, Quine often disputes the clarity or theoretical suitability of the vocabulary, the validity, or even intelligibility of the presuppositions. He wants a fresh start. His aim is not to pose the Big Questions as traditionally understood and give them straight answers in the style of traditional philosophy, but to transpose them into a different key, one in which the questions acquire sufficient clarity and tractability to admit of comparatively much more definite and defensible answers. And some questions, as we will see, are simply dismissed.

This "new key" is what Quine calls "Naturalism" (though arguably the point of view was only assumed *after* the composition of the widely read essays in *From a Logical Point of View* of 1951, and he himself used the name only in the 1960s). And it is a view more exacting than those of some others working under that name. A good start in appreciating what Quine means can be made by considering how Quine re-conceives the sorts of Big Questions with which we began. Philosophers have given the metaphysical question "What exists?" some pretty exotic answers in the history of philosophy: True existence is accorded not to tables and trees, but to Platonic Forms, Leibnizean Monads, Berkeleyan Spirits, The All-Encompassing One. Such answers often have it that the *kind* of thing whose existence is announced by philosophers is something whose existence nonphilosophers would never have suspected. By contrast, Quine's naturalism interprets a metaphysical question such as "What exists?" as a *scientific* question, one that is distinctive only because it is uniquely general (as compared with the question, say, "What animals exist on Svalbard?") and calling for a disciplined answer. Meanwhile the epistemological question "What is knowledge?" becomes by and large a question of *psychology*, where this is understood as a branch of biology: What is it about the neurology and behavior of an animal that constitutes its having knowledge?

In these ways, Quine seeks to convert philosophy into something continuous with, and indeed included in natural science. Not only the answers but the questions are to be constrained by scientific standards, not by traditional philosophical ones. Sound philosophical reflection shows that "[w]e must abandon the goal of first philosophy" (*TT* 67), says Quine. Similar pronouncements have been issued before—for example by David Hume—but perhaps never so rigorously as by Quine. A principal task of this book will be try to understand this naturalistic conception of philosophy, and in particular, to understand the ways in which Quine's naturalistic answers may be said to constitute answers to specific philosophical questions. But perhaps the larger and more philosophically urgent task is that of trying to understand *why* Quine holds that his naturalistic transposition of philosophy and rejection of the tradition is justified. That sort of question has to be answered in general terms, but also in specific terms. For example: Why does Quine think there is no need to solve the famous Humean problem of *induction* (how do we know that unobserved phenomena can be predicted on the basis of observed phenomena)? Why does Quine think there is no such need as that of explaining why mathematical truths are necessary truths? What justifies Quine's emphasis on language, when so few philosophical questions are, on the face of it, about language? On these and many other questions, the trick is to see why Quine is not merely ignoring long-standing philosophical quandaries, throwing the baby out with the bathwater.

Quine, as indicated above, did not begin his philosophical career with a mission to develop and defend a comprehensive philosophical doctrine of naturalism (unlike Hume, who apparently did). He came to do so in steps, even if some of them were giant steps in the seminal years of his career, between the end of the Second World War and the 1960 publication of his watershed book, *Word and Object*. And in order to see how Quine came to see a doctrine of naturalism as the right way to approach philosophical problems, and as the correct philosophy in itself, we need to have some understanding of the state of philosophy as it presented itself to Quine at the outset of his career in the 1930s. As we will see, the central figure in this—the "towering figure" as Quine put it—was the German Rudolf Carnap (1891–1970). There were other significant influences on Quine—Bertrand Russell, C. I. Lewis—but unquestionably Carnap is the most profitable to consider in some detail for understanding the mature Quine (see the Further Reading and Historical Notes at the end the chapter). As Carnap's philosophy, at least as Quine understood it, has so many evident and important affinities with that of Hume, we begin with a brief outline of the agenda set by that incomparable Scotsman (we might have discussed Kant as well, but we shall make do only with scattered remarks concerning him). This historical stage setting will do something to show how the problems that Quine explicitly set himself engage with philosophy's long-standing concerns.

Empiricism and the Claims of Science

In seventeenth- and eighteenth-century philosophy it was customary to draw a distinction between knowledge that is *a posteriori*—knowledge that is justified by perceptual experience or observation, and knowledge that is *a priori*—knowledge that is justified not by experience but by means of something else, characterized perhaps as pure thought or reason.

For many important philosophers—Plato, Descartes, and Leibniz are likely examples—metaphysical knowledge is largely *a priori*. The most general and abstract features of reality are knowable by pure thought. The model often held up for such knowledge was geometry, especially as understood since the formative works of the ancient Greek mathematician Euclid. In this tradition, the subject-matter of geometry was held to be actual space, not some mathematical idealization or model of it.[1] All the same, when we know, for example, that the sum of the angles of a triangle is equal to that of two right angles, we do not know it because we have measured a certain number of triangles, and then extrapolated to all triangles. It is not like the knowledge, say, that all polar bears are white. We know it because we have deduced it by valid reasoning from certain "axioms" or "postulates," propositions of geometry that are accepted as self-evident, that is, by something like direct insight into the nature of space— such as the proposition "Between every two points there is a third."

Accordingly, many philosophers accepted that pure reasoning could extend to many other metaphysically interesting topics, such as time, causation, free will, God, the natures of mind and matter and the relations between them, the possibility of eternal life, and even the origins of the world. Hume for one denied all of this. On the basis of a theory of the actual contents of human experience and thought—which he took to be more-or-less self-evident—he argued that there is no such thing as *a priori* knowledge that is genuinely about the world. The human mind is limited to what Hume called "impressions"—roughly, sensory input as we subjectively experience it—their memory traces retained over time as "ideas," and further ideas constructed from these by dissection and recombination. Such in its simplest terms is the Epistemology we now know as Empiricism, in its "classical" form. On this basis, Hume thought we can account for what we would now call Natural Science, but *not* Metaphysics. For, whereas the former begins with observation and constructs theories logically on that basis, the latter speculates about the necessarily unperceivable, *viz.*, such things as Substance, the Cartesian self, a Transcendent God. If such things are necessarily unperceivable, then how can the mind have formed Ideas of them on the basis of Impressions? So much the better, thought Hume, for Natural Science, and so much the worse for Metaphysics. As he famously wrote in his *Enquiry Concerning Human Understanding* (1748):

> When we run over libraries persuaded of these [empirical] principles what havoc must we make? If we take in our hand any volume of divinity or school metaphysics for instance let us ask, Does it contain any abstract reasoning concerning quantity or number? No. Does it contain any experimental reasoning

concerning matter of fact and existence? No. Commit it to the flames for it can contain nothing but sophistry and illusion.

According to Hume, then, there is no non-experiential source of knowledge save mathematics. Furthermore, mathematics concerns only what Hume called "Relations of Ideas" (roughly what would later be called "analytic" truths); it does *not* make any essential reference to anything beyond the realm of ideas, that is, ingredients of the mind. Thus even geometry, according to Hume, does not essentially concern space in the sense in which Descartes and others understood it, as something known *a priori* yet existing "out there," independent of the mind. (Famously, Hume remained steadfast on this point, arguing that since there is a limit to how small a thing can be perceived, it is not literally true that space is infinitely divisible, contrary to the Euclidean proposition that between every two points there is a third.)

Hume published his great early work, the *Treatise of Human Nature* (1739), during a period of general assimilation of some of the great scientific advances of that intellectual revolution known as the Enlightenment (Sir Isaac Newton's *Principia* had been published in 1687). Hume thought that, on the whole, his philosophical scheme successfully distinguishes natural science from speculative metaphysics, vindicating the one as corroborated by experience, and dismissing the other as ill-founded or even meaningless (commit it to the flames!). Since Hume's claims were based largely on his account of the contents of the mind, which was itself based on observation—introspection—Hume's philosophy was thoroughly empiricist in the sense of being thoroughly empirical: it strove to "extend the experimental method to the science of man."

Logic in Logical Empiricism

Carnap, along with Moritz Schlick and others, was at the center of the so-called Vienna Circle at around 1930, developing a general philosophical trend called Logical Empiricism (or Logical Positivism, or simply Scientific Philosophy). The new trend was inspired by developments in logic and mathematics on the one hand, and in empirical science on the other. It was the time, to take the most sensational example, of Einstein and his revolutionary new theories. Like Hume, Carnap sought to vindicate natural science, and to dismiss the claims of metaphysics as nonsense. But Hume's attack on metaphysics was more persuasive than his attempt to vindicate natural science. Let us briefly survey two of what seemed to be the principal shortcomings. As will become evident, a main shift that Carnap brought about—though not only Carnap—was a shift from Hume's emphasis on the mental realm to a very explicit emphasis on *language*.

The most famous is Hume's problem of induction. At the center of natural science are such empirical laws as Newton's Second Law of Motion (F = ma): the force acting upon a body (in a certain direction) is equal to the product of its mass and the alteration of its motion—its degree of *acceleration* (in a certain direction). This law is supposed to apply without exception, at all times, at all places; such is the point of calling it a *law*. But necessarily this purported law has been verified only with respect to a very limited range of cases. The problem is that Hume had demonstrated—with an argument that to this day remains to be decisively refuted—that there is no valid inference from the observed to the unobserved. For consider the principle upon which such reasoning would depend, namely that if all entities or events of an observed sample of a certain kind have a certain property—where the sample is of sufficient size, randomly selected and so on—then *all* entities or events of that kind have that property. Call this the "Inductive Principle." Philosophers had long assumed, or attempted to prove, that something like such a principle is known *a priori* (sometimes in the form of the "Principle of Sufficient Reason" or the "Uniformity Principle"). But the principle, if true, is surely not a *necessary truth*; we can coherently imagine a world in which it does not hold—for example, we can coherently imagine the laws of nature changing overnight, or as differing at faraway places. The Inductive Principle, then, must be a contingent truth. That is to say, it must itself be an empirical law that describes our world. But the establishment of empirical laws, as we have just seen, depends on assuming the Inductive Principle. To attempt to justify the Inductive Principle, then, is to argue in a circle.

Hume's place in the pantheon of the philosophers is secured by his discovery of this problem alone. But his response to it has often been thought inadequate. Hume's way out was to suppose that the human mind is naturally constituted so as to have the sorts of expectations that the Inductive Principle would justify, if it could be justified. This explains why human beings do reason about the unobserved as they do, and explains why that reasoning leads to true conclusions in a world that is in fact governed by laws of nature. But it does not seem to *justify* that reasoning, or do anything to show how we could know that the world *is* governed by laws of nature. It seems to stop short of showing that we have knowledge of empirical laws.

The second main shortcoming—it is decidedly less well-appreciated—lay in Hume's account of mathematics. Set aside Hume's account of geometry. The rest of mathematics, as Hume recognized, is inextricable from natural science: the empirical laws discovered by science are "quantitative" laws, dealing with relations of quantities such as mass, volume, and force; pure mathematics is essential to the content of such laws, and is what make it possible to calculate with them. Hume had described mathematics only rather vaguely as consisting in "relations of ideas." What exactly does this mean, and how do we know that it really would provide a basis for mathematics? The whole idea seems doubtful. Mathematics is the most precise and most certain of sciences. How could it be based upon something so obscure and fleeting as *ideas*, where these are understood as the contents of human consciousness? What would the demonstration of such a basis look like? How could it begin? How do we know that my mathematics is the same as yours? Hume had done little or nothing to address such questions, and it would seem unprofitable to try.

In short, Hume seemed not to have accounted for two sets of principles that had traditionally been thought to be *a priori*, but which are essential to science. Many Scientific Philosophers took these failures to be owed in large measure to the unavailability, in Hume's day, of a sufficiently powerful logic, conceived not only as rules of reasoning but as the primary tool for the analysis of language. For Carnap, in particular, the lack of clarity and gaps in justification in Hume's account should be rectified by formulating human knowledge in terms of precise artificial languages, internal to which would be the rules of reasoning necessary for both mathematics and inductive inference. The features of knowledge traditionally reckoned *a priori* would be explained by the logical features of language. Hence Carnap's favored designation for the new regime: Logical Empiricism.

The new more powerful logic that underlies this idea was engineered primarily by Gottlob Frege and by Bertrand Russell. Frege tried, informally in 1884 with *Die Grundlagen der Arithmetik* (the *Foundations of Arithmetic*) and formally in 1893 with *Grundgesetze der Arithmetik* (the *Basic Laws of Arithmetic*) to demonstrate the thesis of Logicism, that mathematics—mathematics exclusive of geometry—was really just logic, that Mathematics despite perhaps appearances has no non-logical content. True, this required a re-conception of the scope of logic, but there is little dispute that most of the gained ground was indeed logic. But unfortunately not all. The sore point was Axiom V of the *Basic Laws*—which says that predicates are true of the same things just in case their corresponding sets (their extensions) are identical. Not only was this demonstrably not a truth of logic, or even simply false; it is inconsistent. Such was Russell's horrible discovery. Consider the set of all and only those sets which are not members of themselves. If this set is a member of itself, then it is not; if it is not, then it is.

One can derive such a contradiction in Frege's system. Frege tried to institute a quick fix but eventually gave up on the thesis of logicism, but Russell, along with his colleague Alfred North Whitehead, persevered, coming up with the great *Principia Mathematica* of 1910 (and 1912, 1914). Although much more complicated than Frege's attempt, the system of *Principia* seemed consistent and mathematics seemed derivable within it. Whether or not it is properly speaking logic is a further question; as we'll see much later Quine changed his mind on this, going from yes to no.

For our purposes, two features stand out.

First—and this is more Frege than Russell—the existing Logic, and indeed Mathematics itself, suffered from not being maximally clear and rigorous. For some problems, especially the problems which Frege set for himself, such clarity is vital. Reasoning, or proofs, must be absolutely "gap-free," such that it is demonstrably impossible for any premises, any "content," should be smuggled in without explicitly being recognized as such (only then is it possible for a stupid machine—a computer—reliably to check a proof for its validity, a possibility of which Turing would make so much). Reasonably convinced that his system— his "Concept-Script" or *Begriffsschrift*—achieved this, Frege was in a position to claim, even if falsely, that he had demonstrated his thesis of Logicism. For the premises in the relevant proofs were to be the axioms of logic themselves, axioms which are presupposed in all discourse, whatever its subject-matter: "The task we assign to logic," declares Frege, is that of "saying what holds with the utmost generality for all thinking, whatever its subject matter" (Frege 1979, p. 128). The inconsistency described above manifestly does not affect the point about rigor; indeed the system minus Axiom V is consistent and the first-order part is complete. For this Frege is rightly regarded as the inventor or discoverer of modern predicate logic or quantification theory.

The second point concerns the power of Logic. Logic until 1879—the publication year of Frege's seminal *Begriffsschrift*, the first presentation of his Logic—was dominated by Aristotle's logic of the syllogism, which dealt with "categorical" inferences such as "Some A are B, all B are C; therefore some A are C." In modern terms, this logic deals only with one-place predicates ("categories") such as "_ is wise," not many-place predicates, i.e., "relational" predicates such as "_ loves _." Frege and Russell had developed logical systems that demonstrate the validity of such inferences, a simple example of which is the relation "_ ate _," as in "Everyone ate a mushroom; all mushrooms are funguses, therefore everyone ate a fungus." These systems rapidly superseded the far weaker logic of the syllogism.

Crucially, full predicate logic made it possible to give purely logical proofs of propositions about *order*—propositions describing, for example, the relational structure of the collection of natural numbers 0, 1, 2 ... and so on. This was important for the aforementioned thesis that mathematics is reducible to logic. Frege and Russell had seemed to have shown, first, that mathematical reasoning is a matter of pure logic, and does not, as Kant and many philosophers after him had held, depend on an understanding of order as given by our understanding of time or space, and hence as depending in some way on the structure of perceptual experience; second—and strictly speaking this is more Russell than Frege, because of the inconsistency described above—that the vocabulary of mathematics is definable in terms of the vocabulary of logic (details in Chapter 6).

What neither Frege nor Russell had done, however, was to provide a satisfactory explanation of our knowledge of logic itself. It may seem obvious that knowledge of logic is not based upon experience and is therefore *a priori*, but that does not explain what knowledge of logic *is*; it does not tell us what positively constitutes such knowledge. Frege said that logic is "what holds with the utmost generality for all thinking," but that is merely a negative characterization. Why does logic have such status? It was on this question that Carnap was to make his distinctive mark.

Linguistic Frameworks, Analyticity, and Tolerance

One of Carnap's main moves was a shift toward an explicit attention to language. For the early Carnap, logic is to be explained in terms of the "syntax" of a language, envisaged as an entirely formal matter, that is, having to do only with typographical shapes and their combinations. The syntax of a language comprises the vocabulary of the language—essentially a list of simple expressions—plus two sorts of rules. The first, the "formation rules" specify which combinations of simple expressions constitute the sentences of the language. The second, the "transformation rules" are of two kinds. One kind allows some sentences to be written down outright—a rule, for example, might allow us to write down "p or not-p" with any sentence substituted for "p" (such sentences would correspond to what traditionally are called axioms). The other kind determines the relation of logical consequence for the language. They might tell us, for example, that if we have "if p then q" and "p", then we may write down "q". The sentences that can be written down outright along with their logical consequences are the "analytic truths" of the language. Different languages may have different rules, hence different analytic truths. But the rules themselves do not admit of being right or wrong, true or false, any more than the rules of chess are true or false; indeed, since we are free to invent new languages as we please, they are *conventions*. Analytic truth is a matter of convention, the conventions of language. The conventions determine the meanings of the logical connectives "and," "not," "every," and so on, in the sense that they always tell us what statements involving those connectives can be logically deduced from other statements, and what statements can be deduced from them, as well as that certain truths—for example any of the form "a is F or a is not-F" are analytic. Crucially—and this was left hanging in the previous section—if the language is one that deals with empirical matters, then normally it will contain a logic of inductive reasoning: Hume's problem of induction simply cannot arise in such a language, since the validity of the inductive principle will simply be a convention of using the language.

Carnap attempted an early but detailed implementation of the idea of Logical Empiricism in an early work, *The Logical Structure of the World* ([1928]; henceforth the *Aufbau*). The aim was to show that empirical knowledge could be represented in a language whose basic terms refer only to subjective experience, understood as momentary perceptual states of the subject: by virtue of definitions and related devices, all statements in such a language "about" material objects reduce to statements referring only to those momentary perceptual states. Such is the idea of "radical reductionism," Logical Empiricism at its purest (and perhaps most naïve).

This aspect of Carnap's program might sound a bit old hat, as if Carnap were merely repeating Hume's ideas (or more accurately Berkeley's), made explicitly linguistic and dressed up in flashy technical devices from modern logic. In later chapters we will see more of what these technical devices are, and why they are philosophically so important. All that need be stressed at this point is (1) the profound difference made by the shift from Hume's emphasis on experience to Carnap's precise re-conception of the problems in terms of language; (2) the sheer complexity and ingenuity of Carnap's constructions, many of which— though certainly not all—he actually carried through in exact and rigorous detail. Setting his lack of the resources of modern logic aside, Hume and Berkeley too had thought that talk of enduring bodies was really only a kind of convenience, that all we really talk about are the impressions that we take, in some way, to be "of" them. But the sort of reduction that they envisaged turned out to be *far* more complex than Hume or Berkeley is likely to have suspected or, in view of the relatively benighted state of logic in their day, can even have conceived. Even Russell—who did command the requisite logical devices, and whose early attempts in this direction inspired Carnap—managed comparatively little actual implementation of such a program. A likely comparison might be that of the relation of Democritus, the ancient Greek who boldly asserted that matter is made of atoms, whatever they are, to twentieth-century physics, which gave us an enormously complex and rigorous theory of what atoms are, and of how they combine to form the various compounds that we identify as matter.

Such was the signature application of Carnap's general linguistic strategy in philosophy. Now for two more general features of it, both of which were essential to Carnap's philosophical vision.

(1) The first is Carnap's celebrated "Principle of Tolerance." The foregoing sketch of the *Aufbau* might suggest that Carnap believed that our knowledge really does not concern anything but sense-experiences, or even in the Berkeleyan manner that there are really no such things as material objects "out there," independent of our experience. Carnap might have held such a view when writing the *Aufbau* (in 1928), but he swiftly came to a more sophisticated view, as for example in *The Logical Syntax of Language* (in German, 1934). From this more sophisticated and slightly later point of view, the *Aufbau* language is just one language. A language embodies a set of conventions, and one is always free to adopt a different set of conventions, hence a different language. Thus Carnap writes:

> In logic, there are no morals. Everyone is at liberty to build up his own logic, i.e., his own form of language, as he wishes. All that is required of him is that, if he wishes to discuss it, he must state his methods clearly, and give syntactical rules instead of philosophical arguments.
>
> (*The Logical Syntax of Language*, §17)

The *Aufbau* language is valuable for exploring a certain set of epistemological questions; but other languages—in particular, ones that make direct reference to physical objects—might well be more valuable for other purposes. In fact, when it comes to choice of language, *there is no right or wrong*. For being reasonable, of course, is at least partly a matter of being logical. But logic—deductive or inductive—is for Carnap a matter of the language one is using, its rules. Thus there is no standard for what is reasonable that is not provided by the language one is using: one cannot be criticized for using a given language without presupposing standards that are foreign to it. The attitude toward a person's choice of language should be that of tolerance. One may find that this language rather than that is more useful or desirable for certain purposes, but this is a practical matter, not a theoretical matter.

(2) The second general feature is closely related to the first. It was implicit in Carnap's earlier work, but only reached full explicitness in his famous 1950 paper "Empiricism, Semantics and Ontology." Standard ontological questions include "Do numbers exist?," "Do material objects exist?," and such like (Carnap 1956). Take the question of numbers. In a language that includes the truths of elementary arithmetic as analytic truths, it is analytic that there is a number between 5 and 7. It thus follows trivially that *there is a number*, i.e., that at least one number exists. But of course, the philosopher who asks "Do numbers exist?" will not be satisfied with the observation that the existence of numbers is a convention of certain languages; the intention was to ask a difficult metaphysical question, calling for profound philosophical inquiry. According to Carnap, however, the philosopher is confused. The question *Do ... exist?* can be asked as either an "internal" question or an "external" question. As an internal question, such a question will be decided according to rules internal to the language—either as a matter of analytic truth as in our example, or as a matter calling for empirical confirmation. As an external question, the question is one about choice of language: shall we use a language that includes such terms (e.g. for numbers), or not? As we have just seen, such a question is not a theoretical one at all, but a practical one, one that depends on our interests in choosing a language. Similarly for such questions as whether physical objects are real, or whether only sense-experiences are real. It is characteristic of philosophical existence questions that they are recognized as not being internal and hence not standard scientific questions, without its being recognized that if they are not, then they are not theoretical questions at all. All theoretically significant questions, for Carnap, are internal questions, to be decided according to the standard scientific procedures embodied in the language used.

The internal-external distinction was Carnap's mature development of his earlier characterization of metaphysical questions generally as "pseudo-questions." More generally still, it is fair to say that for Carnap, philosophy as traditionally practiced was a kind of jungle of linguistic confusions. The correct procedure in philosophy consists of the development and analysis of formal languages, that is, languages with a precisely specified syntax. Under that regimen, traditional philosophical problems would simply dissolve—they would be shown to be external questions, or perhaps incapable of formulation in any well-behaved language (some purported philosophical propositions, Carnap argued for example against Heidegger, are nonsense because they could not even be stated in such a language). This anti-metaphysical point of view, perhaps together with his interest in radical reductionism, is what marks Carnap out as a logical positivist—even if Carnap's actual philosophy is much more sophisticated than that popular phrase tends to suggest. In general, the position may be summed up by saying that for Carnap, traditional philosophical disputes are merely *verbal*: what look like profound philosophical disagreements are mere differences in the meanings attached to words, which are in the final analysis nothing but different conventions concerning the use of words.

The concepts of *convention* and *analyticity*—as well as the general idea of tolerance—bear heavy burdens in Carnap's grand vision. Indeed the role they play in Carnap's vision of knowledge is a "constitutive" one in something like the way that *a priori* structures—the categories and forms of sensibility—are so in Kant's. Just as for Kant, those structures are what make experience possible in the first place, so for Carnap, there is no cognitive significance except in relation to and conditioned by the rules of the language one is using. Thus when Quine, as we are about to see, argues that convention and analyticity cannot play the roles that Carnap marks out for them, he is not only arguing, as he explicitly claims, that there are no firm boundaries between the *a priori* and the empirical, or the theoretical and the practical, or the philosophical and the scientific; he is questioning the very idea that there is a peculiarly philosophical task of explaining what it is that makes knowledge possible in the first place. To re-quote Quine, there is no "First Philosophy," in the sense of Descartes, a standpoint that is categorically prior to human knowledge as a whole. Philosophy takes place in *medias res*, that is, in the middle of things (see QQ).

Further Reading and Historical Notes

The influence of C. I. Lewis and Russell was at its strongest on Quine's early development, when he was a graduate student at Harvard. Russell is of course relevant for Quine's understanding of logic: Quine's PhD thesis was *The Logic of Sequences: A Generalization of Principia mathematica*. For the influence of C. I. Lewis (e.g. Lewis 1929), see Ben-Menahem 2006, Verheagh 2018, and especially Sinclair 2022. It would help to have some familiarity with Hume's *Treatise of Human Nature* (1739) or his *An Enquiry Concerning Human Understanding* (1748). For Quine's own very interesting take on Hume, see his lecture notes, CCE 36–136. Pick and choose from Ayer's collection *Logical Positivism* 1959 to gain a feel for Logical Empiricism/Positivism. For more substantial fare on Carnap, see his *Aufbau* (1928), *The Logical Syntax of Language* (1934), and *Meaning and Necessity* (1956), which contains the important 1950 essay "Empiricism, Semantics and Ontology." I have tried to present Carnap as Quine understood him, making no attempt to present other interpretations and skirting over questions of his development. There is substantial scholarship on Carnap—especially on his relation to Kant—by Michael Friedman 1999, Alan Richardson 1998, J. Alberto Coffa 1991, Andre Carus 2007, and Thomas Uebel 2007. The importance of tolerance in Carnap's philosophy has been penetratingly explored by Hylton 2023.

Convention, Analyticity, and Holism

Quine completed his Harvard PhD dissertation on Whitehead and Russell's *Principia Mathematica* in 1932, and, with the financial support of Harvard, visited Europe right after. The high point of these travels, at least from our point of view, was his visit to Prague, where Carnap was situated. Before arriving in Prague, in Vienna, he read Carnap's *Aufbau* of 1928; and in Prague, as Carnap was just then completing it, his *Der logische Aufbau der Welt* (*The Logical Syntax of Language*), in which the roles in his philosophy of syntax and convention were developed explicitly and precisely as outlined in the last chapter.[1] Quine was on the one hand excited by Carnap's scientific philosophy, and with it his strategy of explaining the *a priori* in terms of language. However, he was evidently uneasy with Carnap's appeal to the notion of convention, publishing, at age twenty-six, a penetrating critical discussion of the matter in his 1935 paper "Truth by Convention" (*WP* 77–106). The criticisms of convention would transmogrify in the following fifteen years into a fully general criticism of the idea of analytic truth, which he wrote up in his famous 1950 paper "Two Dogmas of Empiricism" (*FLPV* 20–46). Quine also found structural problems in the *Aufbau* reductionist program. These conclusions, for Quine, all pointed the same way, namely toward a thesis of epistemological "holism": this not only denied that human knowledge is reductionist in character, but erased the supposed epistemological boundary between the *a priori* and the empirical. He was by no means a mere observer. Throughout this period, Quine was at the same time a logician and set-theorist of the first rank—publishing several works including the important "New Foundations for Mathematical Logic" in 1937 (in *FLPV* 80–101), putting money where his mouth is.

Our primary task in this chapter is to understand these attacks on convention and analyticity, and to understand the holistic conception of knowledge with which Quine replaces reductionism and the *a priori/empirical* distinction. A secondary task is to see holism as a step toward Quine's subsequent naturalism, which will, perhaps ironically, set the stage for the scaling back, in his later philosophy, of not only holism but of the attack on analyticity.

"Truth by Convention": Preliminaries

The aim of Quine's "Truth by Convention" is to show that no such thing really makes sense, at least not in a way that would make good on the idea that knowledge of mathematical and logical truth can rigorously be explained in terms of the adoption of conventions. (And we should take care to note that convention was thought by many other philosophers besides Carnap—Schlick, Reichenbach, and philosophically inclined mathematicians such as Poincaré—to explain the *a priori* as well as the adoption of general principles of physics.[2]) Because the notion of convention is so closely allied to that of *definition*—a definition seems to record a convention or stipulation about how to use a word—we need first to say a bit more about the notion of definition. We also need to say a bit more about what is meant here by "logical truth."

A definition strictly so-called, as understood by mathematicians and philosophers, is the introduction of a shorthand or abbreviation for some more complicated expression or form of expression that recurs often enough, or is otherwise sufficiently of interest, that it is useful, or even psychologically indispensable, to introduce a simpler expression to stand in its place. That such an expedient is really only a practical one is standardly understood to require the satisfaction of two conditions. First, the definition must be "eliminative," i.e., the defined term must always be eliminable from statements of the relevant language without loss of content: it must always be possible, by applying the definition, to transform a statement containing the defined expression into a statement not containing it, without changing the statement's truth-value. Second, the definition must not be "creative," in the sense of adding to the theory's essential strength: Adding the definition to a theory must not make it possible to prove any new statements except ones containing the defined term—where these are provably equivalent to statements not containing it which, in turn, were already provable in the theory before the definition was added (sometimes called the requirement of "conservativeness").

Definitions come in two styles, "Explicit" definitions and "Contextual" definitions.[3] Explicit definitions are familiar from ordinary language. For example the definition of "mare" as "female horse" may be written like this:

Df.: x is a mare iff x is a female and x is a horse.

(As in standard practice, I will sometimes use "iff" for "if and only if"). The key is that explicit definitions introduce, for some part of speech that is smaller than a sentence, an expression that is equivalent to it (so the two sides are inter-substitutable without changing the truth or falsity of any sentence.)

Contextual definitions do not do this. They provide a recipe for converting whole sentences containing the defined expression into sentences not containing it, *without* supplying an expression that is equivalent to it. As it is a case that will figure prominently in other sections of this book, let us look in detail at the example of Russell's definition of "definite descriptions."

Definite descriptions are expressions of the form "the F," such as "the capital of France" or "the man wearing yellow slacks." They are much like proper names such as "Paris," in that we can attach predicates to them such as "_ is south of London" to produce significant sentences. In some sense the role of both a proper name and a definite description is to stand for an object, in such a way that such a sentence is true if and only if the predicate is true of the object. There are important differences, but this much justifies the usual practice of speaking of proper names and definite descriptions alike as "singular terms." Definite descriptions are formed from predicates, possibly complex, such as "__ is a capital of France" or "__ is a man wearing yellow slacks." We shall henceforth, as is the custom, use variables such as "x" rather than blanks, writing "x is a capital of France" and "x is a man wearing yellow slacks." And even more artificially, we can represent the operation of forming a definite description from a predicate as that of affixing "the x such that" to such a predicate, yielding "the x such that x is a man wearing yellow slacks."

If we now represent two arbitrary predicates as "F" and "G"—i.e. "x is a capital of France," "x is fat," "x is fat but will not like the pancakes", etc.—it is clear that any statement containing the definite description "The F" can be represented as having the form "The F is G." We can thus give Russell's definition as follows.

Df: The F is G iff (1) there exists an x such that x is F; (2) x is G; (3) for every y, if y is F, then y = x.

In plainer words, for the truth of "The F is G," it is necessary and sufficient that there is something that is uniquely F, and which is G (if there is more than one F, it is not strictly true to say "*The* F is G").

The definition is really a definition of the operator "The," or rather "The x such that ..." (it can easily be extended to cover cases like "Russell's mother"). But the definition does *not* provide an expression that is equivalent to "The," or "The x such that ...." It only tells us how to convert a sentence containing the description operator into an equivalent one not containing it. This is what is meant by speaking of a "contextual definition." Such a definition does, however, satisfy the requirements of being eliminative and non-creative, as explained above. The precise value of this definition in particular will emerge later; the point now is just to see how the requirements of eliminativeness and non-creativeness can be realized.

Early in his career, Quine accepted that Russell had succeeded in showing that all truths of pure mathematics are truths of logic. We can now see exactly what that means. It means that every truth of pure mathematics is an abbreviation of some truth of pure logic, in the sense that by applying definitions, explicit or contextual ones, each truth of pure mathematics can be converted into an explicit truth of logic. When written out basic logical notation, the truths of logic with which truths of mathematics are thus identified, are typically very complex; thus it is no wonder that a great deal of difficult logical analysis was required before this could be seriously contemplated, let alone accepted (notoriously, and comically, a proof of "1+1=2" appears not in Volume I but at Volume II p. 86 of *Principia Mathematica*).

And what exactly are the truths of logic? For Quine, they include first of all simply those truths that contain only logical vocabulary. In English, the question of its exact logical vocabulary is perhaps rather a hazy one, but included are such expressions as "every," "there is," "if-then," "or," "not" (*PL* 58–9), and, crucially for the idea that mathematics is logic, "class" (or "set") and the relational predicate "is a member of," in the sense relevant to classes (the early Quine accepted this crucial point; Quine would later change his mind, as we will see). Also included are devices of "cross-reference" such as the pronoun "it," or the variables "x," "y," and so on, to work in concert with devices of quantification such as "every" and "any." This yields such truths as "For any classes x and y, there is a class z such that for all w, w is a member of z if and only if w is a member of x or w is a member of y"—that is, a sentence asserting the existence of the union of any two classes.

However, truths restricted to this abstract vocabulary are not the only logical truths. A truth such as "For every x, if x is a snake then x is a snake" is also a logical truth, despite the presence of the non-logical word "snake." What makes it a truth of logic rather than a truth of zoology is that the word "snake" occurs *inessentially*: we can replace the predicate "x is a snake" at all occurrences with any other predicate whatsoever, and the result remains true. This is not so of "For every x, if x is a snake then x is a reptile," which goes false if we substitute "x is a dog" for "x is a snake." The truths of logic, then, are those truths which contain only logical vocabulary *essentially*, as Quine puts it.

"Truth-by-Convention": Quine's Objections

Quine's first point as against the idea that convention creates truths is that definition—which might naturally be pointed to as a clear case of truth-by-convention—does not *create* truths. Not out of thin air. What it does, rather, is to *transform* truths that are explicitly truths of logic into ones that are not (*WP* 87–8). According to the above definition of logical truth, "Every mare is female" is not a truth of logic (since it would go false if we substitute, say, "mouse" for "mare"). It seems natural to express the idea by saying that since by definition "Every mare is female" means the same as "Every female horse is female," they express the very same *truth,* that is the same true *proposition,* which cannot itself be said without confusion to be true by definition. But that is not Quine's point. Quine's target is the idea that the truth of some statements—and in particular that of all logical truths—might be explained entirely as a matter of convention. Since the explanation of "Every mare is female" appeals to convention plus the fact that "Every female horse is female" is a logical truth, we have not explained the truth of the former as entirely a matter of convention unless we can explain the logical truths themselves in terms of convention.

So the idea that definition creates truth-by-convention provides at most a conditional explanation of truth as convention: given an explanation of logical truth, some truths might be explained in terms of convention plus whatever explains logical truth. But definition cannot explain logical truth itself. Definitions may reduce non-logical truths to logical truths; also some logical truths to others, when the definitions involved are definitions of logical expressions in terms of others. But since not every logical expression can be defined—for in terms of what would the last one be defined?—logical truths must remain whose truth cannot be explained in that way.

Now Carnap's actual strategy, as we know, is simply to specify some sentences of a language as true, as in "Let s be true!," and to give rules for deriving further sentences from the sentences so specified. All such sentences are to be understood as true by stipulation, including the logical truths.

To this idea Quine poses two objections. The first, perhaps less serious objection (*WP* 100–2), is simply that if the theorist has the power to specify certain sentences of a theory as true-by-decree, then what is to stop any theorist, of whatever domain—physics, biology, or whatever—from taking the same approach? Why should the physicist not decree, for example, that Einstein's principles of relativity are henceforward to be understood as true by convention? True, such a scientist might find it necessary to change those conventions from time to time, but that is not decisive, as the definitions used in science certainly do change with time, in response to changing theoretical pressures. But surely, we might well think, something is fishy: it cannot be quite that easy to change the whole epistemological basis of a science!

Carnap might have replied that something's being fishy is not much of an argument. Indeed some theorists did think that there was an element of convention in the laws of physics. But we will return to this issue in discussing "Two Dogmas of Empiricism" below. The second objection (*WP* 103–5) is in any case more substantial, and is widely regarded as decisive. Conventions, as Carnap understands them, must be *stated*. As a telling example, Quine considers:

> (1) For every x, y, and z, if z is the result of putting x for "p" and y for "q" in "If p then q," and x and z are true, then y is true.[4]

This tells us that if we have a true conditional statement with a true antecedent, then the consequent of the conditional is to be true (for example, suppose that "If Mary is tall then John is tall" and "Mary is tall" are both true, then so is "John is tall"). Suppose now that x, y, and z are as stated in the hypothesis of (1), i.e., we have:

> (2) z is the result of putting x for "p" and y for "q" in "If p then q," and x and z are true.

It seems we can infer

> (3) y is true.

Yes, *but only by using the logic of if-then*. That is, the fourth English word of (1) is "if," and the third English word from the end is "then"; we know that given (1) and (2) we can infer (3) because we understand the English expression "if-then." But this understanding is not provided by (1); rather it is presupposed by it, in the sense that we cannot grasp the import of (1) unless we already understand "if-then." More generally, the statement of conventions cannot be what determines logical truths or logical relationships, because it is only by virtue of logical relationships that logical truths and logical relationships are derivable from them. As Quine puts it:

> In a word, the difficulty is that if logic is to proceed *mediately* from conventions, then logic is needed for inferring logic from the conventions. Alternatively, the difficulty which appears thus as a self-presupposition of doctrine can be framed as turning upon a self-presupposition of primitives. It is supposed that the *if*-idiom, the *not*-idiom, the *every*-idiom, and so on, mean nothing to us initially,

and that we adopt the conventions … by way of circumscribing their meaning; and the difficulty is that communication of [the conventions] themselves depends upon free use of those very idioms which we are attempting to circumscribe, and can succeed only if we are already conversant with the idioms.

(WP 104)

A clarification we might add is that of course, if we are explaining a new language or a language not already known to the pupil, then our explanations of the logical expressions of that language do not presuppose an understanding of the logical expressions of *that* language. But in order to answer the epistemological question *What constitutes knowledge of logic?*—or rather to explain what makes something a logical truth—we should have to be able to do the trick in a way that applies to our grasp of logic even as expressed in the very language we are using in the explanation. Quine's point is that convention cannot do this, on pain of circularity.

The First Dogma of "Two Dogmas": Analyticity

Convention or stipulation was a way of explaining the idea of analyticity. In "Two Dogmas of Empiricism" of 1950—and as noted the main ideas had been festering long beforehand—Quine launches a more general attack on the idea of analytic truth (the first dogma), along with a related attack on the thesis of reductionism (the second dogma), as an account of the actual structure of human knowledge. We begin as Quine does with analyticity.

The structure of Quine's argument deserves some comment before we consider its detailed substance. The conclusion of the argument is that there is no such thing as analytic truth—or more cautiously, that there is no firm boundary between one kind of statement and another that has the epistemological significance that the purported distinction between analytic and synthetic statements is supposed to have. But, as we often say, it is hard to prove a negative. One way to prove that something doesn't exist is to show that it is internally contradictory, or that some kind of contradiction follows from the supposition that it does exist. That is how we disprove the existence, for example, of the set of all sets not belonging to themselves, or the village barber who shaves all and only the villagers who don't shave themselves. Quine's argument is not like that. His argument, rather, is more like one in physical science whereby, for example, the existence of a certain force is disputed on the grounds that it cannot be explained in terms that do not simply presuppose its existence, *and* that the phenomena which it was invoked to explain can be explained without it. Thus after trying out several ways of explaining the concept of analyticity and finding that they fail to do so informatively, Quine declares that the sensible thing is to give up—to "stop tugging at our bootstraps"—and conclude that the existence of the analytic-synthetic distinction is "an unempirical dogma of empiricists, a metaphysical article of faith" (*FLPV* 37). He then explains, by means of his doctrine of epistemological holism, why there should seem to be such a distinction when there isn't; the supposed evidence for the distinction can otherwise be accounted for.

Some—such as Timothy Williamson in *The Philosophy of Philosophy* (2007, p. 50)—have found the first part of the argument to be question-begging, the charge of a dogma or article of faith to be unwarranted and unfair: What has Quine to say to someone who finds analyticity, or at least one of the concepts such as synonymy that Quine tries out in possible explanations of it, to be in perfectly good order as they stand? Holism is in a sense his answer in "Two Dogmas," but a more satisfactory answer will emerge later; we will set it aside for our next chapter.

Thus to the substance of the argument. Analytic truths such as "No bachelor is married" are standardly said to be true by virtue of the meanings of words. Meaning, Quine points out, is often thought to be more fine-grained than *reference* (*FLPV* 21). The singular terms "The Morning Star" and "The Evening Star," as Frege pointed out, refer to the same object, namely the planet Venus, but they differ in meaning (or sense, in Frege's terms). Similarly, the predicates "x is a creature with a kidney" and "x is a creature with a heart" are (let us assume) co-extensive—they refer to just the same things—but differ in meaning. But what is meaning? The term "means" is a verb, but "meaning" also shows up as a noun, as in "The meaning of _ is ..." or "_ has a meaning." Quine grants that the apparent reference to special objects, namely meanings, is not endemic to the notion of meaning as such—that it is sufficient, for the concept of meaning to be theoretically serviceable, that the word be restricted to the context "x and y are alike in meaning." This is the concept of "synonymy."

The idea that analytic truth is truth-by-meaning, then, can be cashed out as its definability in terms of logical truth plus synonymy: an analytic truth is one that can be transformed into a truth of logic by substituting synonyms for synonyms (*FLPV* 23). For example since "bachelor" and "unmarried man" are synonyms, we can transform "No bachelor is married" into the logical truth "No unmarried man is married."

But this is not much progress in itself: one who is dissatisfied with the idea of analytic truth is not going to be reassured by its equation with truth-due-to-synonymy, especially not if synonymy, as just described, is what is really essential to the concept of meaning. For analytic truth was supposed to be truth-by-meaning; the circle is small and unexplanatory. We need some kind of independent grasp of the concept that is supposed to be wearing the trousers, namely synonymy. Nor is it helpful, as Quine points out, to say that synonymy is a matter of *definition*; a definition, in the sense in which the lexicographer gives definitions, is at most a *report* of synonymy. Its existence does not afford any insight into what synonymy *is*.

A more promising suggestion is that two expressions are synonymous just in case every true sentence containing one remains true when the other is substituted for it (*FLPV* 27f; i.e., the two expressions are interchangeable *salva veritate*, i.e., saving the truth-value). This is promising because the concepts of substitution and truth are already assumed by logic, a science which Quine assumes is in good order.

No two expressions are interchangeable *salva veritate* in *all* contexts; we cannot substitute "female horse" for "mare" in "There are four letters in 'mare'" (*FLPV* 28). But Quine sets this sort of context—the case of quotation—aside. A more urgent problem is this. Assume as before that "creature with a heart" and "creature with a kidney" are co-extensional, true of all and only the same things. In that case, are they not interchangeable *salva veritate*? If so, then clearly the interchangeability condition is too weak, since no one would accept that these are synonymous (*FLPV* 31). In general, in any language in which substituting co-extensive expressions (those with the same reference) preserves truth-value— that is, in any *extensional* language (more on this Chapter 6)—interchangeability does not suffice for synonymy (an example of such a language is the sort of formal language standardly used for the rigorous presentation of mathematics, and which Quine will argue later is sufficient for the whole of natural science). However, English is presumably *not* extensional, because of the presence of expressions such as "necessarily." Thus consider:

(4) Necessarily, every creature with a heart is a creature with a heart.
(5) Necessarily, every creature with a heart is a creature with a kidney.
(6) Necessarily, every unmarried man is an unmarried man.
(7) Necessarily, every bachelor is an unmarried man.

Substitution of co-extensive expressions leads from truth to falsehood in the case of transforming (4) into (5)—for even if every actual creature with a heart has a kidney, there *could* be a creature with a heart but no kidney. Such a creature is possible or conceivable, if unlikely. Going from (6) to (7), however, we move from truth to truth. This is the right result, since in the latter case we substitute synonyms, but not in the first. Thus in a language rendered non-extensional by the presence of such expressions as "necessarily," interchangeability *salva veritate* seems to be a correct criterion of synonymy.

But this is still no advance, according to Quine (*FLPV* 29–30). For what we say when we attach "necessarily" to the front of a sentence, Quine assumes—as did his envisaged audience—is that the sentence is an analytic truth! That is, "necessarily p" is explained as true just in case "p" is *analytic* (Carnap as well as Alonzo Church had written extensively and influentially making just that assumption). Thus to explain synonymy in terms of interchangeability in non-extensional languages is to explain it in terms of non-extensional devices such as "necessarily," which depend for their intelligibility on the concept of analyticity; the purported explanation is circular, since the aim was to explain analyticity in terms of synonymy.[5]

Those acquainted with the writings of Saul Kripke, or indeed with any significant share of analytic philosophy since about 1970, may take umbrage at this last move, on the grounds that necessity and analyticity are not the same thing. For example, virtually no one thinks that "Water is H_2O" is an analytic truth—that was an empirical discovery—but it is widely held to be a necessary truth (any substance, actual or possible, that is not H_2O would be *different stuff*, hence not water). However, for that very reason, it seems that necessity in this sense—so-called *de re* necessity, i.e., necessity in things—is not suitable for the explanation of analyticity: applying the interchangeability test, we would get the right answer for "creature with a heart" and "creature with a kidney," but we would get the wrong result that "water" and "H_2O" are synonyms.

Quine goes on to consider some further details of Carnap's discussions of analyticity, but details are best left to the final section of this chapter, when we consider a little more closely the actual roles of what are called definition and postulation in science generally. Suffice it to say for now that the fact that Carnap is able to *specify* classes of sentences in his formal languages and call them "analytic" tells us nothing about what it is for sentences to *be* analytic, what is involved in calling them "analytic."

The Second Dogma: Reductionism

Phenomenological reductionism is the idea that every significant non-analytic statement is equivalent to some statement or conjunction of statements that refers only to sensory experience. As we noted in the previous chapter, Carnap's project in the *Aufbau* was to go far beyond the mere declarations in this direction to be found in Hume, Berkeley and others, and far beyond their various sketches of how certain key parts of the reduction might go (such as Russell's efforts). For example Berkeley had suggested that sentences seemingly asserting the existence of a persisting, mind-independent physical object could be explained as asserting the recurrence, in certain situations, of similar sensory experiences. But he did so only vaguely or using examples, and, when explaining statements such as "There is a tree in the quad," tended to assume the meanings of such statements as "If I were to look in the quad, I would have tree-type of visual experience." Well, what kind of sensory experience is that? In order to carry out a *reduction*, that would have to be explained without terms like "tree," on pain of begging the question. And what about the quad? Isn't that a physical object? For that matter, what do we mean by "looking"? Doesn't that mean, turning my head, pointing my eyeballs in a certain way? Heads and eyeballs are no less material objects than trees.

Armed with modern mathematical logic and not a little persistence and ingenuity, Carnap makes enormous progress in solving these problems. But as Quine sees it, at a crucial stage in his "construction" of the external world out of sensory experience, Carnap employs a strategy that is incompatible with strict reductionism (*WO* 40, *FSS* 10–14; cf. *TT* 22–3).[6] At an early stage of the construction, Carnap had succeeded in defining terms for sensory qualities as certain classes of experiences grouped by similarity (what Carnap calls the "recollected similarity of experience" is the single undefined non-logical primitive of the system). He is then faced with the task of defining statements of the form q is at $<x, y, z, t>$ where q is a sensory quality, x, y, z, are spatial coordinates, and t a time (the brackets "$< \ldots >$" indicates an "ordered sequence" of objects, i.e., that they occur in the order given). Doing so would amount to a contextual definition, in the sense explained earlier, of the relational predicate "is at." The idea is that statements about ordinary objects such as trees will be statements about collections of sensible qualities in certain regions of space-time. But things like trees, and hence the sensible qualities of which they are "composed" in this way, exist when we don't perceive them, we assume. Furthermore, *no* statement expressing the sensory state of a subject logically implies a statement of the form *q* is at <*x, y, z, t*>, as we know from visual illusions and ordinary perceptual mistakes. So far as the sensory states of the subject are concerned, the qualities could be anywhere in space-time. Carnap's solution to this problem is to impose certain principles whereby sensory qualities are to be assigned to space-time in such a way as to maximize simplicity, continuity and other features.[7] For example, although it would be consistent with one's experience that the tree in the quad does not exist when one does not perceive it, or turns into an elephant when one does not perceive it, the principles rule out such discontinuities or gratuitous complexities. However, these constraints do not tell us how to translate a *single* statement of the form *q* is at <*x, y, z, t*>. They tell us, given a whole—and very large—*collection* of statements about immediate experience, how to assign truth-values to those statements so as to yield the expected overall world. This is especially striking when we consider what happens when we find we had been mistaken about the location, say, of a certain object, because an experience fails to accord with it: in Carnap's terms, an assignment of sense-qualities to space-time points may have accorded well with experience up to a point, but must now be *revised* in order best to satisfy the principles governing such assignments.

What this means, in a nutshell, is that Carnap did not provide a genuine definition of the expression "is at," explicit or contextual: no recipe is provided for eliminating it from a single statement, for translating individual statements containing it into ones that do not. What there is, rather, is a recipe for mapping whole bodies of statements appertaining to experience onto whole bodies of statements appertaining to the world. Thus the scheme does not provide individual translations of statements about the world into statements about experience. Furthermore, according to Quine, this is not just a feature of Carnap's particular attempt at constructing a reductionist representation of human knowledge. The problem that faced Carnap is inevitable: statements about the physical world are "underdetermined" by statements about experience. Considerations of simplicity, continuity and the like are appealed to in generating theories of the world—even the most mundane ones—but they apply only "holistically," that is, only to whole theories, or otherwise large collections of statements.

The failure and untenability of reductionism also rules out another way in which the concept of analyticity might have been explained (*FLPV* 41). Reductionism is often linked to "verificationism," the thesis that the meaning of a statement is the method or set of conditions that would verify it. Given a scheme of phenomenalistic reduction, the meaning of a statement is the occurrence of some combination of sensory experiences: it is called "true" if and only if they occur. Statements are synonymous if and only if alike in the experiences that confirm them. Some statements, however, will be *vacuously* confirmed, that is, confirmed by any combination of experiences. Where E is the occurrence of some sensory experience, for example, the statement "Either E or not E" will be confirmed by every experience; so will "P if and only if Q" if P and Q are confirmed by the same experiences. An analytic truth, then, might be explained as "is confirmed by every experience," "vacuously verified," "contains no empirical information," or something like that. But if reductionism is untenable, then it is not the case that each statement has a set of empirical consequences of its own. If there is no such thing as the empirical import of an individual statement, then no statement, considered on its own, can be said individually to lack empirical import.

Quine famously expresses the holism he counterpoises to reductionism as follows:

> The totality of our so-called knowledge or beliefs, from the most casual matters of geography and history to the profoundest laws of atomic physics or even of pure mathematics and logic, is a man-made fabric which impinges on experience only along the edges. Or, to change the figure, total science is like a field of force whose boundary conditions are experience. A conflict with experience at the periphery occasions readjustments in the interior of the field ... But the total field is so undetermined by its boundary conditions, experience, that there is much latitude of choice as to what statements to re-evaluate in the light of any single contrary experience. No particular experiences are linked with any particular statements in the interior of the field, except indirectly through considerations of equilibrium affecting the field as a whole.
>
> (*FLPV* 42–3; see also *OR* 16–17)

According to reductionism, if our theory of the world logically implies some particular report of experience—e.g., "If X happens, then such-and-such will be observed"—and that report is *false* (X happens but such-and-such is not observed), then some particular theoretical statement, or finite collection of such statements, is thereby *falsified*. We must adjust our theory accordingly. By contrast, according to Quine's holism, an experience contrary to expectation always leaves us with choices. Typically the experience-report will have been logically implied by a whole raft of theoretical statements, in such a way that any of several could be revised to accommodate the unexpected experience; perhaps A should be dropped, or perhaps B instead of A; or perhaps we should keep A and B and drop C. Typically there will be just one or a few that we actually regard as up for testing—the others are more familiar or well entrenched—but the point is that in principle all these others are involved in logically implying the observational sentence, and thus in principle could be revised instead of the one we had in mind (see Hahn and Schilpp 1986, pp. 400, 619–22). Strictly speaking, each of the changes would result in a different theory; more than one theory could accommodate the same data. Furthermore, since the question of which revisions to make is not answered by a statement that is part of the theory, it must be recognized as a "pragmatic" matter: in choosing revisions, we strive for simplicity of theory, economy of basic concepts, intuitive ease of understanding, a minimum of change to our beliefs, continuity or analogy with otherwise accepted theory, and so on, balancing these factors as seems best. But to call such matters "pragmatic"—and this is crucial for understanding Quine on this rather large point—is not thereby to distinguish them from theoretical matters, for such changes are of course changes of *theory*. The pragmatic and theoretical are inextricably interwoven.

If human knowledge is thus like a web—as Quine would call it elsewhere—then the statements that tend to get revised are the ones lying midway between the center and the outer edge. First consider the outer edge. In point of fact, we do not typically speak of subjective experiences: instead of saying "I experience such-and-such silvery sense-data," the scientist observing the thermometer says something like "The mercury has risen." The typical scientific statements most directly conditioned to sensory experience are not reports of experience, but statements about physical objects (this is for good reason; the other scientists are interested in the state of the thermometer, not your subjective experiences). Quine will later call these "observation sentences" (taken up in the next chapter). Thus when experience is at odds with theory, we can, in extreme cases, maintain that the observation sentence that would normally be provoked by the experience is false—some sort of illusion or other anomaly took place. But this is rare, and insisting that it remain rare is part of what is involved in calling oneself, as Quine does, an empiricist.

On the other hand, statements at the center are those whose empirical implications are the most remote, the most diffuse. These are statements of logic and mathematics. They are furthest from having empirical implications of their own because they are involved in all knowledge and all reasoning. The purpose of leaving these undisturbed is that the implications of disturbing them would be so pervasive that only a general crisis in human knowledge could occasion it. It might, in any case, be practically unmanageable. This, according to Quine, accounts for the feeling that such statements are necessary and *a priori*, and for Carnap's idea that they are not so much components of knowledge as its framework.

Quine emphasizes this aspect of holism in a remark near the end of "Two Dogmas":

> Carnap, [C. I.] Lewis, and others take a pragmatic stand on the question of choosing between language forms, scientific frameworks; but their pragmatism leaves off at the imagined boundary between the analytic and the synthetic. In repudiating such a boundary I espouse a more thorough pragmatism.
>
> (*FLPV* 46)

So far as Quine is concerned—and as we'll see in Chapter 4 this aspect is indeed significant—care must be taken once again over his use of the term "pragmatic." There are affinities to be sure, especially between the very early Quine and C.I. Lewis (Quine having learned directly from Lewis as a graduate student), but by this time Quine is certainly not lumping his own philosophy with that of some other names that the word naturally suggests—Charles Sanders Peirce, William James, John Dewey, or indeed C. I. Lewis. The word occurs primarily because Carnap used it, and Quine was merely "handing back" the word to Carnap as he put it (*CCE* 397; see Sinclair 2022 for much more).

A slight wrinkle in the issues between Carnap and Quine, as mentioned before if obliquely, was that Carnap maintains that he *accepts* holism (the idea of holism is attributable to Pierre Duhem, who urged it in his *La theorie physique: Son object et sa structure*—"Physical Theory: its objects and structure" of 1906; hence its occasional name in the literature, the "Duhem-Quine Thesis"). Carnap's acceptance of holism amounted to the idea that one could always revise one's analytic statements to suit the data; it comes down to the freedom to choose amongst alternative sets of analytic truths. But this does not explain what it means to call them "analytic," or why their being so is epistemologically significant. So from Quine's point of view, Carnap's acceptance of holism only accentuates the emptiness of the view.

Holism: Implications and a Partial Retraction

We should not leave "Two Dogmas of Empiricism" without three further comments, which should help to connect it both with the opening remarks of Chapter 1 and with the topics of our next two chapters.

First, we should point out an implication of Quine's holism for the status of philosophy. The status of philosophy has always been rather a sore point for those philosophers who try to set limits on what it makes sense to say or think, such as Hume, Kant, Frege, the early Wittgenstein, and Carnap in his more guarded ways. If we read Hume's enjoinder that we should commit to the flames everything that is neither empirical nor mathematical, then what are we to do with works of philosophy, such as Hume's? Commit it to the flames? In a word, philosophical prose that sets out conditions for making sense usually turns out not to satisfy those conditions, and attempts such as Carnap's to characterize such prose as nevertheless all right because its import is practical rather than theoretical are seldom convincing. Implicit in Quine's holism is that all theoretical discourse including philosophy is in one boat; it is all one great big theory, aimed at making sense of the world around us. Quine would often follow the Viennese philosopher Otto Neurath (1882–1945) in likening human knowledge, our "conceptual scheme," to a ship at sea, that must be repaired from time to time while at sea—hence, on pain of sinking, not too many planks at one time. There is no philosophical dry-dock—no Cartesian "first philosophy," no vantage point superior to empirical science that sets its standards. Philosophy itself, like everything else, contributes to knowledge only insofar as it is empirical, however remotely and indirectly. The "Naturalism" of which we spoke in Chapter 1, and which we will consider more thoroughly in Chapter 4, could be said to be more or less implicit in Quine's holism.

Second, we should address a concern that many readers raise concerning the web analogy. Quine says that mathematical and logical statements lie at the center of the web. But he also says that logic is what holds the web together. How can logic consist of statements *in* the web but also be what holds the web together? To put it another way, if logic is in principle answerable to experience, then it seems it is answerable to experience only by virtue of itself; but in that case, if experience were to entail changes in logic, the change in logic would undo the pressure that entailed the change, rendering the change unjustified. So logic cannot be both answerable to experience and that in which empirical answerability consists.

A reply to this would not become evident in Quine's work until his book *Roots of Reference* of 1974. The reply is that we have to be careful about exactly what the web or network analogy is an analogy for. We will discuss this in detail in the next two chapters, but the point to make now is that Quine does not think of statements as abstract objects standing in an ethereal relationship called logical consequence. To possess a language, rather, is to possess an exceedingly complex set of verbal *dispositions*. The statements that one accepts are those sentences that one is disposed to assent to. Amongst one's verbal dispositions are higher-order dispositions: dispositions to be disposed to assent to one statement if one is disposed to assent to another. For example, one becomes disposed to assent to "That is an animal" if one becomes disposed to assent to "That is a dog." These "sentence-to-sentence links," as Quine calls them, are the glue that holds the web together; the web is a web of first-order verbal dispositions, with the second-order ones holding them together. So there is no circularity or untenable dual role for logic: logical truths are themselves the objects of first-order dispositions—one is disposed to assent to them—but they also correspond to higher-order dispositions.

Third, and finally, we should stop briefly to register that once this outlook on human knowledge had settled, and its details filled in, Quine could see his way to qualify both the holism and the anti-analyticity stance. In the *Roots of Reference* and the paper "Two Dogmas in Retrospect" (1991), he proposed a less radical form of holism, and a definition of analyticity that satisfies him—a definition which purports to identify the intuitive class of analytic truths, but without doing the epistemological work that Carnap envisaged. We'll set this aside for now, returning to it in Chapter 4.

Further Points on Definition, Postulation, and the Limits of Syntax

In this final section we consider some further dimensions of Quine's criticisms of Carnap. First we consider some applications and generalizations of the arguments that we have considered so far; second, a further point that Quine makes against Carnap's appeals to syntax, invoking, in a non-technical way, the famous Incompleteness Theorems of Gödel.

Remember that one of Carnap's key strategies, especially in *The Logical Syntax of Language*, was that the putatively *a priori* elements of knowledge might be accounted for by the explicit stipulation of certain sentences as analytic. Quine posed two sets of objections. First, this does not explain anything unless it is explained what is meant by "analytic"—the mere fact that certain true sentences of a theory have been singled out and called by a certain name, even a suggestive name, does not really tell us anything about their epistemological status. "Two Dogmas" urges that no suitable explanation is forthcoming. Second—quite aside from concerns directly about analyticity—Quine's "Truth by Convention" argues against the very idea that the activity of stipulation creates truths in a way that might account for the traditionally envisaged role and extent of *a priori* knowledge.

Now Carnap's project was not utterly new. The idea was not that there had never really been any *a priori* knowledge until Carnap came along, like Moses with the tablets. Aside from what philosophers have had to say, it eminently arguable that what Carnap described was really only a more rigorous and self-conscious form of something that had gone on since the dawn of mathematics. This is the activity of *postulation*. The mathematician, we suppose, sets out certain statements—the postulates—and develops a theory by logically deriving further statements—the theorems—from those. The result, one might think, is surely a body of knowledge, but surely the status of the postulates is different from that of the theorems: If we want to reject the idea that the postulates are accepted on the basis of some kind of direct insight into the nature of reality, then what else is there to say but that they are stipulated, in some sense made true by our say-so?

As we noted, Quine argues that logic cannot be explained in terms of stipulation or postulation, on pain of infinite regress. However, not all mathematics is logic, at least in one clear sense of "logic." For, although Quine in earlier years would count set theory—those truths in which the epsilon "∈" of set-membership was the only non-logical expression occurring essentially—as logic, he changed his mind later, thus according with the usual view nowadays that the essential occurrence of "∈" is where logic leaves off and set theory, and hence mathematics, if mathematics is reduced to set theory, begins (*PL* 64–6). And unquestionably the actual character of set theory as developed in the twentieth century has had the character of postulation as described above. So it might seem that even if logic cannot itself be explained in terms of stipulation, then still mathematics might be. Or, even if knowledge of theorems logically derived from postulates must be understood to rest partly upon a knowledge of logic that cannot be explained in terms of stipulation, then perhaps knowledge of the postulates themselves can be.

Quine, in effect, argues that the idea of stipulation or postulation (in that sense) suffers from exactly the same sort of problem that analyticity does. First, Quine distinguishes between "discursive" and "legislative" postulation (*WP* 118). A theory, in one sense of the word, is simply a set of truths about some subject-matter. Many theories are *axiomatizable*: this means that there is some finite subset of the theory—or set of statements specifiable by means of a finitely stateable rule—such that all true statements of the theory are logical consequences of those statements, the axioms. But if a theory is axiomatizable at all, then there are many ways in which it can be done—many choices of axiom-sets. There may be, and often is, theoretical interest in finding different axiomatizations of a theory, finding ever more economical or more intuitive ones, and comparing them in other ways. Quine calls this "discursive" postulation because it is aimed simply at finding different ways in which a body of truths may be summed up, conveyed and otherwise thought about. Clearly it affords no particular insight into what makes the statements true, or what knowledge of them depends on. *Legislative* postulation, by contrast, is what "properly hints at truth by convention" (*WP* 118). However, just as we can ask "What exactly is the difference between accepting a truth as analytic and accepting it as obvious?," we can ask "What exactly is the difference between *stipulating* a statement as true and *assuming* it or *supposing* it to be true?" In both cases, avows Quine, however customary or appealing it may be to use the former turn of phrase in describing what one does, this does not show that there is anything more to it than what is conveyed by the latter. What is going on, rather, is that there are times when some purported truths are set out as starting-points from which to develop a theory; but once the theory is developed and more truths known, the designation of certain statements as starting-points is best looked upon merely as an historical fact about the development of the theory, not as marking a separate epistemological category. For at this point, the theory could be rebuilt using different postulates. Thus Quine writes:

> The distinction between the legislative and the discursive refers to the act, and not to its enduring consequence ... conventionality is a passing trait, significant at the moving front of science but useless in classifying the sentences behind the lines. It is a trait of events and not of sentences.
>
> (*WP* 119)

In fact the same point goes for stipulative definition, the case where some theorist states that something of the form "x is F iff x is ..." is to be understood as a definition, thereby introducing the predicate F. The stipulative character of the act may be lost in history without the theory being any the worse for it. And as in the case of postulation, it is unclear why it should matter that the act is called "definition." For example, one often has a choice of so-called definitions, such as "A triangle is a closed figure with three sides" or "A triangle is a closed figure with three angles." We might choose one as a definition, then derive the other as a theorem, or the other way round. But it is hard to see what difference it would make, except possibly as a practical matter. Further, as Quine would point out later, it really is true that statements once characterized as definitions sometimes get revised under theoretical pressure, sometimes even empirical pressure (the case of "Force" might be adduced yet again). Again we may ask what it adds to our understanding of the epistemological status of such changes that we should call them changes in the "meanings" of the expressions involved (see *WO* 57).

A final point that Quine makes against Carnap's and related views springs from Gödel's Incompleteness Theorems. According to the First Incompleteness Theorem, it is not possible, in effect, to axiomatize arithmetic: there is no set of arithmetical statements—either finite or mechanically specifiable according to a finitely stateable rule—from which all the truths of arithmetic can be derived according to formal rules of inference, that is, the sort of syntactical rules that interested Carnap. That is, for any such formal theory that is consistent and whose language is sufficient to express the truths of arithmetic, some sentence of the language will be such that neither it nor its negation is formally derivable from the axioms of the theory. Thus if the language is interpreted so as to express arithmetic, then since either the sentence or its negation is a truth of arithmetic, this means that some truth of arithmetic is not provable in the theory. According to the Second Incompleteness Theorem, for any consistent theory in whose language the truths of arithmetic can be expressed, the consistency of the theory cannot be proven in that same theory: a stronger theory is needed (a theory including statements not provable in the first theory). In a word, something stronger than arithmetic is needed to prove the consistency of arithmetic.

On the face of it, then, it would be impossible to explain our grasp of arithmetic in terms of the syntax of a language, that is, by specifying the sentences, axioms, and formal rules of inference of a language. Carnap tries to get round this by using arithmetic in specifying the analytic sentences of the language, comprising the logical and arithmetic truths. He does this by using Tarski's method of specifying the class of *truths* of a language. Where the language is L, the effect is that the metalinguistic statement "s is an analytic statement of L" is rendered equivalent to some truth of arithmetic stated in the metalanguage (the language used to discuss L). He thus succeeds in specifying, in the metalanguage, a class of sentences as the analytic statements of L. These are precisely the logical and arithmetic truths of L.

Clever, or cheating? Cheating, according to Quine. As noted, in order to explain their epistemological significance, it is not sufficient merely to label a class of statements as analytic. A basic task set for Carnap, as Quine sees it, was to show that our knowledge of arithmetic could be based upon our grasp of the syntax of a language. "Analytic-in-L" is the relevant concept of syntax. However, in order to apply this concept, one has to appeal to an independent grasp of arithmetic. In fact, as Tarski proved, the theory needed to specify the arithmetic truths of L must be stronger than that expressible in L. Therefore one's grasp of arithmetic cannot be said to be explained in terms of one's grasp of syntax. It is the other way round. Not only is mathematics used to specify the syntax, the mathematics used to do so is stronger than the mathematics captured by that syntax. This is all the more striking when we reflect that Tarski's method can just as easily be used, say, to specify the truths of chemistry or biology, expressed in a language. The mere fact that the truths of a language appertaining to some subject can be specified in this way clearly does not reveal anything about their epistemological status (*WP* 125).

Again, the point boils down to the basic point urged in "Two Dogmas": *however* the class of truths comes to be specified, what precisely does it mean to call them "analytic"?

Further Reading and Historical Notes

See Ben-Menahem 2006 for an introduction to the role of convention, as well as its history, and philosophical discussion of it. For Quine's development from graduate school to 1960 see Verhaegh 2018 and 2023; also Sinclair 2022. For the substance of "Two Dogmas," see Hylton 2007 Ch. 3, and Lugg 2012. It is striking, reading over the scholarship of Verhaegh and Sinclair, and also some of the unpublished essays found in *CCE*, how, despite his main interest in these early years being the technical side of Russell and the construction of his own system of set theory—set forth in "New Foundations for Mathematical Logic"— he was uncomfortable with the idea that the concept of meaning could serve as a stable foundation. But he tried to tell us in an essay of 1990 (*CCE* 390): "The distrust of mentalistic semantics that found expression in 'Two Dogmas' is … detectable as far back as my senior year in college."

The Indeterminacy of Translation

From Criticism to Construction

In "Two Dogmas," Quine argues that the concepts "meaning," "analyticity" and "synonymy," and so on constitute a circle, such that one cannot make any explanatory progress by using one to define the others. He then argues that there is really no need for such concepts in characterizing the structure of human knowledge. What he does not do, however, is to address the possibility of a direct definition of one of those concepts in terms from outside the circle; nor the possibility that one of them, though not definable, is a perfectly good scientific concept in its own right, alongside that of "respiration" or "magnetic field" and so on. Quine's most famous book, *Word and Object*, does exactly that. In its crucial second chapter, Quine argues that if we ask what a genuinely objective science of meaning would involve—one that seeks objective assignments of particular meanings to particular words and sentences—then we find that no such thing is possible. More exactly, the sorts of meaning-ascriptions that we would naturally or intuitively expect are not such that a fully developed linguistic science would validate as objectively correct. Not that it would validate other ones of the same kind; the conclusion rather is that there are no facts of that kind. The assignment of particular meanings must ultimately remain a matter of intuition or convenience, not a matter of scientifically discoverable objective fact.

This finds its signature expression in the conclusion that *translation* is *indeterminate*. Roughly, the thesis is that given an expression E from the foreign language, then (assuming E is translatable into English at all) there will be expressions E* and E** of English such that *from the point of view of empirical science,* E* and E** are both adequate translations of E, but which are not equivalent to each other, not in any sense approaching the intuitive idea of synonymy or sameness of meaning. In the case where the expressions are sentences, it might even be that E* and E** are each other's negations, so that if one is true then the other is false! The empirically objective relation "*x* is translatable as *y*," then, does not capture the intuitive idea of "sameness of meaning." For we naturally assume that the relation "*x* means the same as *y*" is both symmetrical and transitive: it runs in both directions if it runs in either, and if *x* means the same as *y* and *y* the same as *z*, then *x* means the same as *z*. So if E means the same as E*, and also means the same as E**, then E* means the same as E**, contrary to the supposed fact that E* does not mean the same as E**.

Before examining the details of Quine's argument in Chapter 2 of *Word and Object*, we should say a little about the book as a whole. Whereas his philosophical writings had often to this point been critical—critical especially of Carnap's program—much of *Word and Object* is aimed at developing a positive vision of what human knowledge is, and of the role that philosophy should play in analyzing, clarifying, and enhancing it. Central to this conception is a certain implication of his denial of an epistemologically significant analytic-synthetic distinction: If there is no such thing, then there is no difference in principle between *possessing language* and *possessing knowledge*; they can be distinguished for ordinary purposes, but there is no one without the other. Thus the exploration of human knowledge that Quine undertakes in this book—and in subsequent books and articles—is substantially an exploration of what is involved in possessing a language. On the one hand, the possession of a language, for Quine, is understood as the possession of an exceedingly complex set of verbal dispositions. Such is a key component in what Quine would a few years later call "Naturalized Epistemology" (and "Naturalism" more generally). Quine says a great deal here, and even more in subsequent writings, about the character, acquisition, and structure of such dispositions. On the other hand, since language is the vehicle and storehouse of human knowledge, Quine's interest is directed toward those features of language that are most conspicuously germane to philosophical questions about existence and ontology, the relation of evidence to theory, and the nature of reference, i.e., the relation involved in talking *about* an object, which so exercised philosophers such as Locke and Russell. Quine sees philosophy as continuing, into the domain of empirical knowledge, the process of conceptual clarification that took place in the foundations of mathematics that we touched on in Chapter 1. Thus, in reflecting on our conceptual scheme, Quine writes, "one encounters various anomalies and conflicts that are implicit in this apparatus, and is moved to adopt remedies in the spirit of modern logic" (*WO* ix). We will discuss these in Chapters 4 through 6.

In this chapter, we will concentrate on the indeterminacy of translation. We will be especially concerned to understand Quine's responses to certain objections to the thesis and the arguments for it, and also to raise some other concerns that Quine did not explicitly consider himself, or to which his replies may seem merely dismissive. The thesis is in many ways puzzling, and it can easily seem to conflict with ordinary certainties that seem impossible to give up. Much of the task of understanding the thesis lies in seeing why this is not really so, or at least not obviously so. Indeed, we will see that the outright demonstration of the thesis not as important as Quine's conception of linguistic science according to which the thesis is at least conceivable.

Radical Translation

If there are objective facts of meaning, then what sort of facts are they, what would the science be like whose aim is to discover them, and how would such a science discover such facts? The idea is that if there are facts of the form *x means the same as y*, then, in principle, there must be some sort of objective method—a science—capable of discovering what they are. So Quine explores the question of what such a method would be like, finds that such a method would fall well short of discovering facts of that kind, and concludes that there are no such facts.

Quine's first move in this exercise is announced in the very first paragraph of the book's preface:

> Language is a social art. In acquiring it we have to depend entirely on intersubjectively available cues as to what to say and when. Hence there is no justification for collating linguistic meanings, unless in terms of men's dispositions to respond overtly to socially observable stimulations.
>
> (*WO* ix; see also *OR* 26–9, *WP* 221–7)

Quine is asserting that meaning must be *public*, in the following sense: if two speakers were entirely and exactly alike in all their verbal dispositions—their dispositions to speak in various circumstances—then it could not be the case that for any sentence, what one speaker means by it is different from what the other means by it (except in the case of first-person pronouns and related turns of speech, which we will set aside). The reason for this is in principle quite clear: each of us learns to speak only by observing other people and learning to talk as they do—for example, to answer "yes" or something similar when asked, in the evident presence of rain, "Is it raining?" All we can ever have to go on, in determining whether or not we understand other people—determine what they mean—is what they say in what situations. Of course one can remain skeptical nonetheless: perhaps, despite the fact that communication *seems* to proceed smoothly, we never *really* understand each other. Perhaps we only ever understand our *own* language, never that of anyone else!

Wittgenstein, famously, seems to have held that such private understanding or private language is actually impossible: understanding is necessarily something mutual, something corroborated in the public domain. Although Quine is aware of the argument (see *OR* 27) and approves of the conclusion, he does not lean on anything like Wittgenstein's private language argument *per se*. (Although he did say: "Perhaps the doctrine of indeterminacy of translation will have little air of paradox for readers familiar with Wittgenstein's latter-day remarks on meaning"; *WO* 76.) If the language-user reliably retrieves the red one when asked to retrieve the red apple, answers "red" in reply to "What color is that?" said of a red thing, and similar things, then he knows what "red" means in the sense relevant to Quine's inquiry. Something necessarily inscrutable in his mind would not be relevant to meaning, in this sense, even if there were or could be such a thing (*WP* 221–7). As he puts it in his later book *The Roots of Reference*:

> Language, we are told, serves to convey ideas ... Now how do we know that these ideas are the same? And, so far as communication is concerned, who cares? We have all learned to apply the word "red" to blood, tomatoes, ripe apples, and boiled lobsters. The associated idea, the associated sensation, is as may be.
>
> (*RR* 35; see also *SS* 5)

Elsewhere he disparages the "myth of the museum" (*OR* 27), the private inner object being the thing on display.

The intuitive connection of meaning to translation might be simply that meaning is what translation aims to preserve. When actually translating sentences from, say, Russian or Japanese, we typically have the aid of textbooks and dictionaries written by bilinguals, and also bilinguals in the flesh. We can even do it by becoming bilinguals ourselves, without the aid of explicit translations at all, as in the immersion method of language instruction. If we have done this, then we can simply ask ourselves, "How would I say this in Russian?," and so on, and in proportion with our facility in the two languages, an answer will spontaneously come to mind except perhaps in specially hard cases like poetry and slang.

But our ability to do this does not show that Quine's project of describing a scientific method of translation is redundant. For our familiar, ordinary or intuitive ability does not disclose the raw data that goes into translation, and does not disclose the justification for the translations we naturally or intuitively suggest on the basis of that data. A self-conscious science of translation needs to know: exactly what are the data for translation, and exactly how is that data to be used in constructing a translation manual? All this needs to be made as explicit as possible. That is why Quine concentrates on *radical* translation: translation of a language from scratch, about which nothing is known—"translation of the language of a hitherto untouched people," he says. Of course "[t]he task is one that is not in practice undertaken in its extreme form, since a chain of interpreters of a sort can be recruited of marginal persons across the darkest archipelago," but we can "imagine that all help of interpreters is excluded" (*WO* 28). In this way, radical translation is a thought experiment.

The envisaged idea of translation or "Linguistic Science" is a science of linguistic *behavior*. "I hold ... that the behaviorist approach is mandatory," Quine writes; "[i]n psychology one may or may not be a behaviorist, but in linguistics one has no choice" (*PT* 37–8). Accordingly, the notion of "verbal dispositions" will figure prominently: dispositions to speak in a given situation (crucially, both non-verbal situations and *verbal* situations). The demand that the data be specified relatively precisely leads Quine to a very hard-headed notion of "situations." Situations, as we will see in greater detail below, are to be understood as *stimulations of the sensory surfaces*—stimulations of the sensory receptors (nerves in the retina, the eardrum, etc.). Thus Quine writes:

> The recovery of a man's current language from his currently observed responses is the task of the linguist who, unaided by an interpreter, is out to penetrate and translate a language hitherto unknown. All the objective data he has to go on are the forces that he sees impinging on the native's surfaces and the observable behavior, vocal and otherwise, of the native.
>
> (*WO* 28)

This is what is meant by an objective science of radical translation.

Stimulus Meaning and Observation Sentences

Approaching the native in his habitat, we may observe him or her to make some noises which we assume to be speech ("speech" may involve hand signals or other things; set these aside). In order to translate—discover meaning—we must discover some kind of connection between the noises they make and something else that we can observe. No such connection would be revealed by native equivalents of such sentences as "Plants are living things," "We came to this island long ago," and so on. For these are what Quine calls "standing sentences": sentences that, once true, never become false (or once false, never become true). Nothing about the circumstances observable when they are affirmed will tell us what they mean. Something like "We came to this island long ago" might be affirmed in any set of circumstances. What is most immediately useful to the translator, rather, are certain sorts of "occasion sentences." Unlike standing sentences, occasion sentences are sometimes true, sometimes false. These include "I have a pain in my hip," pertaining to a state of affairs that is not public or intersubjective, and "Interest rates are rising," pertaining to a state of affairs that is not observable or perceivable. Set these aside. *The most useful ones are those typically affirmed just when a certain sort of thing or event is observable in the immediate public environment*, such as Native for "It's windy," "The fire is dying out," and so on. For example, if we observe the natives to assent to a certain sound-sequence when it is raining, but not when it is not raining, we can reasonably translate it as Native for "It's raining."

This type of occasion sentence is called an "observation sentence." They constitute what Quine will later call the "entering wedge" of both translation and language-learning.

Stimulus Meanings and Assent

Clearly the translator cannot get very far merely by watching; the native might say "Gavagai!" once when a rabbit scurries past, and this might well mean something like "There goes a rabbit!," but it might mean any number of other things, such as "Dinner!" or "Cute!" In keeping with the lessons of the past two sections, what the translator needs to know is: Would the native assent to "Gavagai?" whenever a rabbit is observed, but not when not? What the translator needs to know is whether or not the native is *disposed to assent* to "Gavagai?" if and only if a rabbit is observed. In order to find this out, the translator must query the native, asking "Gavagai?" in various situations, and recording the native's assent or dissent in each.

To do this, the translator must first translate signs of assent and dissent (*RR* 46–8). Suppose the translator has not definitively settled on the translation of "Gavagai!," but the observed circumstances of its unprompted Native utterance suggest "Rabbit!" The translator tries "Gavagai?" on the native in various circumstances, hoping to bring about conversations like:

[A rabbit is present]
Native: Gavagai!

Translator: Gavagai?
Native: Evet!
(Translator translates "evet" as "yes.")

[No rabbit is present]
Translator: Gavagai?
Native: Yok!
(Translator translates "yok" as "No.")

Confidence in the conjectures—of "Gavagai," "evet," and "yok" will thus increase, and now the translator is equipped with native signs for assent and dissent, enabling him or her to carry out the work much more rapidly.

Remember that the native's language, for Quine's purpose, is identified with the native's present dispositions to verbal behavior. The method of querying is a means of discovering those dispositions (*RR* 15, *PT* 40). And as we said, in seeking correlations between verbal dispositions and situations, Quine is really looking for correlations between verbal dispositions and sensory stimulations. This is Quine's question: What is the *stimulus meaning* of the sentence? This concept, that of stimulus meaning, is not "meaning" in the ordinary sense, but is fundamental to the translator's task. The stimulus meaning of the sentence is the ultimate evidential basis for translating it, but it is not the meaning of the sentence, in anything like the ordinary sense of "meaning."

The translation of "Gavagai," for example, is "There's a rabbit," *not* "Such and such sensory stimulations are occurring."

Stimulations, it should be stressed, are to be understood physiologically, not as "sensations" or "perceptions" in the mentalistic sense (see *TT* 38–42). In the visual case, these will be patterns of neural activity in the retina. In view of this, it is probably worthwhile to be reminded of Quine's overarching purpose in discussing translation. If one's only aim in radical translation were to translate the native language, then it would never occur to one to talk about sensory stimulations and stimulus meanings, and rightly so. If Quine were merely describing what ordinary translators do, then he would not be talking about those things. But that is not the aim. The aim is the more abstract scientific or philosophical one of identifying the ultimate data for translation, and discovering what justifies translations on the basis of that data. And if the native's language is to be conceived as a complex of dispositions, then clearly it does not matter that it is a *rabbit* that causes the native to be disposed to assent to "Gavagai"; whatever those rabbit-caused stimulations are, the same stimulations caused by something else would bring about the same disposition to assent. What the translator ultimately does, then—and even a normal practically minded translator would be doing the same if unawares—is to match the native's dispositions with his own, as far as possible.

At this point we should insert a parenthesis. It might seem that with respect to a native occasion sentence such as "Gavagai!," the translator seeks a sentence of his own language which has the same stimulus meaning. To say that the answer is the sentence "Rabbit!" is to say that the same stimulations that prompt a native disposition to assent to "Gavagai" would prompt the translator's disposition to assent to "Rabbit!," or "There goes a rabbit." But a moment's reflection shows that cannot be right. Not only does my layout of sensory nerves differ at least marginally from those of the native, such anatomic minutiae are surely irrelevant for translation. An alien with very different physiology would not on that account be untranslatable. Quine would sort this out, but only much later; for now we set it aside, and will return to it in Chapter 7.

To resume. Stimulations must be understood as having what Quine calls a modulus, a length. How long? In practice, the translator will decide how long the modulus should be set for particular cases. Although they can never be merely instantaneous—it takes at least a little time to notice even the simplest things—they may be very short as in the case of stimulations typically relevant to "Gavagai." In other cases they will be longer; a very short modulus won't work for a sentence that reports slow movement, for example. Granted that we have settled on the moduli of the relevant classes of stimulations, then, and setting aside the need to relativize the notion to the speaker, Quine defines the stimulus meaning of an arbitrary sentence as follows (writing "prompt assent" as short for "causes a disposition to assent"):

The *affirmative stimulus meaning* of **S** = the class of stimulations that prompt assent to **S**.

The *negative stimulation meaning* of **S** = the class of stimulations that prompt dissent from **S**.

The stimulus meaning of the sentence **S** is the pair of these taken together (strictly, it is the *ordered* pair, thus keeping track of which is negative and which affirmative; the stimulus meaning of the negation of an occasion sentence comprises the same pair as that of the occasion sentence, but taken in reverse order).

Collateral Information

The task of translating observation sentences—of finding sentences of our own whose stimulus meanings match those of the native observation sentences—can be complicated in various ways. Consider again "Gavagai!" A movement in the grass, or a glimpse of a certain rabbit-fly, or even a remark or gesture from another native that is inscrutable to the translator, might dispose the native to assent to "Gavagai!" when it would not dispose the translator to assent to "Rabbit!" (*WO* 37–8). What we want to say, of course, is that these differences reflect not differences in meaning between "Rabbit!" and "Gavagai!", but differences in what we and the natives know about the local rabbits: the natives know, but we do not, that only rabbits would rustle the grass in that way, that those are rabbit-flies. But a little reflection shows that a firm and principled distinction between such "collateral information" and some comparatively pure class of stimulations is a little fanciful—or at least that it could not be formulated in advance of having a scientifically acceptable theory of meaning. For such a distinction would be precisely that between the parts played in native speech dispositions by meaning and by knowledge of the things talked about. As we know from the last chapter, the question of whether there is such a distinction was partly what motivated the question about radical translation in the first place. So even aside from the sheer difficulty of how, in general, reliance on collateral information could be factored out in the assignment of stimulus meanings, it would be unjustified at this stage to suppose that there is any such distinction to be drawn. Ways of recognizing a kind of thing may be very diverse, and no reason has emerged to insist that a certain subset of these must be somehow privileged. Absolute sameness of stimulus meaning, then, is too much to ask for in translating occasion sentences generally, even though stimulus meaning remains the "objective reality that the linguist has to probe when he undertakes radical translation" (*WO* 39). With stimulus meaning defined as above, there might just fail to be an English sentence whose stimulus meaning exactly matches that of "Gavagai!"

However, although in such cases there may not be a simple English sentence to do the job, often a more complicated sentence may do it. Furthermore, collateral information may be expected to vary even within the linguistic community, since the natives will not all have the same information about rabbits and other things, and these may affect their dispositions with respect to occasion sentences. Thus even if the presence of community-wide collateral information is not empirically detectable, variability of stimulus meaning from speaker to speaker can be regarded as a criterion of the effects of collateral information (*WO* 42). And for some sentences, there will be zero or only very small variability, hence zero or only minimal sensitivity to collateral information. These occasion sentences are the ones that should in the first instance be marked out as the observation sentences with the highest *degree* of observationality. In a turn of phrase often used in the philosophy of science, these are the observation sentences that are the least "theory laden" (see *CCE* 409–19 and 473–7; we'll revisit this topic in Chapter 7). A simple example might be "Red!," uttered as a one-word sentence, tantamount to "That's red!" For these sentences, and these alone, concordance of stimulus meaning is the criterion of correct translation.

These constitute the sharpest entering wedge for translation. Moreover it is arguable that empiricists had long supposed their subject-matter to be epistemologically basic: not being sensitive to collateral information, they are the sentences most directly conditioned to sensory stimuli, and perhaps thereby the least susceptible of error (*WO* 44–5). But with two vital differences: first, whereas traditional empiricists took these as reports of *sensation*—where sensation is a matter of having private sense data—Quine takes them as causally correlated with certain *physical stimuli*, and furthermore does not equate their meanings with the stimuli (even if, in typical cases, the meaning of the sentence will concern the presence of something that happens to be the cause of those stimulations, e.g. redness of light in the case of the stimulations that prompt assent to "Red!"). Second, unlike the idea of a direct report of what is experientially given, Quinean observationality is social: the degree to which a sentence is observational depends on the degree to which its stimulus meaning remains constant throughout the linguistic community. As we have seen, this represents a certain tension; we will return to it in the final chapter.

Synonymy and Analyticity Considered Anew

At this stage it is already possible to formulate a version of synonymy: we can say that two sentences are *stimulus-synonymous* if and only if they have the same stimulus meanings (*WO* 46–51). However, since due to varying collateral information the stimulus meaning of many occasion sentences will vary from speaker to speaker, only highly observational sentences are likely to turn out stimulus-synonymous. Thus it may be more useful, for some purposes, to speak of two sentences being stimulus-synonymous *for a given speaker*.[1] This, for example, will usually identify "That's a bachelor" and "That's an unmarried man" as stimulus-synonymous for a speaker, even if different speakers recognize bachelors in different ways, owing to differences of collateral information. We can also define a sentence as *stimulus-analytic* (for a given subject) as one that would be assented to following any stimulus (except those, such as that dispensed by hitting the native over the head, that would prevent the native from assenting to any sentence). Then further: a sentence is *socially stimulus-analytic* if and only if it is stimulus-analytic for the whole community; likewise *socially stimulus-synonymous* for pairs of terms.

How close does social stimulus-analyticity and stimulus-synonymy come to the respective intuitive notions? Not very. They remain "behavioristic ersatz" (*WO* 66). A standing sentence like "All bachelors are unmarried" will presumably be socially stimulus-analytic. But so will a merely obvious and well-known standing sentence such as "There have been black dogs" (*WO* 66). At this point, however, Quine sticks to his guns. Although in these sections of *Word and Object* Quine offers various further remarks on the issue, he remains skeptical concerning the intuition that there *must* be an epistemologically significant subset of the obvious and universally accepted standing sentences of a language that are held true only due to the meanings of words (see also *PT* 55–6, *RR* 78–80, *WP* 129). But one new point is worth mentioning. It is natural to suppose that the denial of a reputedly analytic truth is a clear symptom of not understanding it; or we think, "If he denies this, then he must mean something different by it." In certain cases, such as "2 + 2 = 4," the expressions involved (unlike "bachelor") are so widespread in their use that such a mismatch between speaker and hearer is bound to ramify throughout the language, in such a way that it might be better to regard them strictly as speaking different languages. But this, again, might just as well be said for obvious sentences reporting matters of fact like "There have been black dogs" or "Birds fly" (*WO* 67; for later reflections on these issues see *TT* 43–54).[2] So social stimulus-analyticity perhaps captures the link between analyticity and understanding better than the traditional notion does.

Analytical Hypotheses

So far we have been speaking only of sentences. Obviously we cannot translate a *language* merely by translating some finite list of sentences we have observed; this will not deliver translations of sentences not on the list. We have to translate individual words, and then give rules for combining those into sentences, then rules for mapping those onto sentences of English. Furthermore, we have spoken only of occasion sentences and especially of observation sentences such as "Gavagai!" The methods so far afford no insight into standing sentences such as (the Native equivalent of) "Birds fly." These require translation of individual words.

Translating Terms

It might be thought that by translating "Gavagai!" as the one-word sentence "Rabbit!"—used in the sense of "There's a rabbit!"—we had thereby translated "gavagai" as the general term "rabbit." However, this would be a correct translation of a general term only if "gavagai" and "rabbit" have the same extension (are true of just the same things). The stimulus-synonymy of the one-word sentences "Gavagai!" and "Rabbit!," even if exact, would fall far short of establishing this. The reason is that the stimulations that prompt "Gavagai!" occur not only in the presence of rabbits, but also in the presence of certain other things present if and only if a rabbit is present, in ways much more closely connected with rabbits than, say, the rabbit-fly. These include an undetached rabbit-part (a part of a rabbit that is connected in the usual way to a whole rabbit); a rabbit-stage (a temporal part of a rabbit: think of a physical object as having not just three spatial dimensions but also a temporal dimension, so that we can speak of its temporal parts—e.g. the rabbit from 9:00 a.m. to 9:01a.m.—just as we do its spatial parts such its leg, ear, etc.); and many others, even if more artificial. Such things might seem unnatural, but what seems unnatural to us might be natural to the native, for all we know.

Suppose the native *points* at a rabbit and volunteers "Gavagai!" How can we tell that the native is pointing at, and referring to, the rabbit, and not just an undetached rabbit-part or rabbit-stage? More exactly, what is the empirically verifiable difference between them? We might ask the native, pointing at the ear, now at the leg, whether the one is the same *gavagai* as the other; similarly, pointing at the rabbit at one moment, and at the same rabbit a few minutes or days later. If the answer is yes to the first and similar questions, then presumably the native is not talking about rabbit-parts; conversely if not. Similarly for the possibility of rabbit-stages. However, in order to ask the native these questions, we need to know how to ask them in Native. We must have identified the Native equivalent of "Is this_ the same as that_?." "Is the same as" is the notion of *identity*. Let us thus turn briefly to the question of translating this and other "logical particles" as Quine calls them.

Logical Particles

The simplest kind of logical particles are the truth-functional connectives such as "not," "and," "or," and so on; these among other things join whole sentences to form compound sentences. They can be translated as follows. Suppose we have translated two simple occasion sentences A and B. For some simple Native expression #, we can translate it as negation just in case the natives assent to A if and only if they dissent from #A: the stimulus meaning of the negation of a sentence is just the converse of the stimulus meaning of the sentence as mentioned. We can translate another expression @ as conjunction ("and") just in case the natives assent to A@B if and only if they assent to both A and B individually. The stimulus meaning of a conjunction is the logical sum of the stimulus meanings of the conjuncts. Similarly for other truth-functional connectives (in fact there is more complexity—see *RR* 75–8—but we needn't go into the matter further for these purposes).

Quine points out that if this sort of thing is the correct procedure for translating logical connectives, then the idea, sometimes fancifully entertained, of non-logical people, is not an empirical possibility (*WP* 109, *WO* 57–9). For suppose the natives regularly affirm A@B but dissent from B. Might this be a case of affirming a conjunction but denying one of its conjuncts, hence of refusing to accept a logical consequence of their own beliefs? No, because acceptance of A@B without acceptance of B would be the strongest possible evidence that "and" is not a correct translation of @. Such is the simplest dimension of the so-called Principle of Charity that would figure so prominently in the work of Donald Davidson: in general, translation is impossible except under the assumption of the rationality of the subjects translated, and is justified only insofar as it does not impute gross failures of reason or perception to the natives (*WO* 59; see also *OR* 5–6). We will return to this point presently.

Beyond the truth-functional logical particles are those used to form so-called categorical statements such as "All men are mortal." These are such expressions as "all," "some," "there is," "any," "each," and so on. These devices do not simply join whole sentences, but occur within sentences that do not have other sentences as proper parts. Thus consider for a moment the problem of finding the Native equivalent of the English categorical form

All S are P.

By analogy with the procedure for strategy for truth-functional connectives, we might suppose that a Native form

*S ◊ P

can be translated that way so long as the stimulus meaning of S is in some sense included in that of P. This will not work, however. For as we noted, the stimulus meaning of "Gavagai" does not distinguish between "rabbit" and "undetached rabbit-part"; in English, the stimulus meanings of those two would coincide. The proposed rule of translation, then, would have us expecting the natives to affirm the Native equivalent of:

All rabbits are undetached rabbit-parts.

But of course they wouldn't. The problem is that unlike the case of the truth-functional sentence connectives, translation of the Native devices of generality—of "quantification"—depends on the translation of particular *terms* such as "gavagai." We have, in effect, to assign *reference* to particular sub-sentential linguistic expressions. But now we seem to have come full circle. For we already found that, in order to distinguish "rabbit" from "rabbit-stage" and the like, we have to identify the Native expression for identity, that is, their equivalents of "is the same as" and the like. Of course "x is the same as y" is true if and only if the expressions put for "x" and "y" have the same reference. So in general, it looks as if the problem of identifying sub-sentential expressions, translating them, and identifying logical devices of identity and quantification constitute one unitary problem: there is no translating the terms without translating the logical devices, and no translating the devices without translating the terms.

So let us return to the problem of translating particular words. The translator looks for sequences of phonemes that recur frequently as parts of sentences, and supposes these to constitute individual words. Their recurrence in occasion sentences may afford definite clues. For example if "Begogavagai" has been translated as "There's a black rabbit" and "Begobavagai" as "There's a black dog," then "black" is a good guess for "bego." Having translated a number of words in this and similar ways, the translator may begin constructing a grammar for the native language; on that basis, he may construct what he believes to be as-yet unwitnessed Native occasion sentences, and query the native with those. "Begoravagai?," might be tried, expecting this to have the same stimulus meaning as "There's a black cat." If the native verdicts with respect to the native sentence in various circumstances agree with the translator's with respect to the English sentence in those circumstances, the hypothesis is corroborated.

The translator may also try out translations of standing sentences: the corroboration sought here is simply that the native verdict with respect to the native sentence should agree with the translator's with respect to the English sentence. Given data about stimulus meaning, the whole system of word-word correlations and mappings of grammatical structures of the one language onto those of the other is what Quine calls a system of "analytical hypotheses." The more that such analytical hypotheses successfully predict the coincidence of verdicts of standing sentences and stimulus meanings of observation sentences, the better confirmed the translation manual.

Imputing Belief

Perfect coincidence is not to be expected, for it is certainly possible that X is a good translation of Y, yet the translator denies X when the native affirms Y. This is because the native and translator might sometimes have different beliefs. Obviously the native, being human, can be expected to make occasional mistakes of the ordinary variety; for example he might assent to "Gavagai!" when it was a cat, not a rabbit. If a substantial body of other observations support the translation as "Rabbit!" and not "Cat!," then the episode can be discarded as a native mistake. But more dramatic falsehoods, or at least divergences of belief between translator and native, cannot be ruled out. For example, the translation manual might all be working extremely well except for one thing: it translates a certain Native sentence, persistently affirmed, as "All rabbits are reincarnated humans"; if changing the manual so as to translate this as something true, or at least something less eccentric, would result in worse disturbances elsewhere in the translation manual, then the translator might have to attribute that belief to the natives.

Indeterminacy of Translation

Having described a method of translation, Quine notes the seeming scantiness of the hard data that informs translation, and the degree of ingenuity required of the translator in coming up with analytical hypotheses. He then observes that analytical hypotheses are not directly answerable to any data: they generate testable consequences in the form of expected stimulus meanings of observation sentences, and assent, dissent, or abstention from standing sentences, but there is no more direct way of confirming them. Thus if there were two systems of analytical hypotheses with the same testable consequences, then there would not be a factual disagreement between them: they are necessary for translation, but go beyond the behavioral facts (*WO*

69–72; see also Hahn and Schilpp 1986, p. 367). And he concludes that there is no categorical way to rule this out, that is, that translation is "indeterminate": the method described could lead to two translation manuals that predict the same behavioral data yet disagree over the translation of at least some Native sentences. Disagree in what sense? In the most extreme: one manual might translate a Native sentence as one English sentence, where the other translates it as another which not only has the opposite truth-value as the first, but which is logically incompatible with it.

Quine advances three further reasons for this infamous conclusion. We will consider the reasons in their ascending order of prominence in Quine's writings, then reflect on what the indeterminacy thesis means—and perhaps more urgently, what it does not mean.

Translation and Belief

The first further reason is one that Quine does not make much of in *Word and Object*, but which we have touched on before, and which became a centerpiece of the philosophy that Davidson was first developing around the time of *Word and Object* (Davidson read drafts of *Word and Object*, and would begin to publish his own contributions to these issues shortly after; see Davidson 1984, p. 27). This is that translation inescapably involves the application of *normative* ideas. As we noted, there will always be a trade-off between translation and the attribution of belief (Davidson would call this the "interdependence" of meaning and belief). Sometimes, the price of smooth translation will be the imputation of false belief; but if the belief is *too* weird, then the price is too high: we had better revise the translation. For otherwise we could just as well translate in such a way that *all* Native standing sentences come out false or even preposterous. But it seems impossible to formulate a precise rule for managing the balance in all cases, from the Martian to the Sherpa to the Dane; surely this will have to be a matter for the translator's judgment, a matter of how the matter strikes him in the particular translational problem that confronts him. Moreover, the concepts used in describing problem cases—*weird, bizarre, irrational*, and so on—are not only vague in the sense of being uncertain of application, they have no analogues in science generally. In general, the maxim that we must not attribute weirdness— severe irrationality or failure of perception—is a "normative" idea, an idea describing what agents ought to do or think. Such concepts are never used in describing, say, jellyfish or planets.

Pressing from Below: The Inscrutability of Reference

For the second further reason, return to the problem of the rabbits and rabbit-stages. Considered as one-word sentences, the stimulus meaning of "Rabbit!" and "Rabbit-stage!" are the same. Thus either would be suitable as a translation of "Gavagai!" The fact that the stimulus meaning of "Rabbit!" matches that of "Gavagai!," then, does not imply that "rabbit" and "gavagai" are synonymous or even co-extensive *terms*. To find out whether the term "gavagai" has the same reference as "rabbit" or "rabbit-stage," as we have seen, we need to fix a translation of some Native expression as "is the same as." We need to know when we have one gavagai or two. Thus suppose we have identified the Native construction "ipso" as a candidate for the "is the same as," and "yo" as a demonstrative pronoun, like "that" in English. The Native, we find, affirms:

(*) Yo gavagai ipso yo gavagai.

He affirms this, we find, when we point at the same rabbit the whole time, no matter how long we wait between the first "yo gavagai" and the second, and affirms it however many times we repeat it, so long as we are pointing at the same rabbit. Unless "gavagai" means a *very long* rabbit-stage, this seems to confirm the hypothesis that "gavagai" means rabbit, not rabbit-stage.

But in fact the rabbit-stage hypothesis is by no means ruled out. Here are two translations of the sentence (*) above:

(1) That rabbit is the same as that rabbit.
(2) That rabbit-stage is part of the same animal as that rabbit-stage.

According to (1), we assume the following translations of sub-sentential parts:

(1*) "gavagai"—"rabbit"
     "ipso"—"is the same as"

Whereas according to (2), we assume:

(2*) "gavagai"—"rabbit-stage"
     "ipso"—"is part of the same animal as"[3]

(1) and (2) have the same stimulus meanings, but they also have the same *truth-conditions*: we have the same rabbit just in case we have rabbit-stages that are part of the same animal (*OR* 4). So clearly the native's speech-dispositions will not fix the reference of the term "gavagai." Of course, the expressions involved in (*)—"gavagai," "ipso"—have uses in the rest of language, so the translations of these will have ramifications for other translations. But presumably, just as

the data left us with choices in assigning references to the parts of (*), so these choices can be compensated for where other choices emerge in connection with other parts of the translation manual (*WO* 71–2; see also *OR* 1–3, 30–5). At least, it cannot be ruled out.

Such is the thesis of the "inscrutability of reference" or what Quine would call the argument for indeterminacy which "presses from below": native speech-dispositions—even if we allow that they do fix the truth-conditions of whole sentences—do not determine the references of terms, i.e., the translation of referring terms. Different assignments of reference can be compensated for by different analyses of what Quine calls the "referential apparatus" of a language: its system of quantifiers, pronouns, and copulae, that is, the "is" of identity and the "is" of predication. The apparent impossibility of deciding between such reference-schemes does not mean that the facts about reference are unknowable. It means that there is no factual difference between them; they constitute, if you like, different ways of construing the same facts.[4]

None of this, it should be stressed, suggests that the translator would be utterly unjustified in preferring (1) to (2). In fact, a real translator would never think of (2), and rightly so (*OR* 3–5). For (1) is of course the more practical and more natural hypothesis. But this does not affect the point: the translator need not choose the natural or easy hypothesis in order to fit the theory to the data.

In later writings Quine would come to deny that the inscrutability of reference entails the indeterminacy of translation (*PT* 50, *SS* 75). The reason is simply that the sorts of jury-rigging of reference described above does not affect the truth-conditions of sentences taken as wholes, and thus cannot by itself yield translations of a given sentence that differ in truth-value. The point might seem merely terminological, since obviously the inscrutability of reference means that the translation of referring *terms* is indeterminate. But there is a more substantial point behind the restriction of the indeterminacy thesis to sentences. According to Quine, but plausibly according also to Frege who wrote that we should "never … ask for the meaning of a word in isolation, but only in the context of a proposition," sentences are the primary units of meaning (*TT* 68–70, *FSS* 6–7, *PT* 56–7; Frege 1953 [1884], p. 71). There is no way to "get at" the meanings of terms except via their effects on the meaning of sentences. If so then if the translation of sentences were determinate, it would be misleading to speak of the indeterminacy of translation just on the grounds of indeterminacy at the level of referring terms. Indeterminacy of translation at the level of whole sentences is more radical.

Pressing from Above: Underdetermination of Theory

Thus the third further reason. In an alternative terminology that Quine used for a time, an argument that "presses from above"—for the indeterminacy of translation of sentences—is a very different animal from one that "presses from below"—for the inscrutability of reference. It derives from the general epistemological holism which Quine had spelled out in "Two Dogmas." Holism implies that, given the set of empirically testable consequences of a theory—*all* of them, past, present, and future—the discovery that one of those consequences is false leaves open any number of adjustments to the theory that would restore the theory's harmony with observation. This suggests that theory is "underdetermined by data": in principle, for any given set of empirical data, more than one theory could account for it equally well.

In formulating a set of analytical hypotheses, the translator is in effect ascribing a theory to the native. For every sentence the natives are disposed to assent to, the translation manual pairs it with some sentence of English, either true or false. The standing sentences accepted by the native constitute—in a broad sense of the word—the native theory. As we saw, there is not much direct evidence for the translation of standing sentences. All that is known about them is that some are accepted and some rejected, and that they contain parts that recur in occasion sentences which, insofar as they are observational, can be translated via stimulus meaning. What is wanted from the translation of standing sentences, then, is that the ones accepted by the natives should come out as logically implying accepted observations, and not as implying rejected ones. What this comes to, for the translator, is that the translations of natively accepted standing sentences should logically imply—in English—the translations of natively accepted observation sentences. That set of English translations of Native standing sentences is our English version of the Native theory.

But if theory is underdetermined by data, then some other set of English sentences could logically imply that set of English equivalents of natively accepted observation sentences. To formulate such an alternative theory would establish the existence of an alternative set of analytical hypotheses for the translation of Native into English: since the alternative theory in English would logically imply the correct set of testable consequences for a translation manual, the completion of the new set of analytical hypotheses could meet no further empirical obstacle, and all that would remain would be the combinatorial puzzle of mapping vocabularies and grammatical structures, in principle no different from that which led to the first translation manual.

This last argument—one that "presses from above"—may be summed up by saying that epistemological holism implies the indeterminacy of translation (see especially *OR* 80ff; also Hahn and Schilpp 1986, pp. 155–6). In fact this argument was not given in *Word and Object*, but in a later paper of 1970, "On the Reasons for the Indeterminacy of Translation" (*CCE* 209–14; see also his "Reply to Chomsky" in Davidson and Hintikka 1969). Indeed, in *Word and Object*, he used the indeterminacy of translation as reason to infer the underdetermination of theory (*WO* 78)! Still later, Quine began to have some doubts about the intelligibility of the underdetermination thesis itself; we will return to this in Chapter 7.

Reflecting on Indeterminacy

The thesis of the indeterminacy of translation can be hard to understand and hard to accept. It seems to deny not only ordinary certainties about our grasp of language, but also some key findings of the linguistics and cognitive psychology of the past fifty years. But it does become easier to accept—it seems less bizarre or outrageous—once it is understood more thoroughly. In this section, we try to come to terms with just what its repercussions really are, and try to see why, from Quine's point of view, it should not really be alarming.

What the Thesis Means

It is important first to be clear what is meant by Quine's claim that there is no "fact of the matter" about correct translation. Quine's naturalism seems to dictate that facts are physical facts: there cannot be an intrinsic factual difference between two states of affairs if there is no physical difference between them. Thus Quine at one stage would construe the claim of "no fact of the matter" as meaning that incompatible translation manuals may be equally compatible with the physical facts (*TT* 23; also "Reply to Chomsky" in Davidson and Hintikka 1969, and *CCE* 209–14). However, this can seem dogmatic, as if meaning must be rejected because it is not a physical property like heat. In later remarks, as well as in *Word and Object*, Quine does not put it that way. As explained at the beginning of this chapter, the claim is more broadly that there is nothing that natural science as we know it could identify as a kind of objective fact that determines translation in the way that we intuitively expect (again *TT* 23; but also Hahn and Schilpp 1986, pp. 187, 429–30; *QQ* 290).

He is certainly not saying that there is no such thing as *good* translation. As we have noted, one translation may be preferred over another because it is more convenient, even if its factual justification is not superior (see *OR* 3–5, 34, 46). Nor is he saying that translation or radical translation is *impossible*. Quite the opposite: the claim is that translation is in principle *too easy*, in the sense that incompatible yet perfectly acceptable translation schemes are possible.

It is of first interest that Quine retreated more recently to characterizing the thesis of the indeterminacy of translation as "speculative," as a "conjecture" ("Indeterminacy of Translation Again" *CCE* 341–6; "Indeterminacy Without Tears"; *CCE* 447–8; "Reply to George," Orenstein and Kotatko 2000, p. 409). For what matters is the *conceivability* of the thesis—that the thesis that alternative translations are in principle available is consistent with a clear-eyed survey of the facts in which radical translation consists. It's the character of the facts of language, of a science of meaning, that are most important to appreciate; the conjecture of indeterminacy merely dramatizes those facts, the situation of the scientist.

Still, it is important to appreciate just how far the fully fledged indeterminacy thesis goes. The most striking consequence is that two translation manuals could be equally empirically adequate in the ways described above, where one of them translates a certain native sentence S as S*, and the other as S**, where it is a logical truth that S* if and only if not S**. A first thought in reply might be that this could surely be ruled out by the need to translate accepted native sentences by English sentences we accept, and rejected ones by rejected ones. Since one but only one of S* and S** is true, find out whether or not the native assents to S, then prefer the translation manual that matches the native's assent to S to the true member of the pair S*, S**, or the native's dissent to the false one. The problem is that this will not in general be both available and efficacious. It may not be available, because the native may simply have no opinion about S: it may be too complicated, or pertain to things he knows nothing about, or involve distinctions he thinks too fine. Alternatively, it may be we who are undecided: we may have no opinion as between S* and S**. But even where we can seek agreement in this way, it may not be efficacious: as we saw, the translator's task is inescapably holistic, in that the translations of individual expressions including sentences are interdependent. Decisions about individual sentences have repercussions for other sentences. Thus, the price of insisting on agreement with the natives in the one case may be disagreements in others; if so, then according to the principle of charity, the price may be too high: according to the need to optimize agreement overall, the insistence should be withdrawn (*WO* 69).

In later comments—"Indeterminacy of Translation Again" (1987) and "Indeterminacy Without Tears" (1994)—Quine proposed another sort of test for indeterminacy: If one translation scheme which is adequate on its own cannot be used in alternation sentence-by-sentence with another equally adequate scheme (without producing bafflement), then we have a case of the indeterminacy of translation. This is preferred as a way of putting the point, presumably, because it does not avail itself of semantical concepts at all—no reference, truth, or negation—and trades only on behavior.

Understanding

The possibility of translating a sentence into sentences with opposite truth-values is the most striking illustration of the thesis that there might be equally correct translations which "stand to each other in no plausible sort of equivalence however loose" (*WO* 27). As we noted earlier, it follows, according to a kind of back-and-forth argument, that even a sentence of one's own language could be "translated" into one's own language into a sentence that one would by no means intuitively recognize as meaning the same. It could even be a sentence that is logically incompatible with it. This can easily seem outrageous. I sincerely and non-ironically say P, but you could correctly understand me as saying not-P??!!?? Not quite. Remember that Quine's task was to discover the objective basis of translation—not to explain how to *understand a speaker.* Understanding is largely an intuitive practical thing, and getting someone to understand something is largely a matter of human skill. It follows from Quine's thesis that there could be some convoluted permutation or recombination of English which would count one sentence as translating another where we would never dream of counting them synonymous. And we saw that real examples of this are likely to concern relatively abstruse matters. Furthermore, communication *within* a language is best served by something that is unavailable in the case of translation between languages, namely actual sameness of linguistic dispositions: we are both disposed to accept "Rabbits are skittish," and so on. Our mutual understanding consists in the sharing of such dispositions, an interactive practical matter. The matching corresponds to what Quine calls "homophonic" translation, the translation of each expression as itself. Someone who spoke according to a non-homophonic translation of English will be unlikely to be understood by a normal English speaker. We could, equivalently, describe him as speaking English but holding a different theory, or as speaking a different language.

Likewise, it does not follow from Quine's thesis that one *does not know what one means*, or does not really understand anything, in the ordinary sense of "knowing what one means" or "understanding." Having a language, for Quine, is having a complex set of verbal dispositions. If knowing what a speaker means is being able to translate the speaker, then one can easily do it with respect to oneself by using the homophonic method: since one has the dispositions one has, a given sentence must always have the same stimulus meaning as it has for oneself, and so on. On the other hand, if knowing what a speaker means is *understanding him* in the practical sense as described above, then it should be conceived as a kind of skill, that is, a matter of knowing-how (to do something) rather than knowing-that (something is true). In that case, one cannot fail to understand one's own language: if having a language is having a set of verbal dispositions, then that is just what it is to have the relevant know-how. Having the know-how is what understanding is. The idea will sound such much like the Pragmatism of Dewey, or like an Ordinary Language philosopher such as (purportedly) Austin, or like the later Wittgenstein; Quine explicitly accepted the affinity (*OR* 27).

Bilinguals

For the same reason, it is irrelevant to Quine's thesis that two radical translators whose aim is simply to translate the native language would probably come up with similar translation manuals. It is also irrelevant that a genuine bilingual, though in some way authoritative, would not have to translate in the self-conscious way that Quine describes; nor that two such bilinguals might well agree for the most part in their translations (*OR* 5, *TT* 54). For, again, the distance between Quine's concern and questions about actual understanding cannot be over-stressed. Given a sentence of the one language, what the translating bilingual does, roughly, is to ask himself what he would say in the other language to get the same effect. Since he knows how to speak both languages, an appropriate sentence will typically come to mind. He need have no more idea of the objective data for translation, and of what justifies it, than one does just by virtue of the ability to speak one's own language. The bilingual's ability to translate stands to the Quinean translator's task in much the same relation that a golfer's ability to sink a putt from 20 feet stands to the physicist's task of calculating the precise angular momentum with which a clubhead of a given size, shape, and mass must strike the ball in order to knock it into the hole. The bilingual in some sense "chooses" a set of analytical hypotheses, but only in the sense in which the golfer chooses a precise angular momentum—not necessarily in a way that he could specify in the theoretical vocabulary relevant to the problem.

Linguistics

It is important also to acknowledge that the fact that some translations are "natural" and some are not is by no means a trivial fact, of no theoretical relevance or interest (see *OR* 3–5). On the contrary, the tremendous advances in linguistics begun largely by Noam Chomsky show among many other things what is theoretically substantive about the naturalness of some translations over others.[5] I will revisit the topic in slightly more depth and generality in Chapter 7; here I want specifically to sketch Quine's attitude toward the uneasy encounter between the indeterminacy of translation and the science of linguistics as Chomsky conceives it.

The basic Chomskyan thesis is that the human brain has evolved to be disposed to acquire languages of a certain general kind according to a certain abstract grammatical template which comprises such categories as phrase, noun phrase, verb phrase, and so on, along with certain possibilities of analysis and combination. The infant language-learner approaches the data—the verbal behavior of people around him or her—constrained to assimilate the perceived language going on to that template, that is, to the categories and principles of Universal Grammar, as it is now known. The assimilation is mirrored in the transformational grammars drawn up by linguists, which map actual human languages onto this so-called deep structure (this is a famous but now superseded way of describing it; the changes won't matter for our purposes). In this sense, grammar—abstract grammar common to all known languages—is innate, pre-wired into the human brain as part of its evolved biological endowment.

Arguably, then, what makes one translation manual more natural than another might well be that the transformational grammar it implies is simpler than that implied by the other: since according to the Chomskyan outlook, grammatical transformations are actually realized in the human brain during language-processing—that is, during linguistic performance and understanding—we should expect, modulo certain caveats, the linguistic structures requiring simpler transformations to be those that subjectively seem more natural or familiar (see Hahn and Schilpp 1986, pp. 186–7). Now as Quine points out (*WO* 76), the grammatical similarities amongst such languages as English, German, Dutch, and so on are largely due to their having common ancestors, and to their constant interplay down through the centuries. No wonder they map onto each other so readily. But further—despite some legends to the contrary—even *across* such language-families, human languages all prove to be intertranslatable, and bilinguals do not become actual schizophrenics.[6] Thus, if the theory of Universal Grammar is right, then even where the remotest languages are concerned, there is reason to doubt that two radical translators working independently will come up with dramatically different manuals. The translators will naturally and quite rightly read as much familiar structure and semantical categorization as they can into the native language, not just because they are lazy.

All the same, Quine can resist. However complicated or otherwise bizarre a translation manual that meets Quine's empirical criteria—however far it departs from what would yield the simplest Chomskian grammatical transformations—it does not thereby misrepresent anything that can rightly be called *meaning* (*WP* 56–8, *CCE* 271–2). For meaning, recall, is assumed to be something public, something that can be recovered from linguistic behavior (which boil down to assent and dissent). The cognitive processing of grammatical transformations, however essential their natural human form may be for actual human understanding of language, is of no concern for the detection of meaning. To make this vivid, suppose there were some genetic disease that causes the human brain to process language in an abnormal way; drastically different from what goes on in a normally functioning human language module, and perhaps more complicated. Those with the disease do learn to speak as everyone else does, but perhaps it takes them longer; their language processing is more circuitous, it takes them longer to catch on to the linguistic classifications that normal humans learn readily, and so on. Once they learn the language, however, they speak like everyone else. If so, then it makes no difference to the translator whether the person being translated has the disease or not. If two people have the same verbal dispositions, only one of which has the disease, then a translation manual that works for one of them will work equally well for the other, and would be equally correct with respect to either. If so then the psychology of language-processing, though of profound theoretical interest in its own right, is irrelevant to questions of semantics, at least as regarded in Quine's way, via the critical methodology of radical translation.

More on Indeterminacy and Underdetermination

I have minimized the incompatibility between Chomsky and Quine, but Chomsky himself does not accept that Quine's "linguistic behavior" comprises a suitable field for the study of language, and Quine has some serious reservations about some central claims of Chomsky's. The issues between Chomsky and

Quine would require another book adequately to explore—and I'll revisit them in the final chapter—but Chomsky did make a certain objection that is worth pausing over here, one that has a general and thoroughgoing philosophical angle (Davidson and Hintikka 1969, pp. 53–68; for Quine's reply see Davidson and Hintikka 1969, "Reply to Chomsky," pp. 302–11).

We said that, according to Quine, translation is holistic: translations of individual standing sentences cannot be empirically justified except insofar as they are given by a whole translation manual that is empirically justified as a whole. However, this does not in itself distinguish translation from other sorts of theory. As we saw, Quine himself holds that the confirmation of theories in general is always holistic. No non-trivial theory is empirically determined by data: any theory could in principle be replaced by another that has the same observational consequences. So why, then, isn't the purported possibility of alternative translation manuals just a special case of the underdetermination of theory? The underdetermination of physics by its data doesn't lead Quine to say that there is no fact of the matter about physics, so why pick on translation?

Despite the presumed underdetermination of physical theory, there is no temptation to say that, this being the case, it is not really a fact that water molecules contain two hydrogen atoms. The reason is that we must always, as Quine puts it, *occupy* a theory. According to Naturalism, we must always speak from the point of view of a theory. It is not as if we could possess a language, yet remain undecided as to what to say, what to assert (compare the situation of Descartes at the end of Meditation I). To possess a language is to possess verbal *dispositions*, hence dispositions to *say* or to *assent* to certain things. The sum of what we would be disposed to assent to comprises our theory, in the broadest sense. To possess a language is thus to possess a theory. Our theory of nature, our scientific account of how and what the world is—with caveats as will be seen—is a physical theory: reality is physical, consisting of energy and matter in space-time. Our attitude toward this theory, or Quine's attitude at least, is fully realistic: there really are electrons, protons, neutrons, anti-protons, quarks, and all the rest of it (we will discuss Quine's realism further in Chapter 5). Theories that deal with reality at higher levels of organization—chemistry, biology, geology, and so on—are not logically determined by physics or reducible to it, but the processes and structures they describe are realized by, made up of, the entities dealt with directly by physics, and a central aim is always to explain higher-level phenomena in terms of lower levels, as in the explanation of biological phenomena in terms of chemical phenomena (biochemistry). But now consider, as Quine puts it, *all* this truth—all true statements expressible in the language of physics and the higher-level physical sciences, including those pertaining to the future. Translation remains undetermined: as even Chomsky accepts, different sets of analytical hypotheses could fit the facts equally well. But if physical fact does not determine translation, then nothing determines it, since reality is physical (again in a more elastic sense of "physicalism," where "the physical" is whatever is continuous with or implied by paradigm physical objects; see *WO* 75-6; also *CCE* 209-14, and "Reply to Chomsky" in Davidson and Hintikka 1969, pp. 302-4).

It would be tempting to summarize this by saying that the truth of physicalism is a premise in the argument for the indeterminacy of translation. And then one might worry that this merely begs the question, or that it assumes an insupportably austere metaphysical view: why isn't semantics simply one of the higher-level sciences? But perhaps the best way to see the matter—or rather the best way to see it as Quine does—is not to look for a kind of proof that translation is indeterminate. That reality is physical—in the sense that physics, replete with quantum theory and perhaps more, supplies the most basic description of reality—is for Quine an empirical discovery, at least in the sense that reality's being physical is something that scientific method assumes as its best working hypothesis. In view of this, the question to ask should be: given that translation is undetermined by physical fact, what is to be *gained* by supposing that some translation manuals—the ones we find most natural or convenient, or the ones that best run along the rails of our native language-processing— report the semantical facts, whereas others, despite being equally empirically confirmed, do not? In making such a supposition, we are not thereby afforded any further *explanation*, any further insight into what everyone agrees are the underlying facts. The supposition, we might say, would be gratuitous: semantics would be counted as factual only by courtesy. As Quine puts it, "we could posit [fixed meanings] out of hand, but they would be nomological danglers" (Hahn and Schilpp 1986, p. 364).

As you might expect, Chomsky thinks that Quine's move is indeed to throw the baby out with the bathwater—to have not only an unjustified prejudice against the mental, but a too-simplistic and outmoded conception of what the mental is and how to theorize about it (e.g. Chomsky 2000, pp. 57–61). He denies what was just said about explanation and underlying facts. The conflict is deep, not superficial; we shall return to it in Chapter 7.

Lexicography

Finally, we should point out that the negative status of meaning which the indeterminacy thesis implies does not imply that the ordinary use of the word "meaning" is somehow nonsense or illegitimate, is if the lexicographers of the world are all a lot of charlatans. On the contrary, Quine himself is quite the enthusiast of what they do, and takes pains to explain it (*FSS* 83, *PT* 56–9, *TT* 203–8, *FLPV* 58–9, Hahn and Schilpp 1986, pp. 365–7, *Q* 130–1). What it does imply is that the use of the word "meaning" and its cousins is more toward the pragmatic end of the pragmatic/theoretical spectrum, even if a very important and interesting one at that. When someone asks "What does that word mean?," our task is to enable that person to use the word in sentences. How we do this will depend on what sort of word it is. In some cases there is some other word that is sufficiently interchangeable with the word in question, and we can just cite that. We can almost always use "help" for "assist," for example; so we say "'assist' means 'help.'" In other cases there is no such equivalent, and we will suggest a few near-misses; or we simply give a few telling examples of the correct use of the word in whole sentences, hoping the questioner will catch on. In still other cases we don't bother about the *word* so much as describing the *thing*; the dictionary doesn't *define* a word like "tiger" so much as describe the animal, perhaps telling us about the size, the stripes, its feline genus, where it lives. So much is exactly of a piece with Quine's denial of a sharp boundary between matters of meaning and matters of fact. Dictionaries, as Quine points out, are not sharply distinct from encyclopedias.

Further Reading and Historical Notes

Indeterminacy of Translation was major topic in the 1960s, 1970s, and 1980s. Some of Quine's replies to commentators—in Davidson and Hintikka 1969, Hahn and Schilpp 1986, Barrett and Gibson 1993, Leonardi and Santambrogio 1995, and Orenstein and Kotatko 2000—are very helpful on the Indeterminacy of Translation. They should inure one to the many misunderstandings abroad. For a longer run-through of the argument for the Indeterminacy of Translation, and the significance of it, see Hylton 2007 Ch. 8. See Severo 2022 for astute observations on the argument that "presses from above"; see Sinclair 2002 and my Kemp 2022 for further details on stimulus meaning. A good question—which I have not taken up in this book as being too involved—is how does the seemingly similar view of Davidson's differ (as in "Radical Interpretation," in his 1984). See my Kemp 2012.

Naturalized Epistemology and
The Roots of Reference

Reciprocal Containment

Empiricist epistemology—the sort we associate with Locke, Berkeley, and Hume, and in its logically supercharged forms with Russell and Carnap—divides into two tasks. The first—Quine calls it the "doctrinal" one—is better known, both for its defining hope and for its apparent futility: the task of justifying our claimed knowledge of the physical world strictly in terms of sense-data, impressions, experience, phenomenology, the sensory given, or some such thing (*OR* 69). Only a few have thought the thing possible, but many have regarded it as a kind of holy grail of epistemology, worth trying if there were any hint of success. The other— Quine calls it the "conceptual" one—differs from the first in that all the above-named have earnestly thought it possible: the task of the conceptual reduction of our purported knowledge of the world to discourse referring only to sense data, the sensory given, or the like. Success in the one would not entail success in the other: one could perhaps imagine the justification without the reduction, but more definitely not the other way round: even if all sentences about the physical world were translated into sentences about the sensory given, the question of which ones were true, and which justified, would remain. "[G]eneral statements," observes Quine, "also singular statements about the future, gained no increment of certainty by being construed as about impressions" (*OR* 72).

The task of conceptual reduction was the one that Carnap explored in the *Aufbau*. As we saw, Quine argued that it cannot be carried out, however desirable it would be if it could (*TT* 22–3). So neither task of empiricist epistemology is viable. Yet Quine by no means concludes that either empiricism or epistemology is a dead-end. On the contrary, he refines the claims and tasks of epistemology so as to make good on the basic claim that the only requirement on knowledge is accord with experience, and to point the way toward positive advances in epistemology, toward a sound theoretical understanding of human knowledge. He never gave up on the idea that "[T]he stimulation of his sensory receptors is all the evidence anybody has had to go on, ultimately, in arriving at his picture of the world" (*OR* 75–6). As we will see, this understanding is largely to be delivered by empirical psychology, even if Quine is most interested in the matters of abstract principle that lie furthest from actual experimentation. This does not, however, mark an abrupt change of subject from the concerns of *Word and Object*. For reasons we have touched on and will get into further below, Quine sees the possession of knowledge largely as consisting in the possession of a language. His psychological concerns focus primarily on the acquisition and structure of the human language-capacity, and dovetail neatly with the linguistic categories developed in chapter 2 of *Word and Object*. They also develop them further.

This chapter will introduce the reader to Quine's psychological work, his "Naturalized Epistemology"; we will also go back over some of his key linguistic concepts, but from a different angle, largely the one that Quine takes in his book the *Roots of Reference* (1973). It is epistemology *naturalized*, of course, because epistemology is now being conceived as a branch of natural science. Its interest lies partly in its actual details, especially in Quine's account of what constitutes *reference*, the capacity to talk about objects in the world; but also partly in the further philosophical issues it throws up concerning scientific method and the relation of philosophy to science. Naturalized Epistemology and more generally Naturalism—Naturalized Philosophy—were definitely up and running by the time *Word and Object* of 1960, but took hold in Quine's thought only gradually, and certainly were not called by those names until "Naturalized Epistemology" of 1968 (see also "Five Milestones of Empiricism" of 1975, and the chapter "Naturalism" of *FSS*; see Verhaegh 2018 for further details of Quine's development).

Before entering into these matters in earnest there is one matter of principle that needs to be cleared up, a certain principle of naturalism. A central question of epistemology, especially as handed down from Descartes, has been the question of what justifies our presumed knowledge. Quine claims to be an empiricist, and as noted says such things as that sensory stimulation is all we have to "go on" on arriving at our knowledge of the world. So he seems to accept in some way the challenge posed by the first task described above. Yet psychology—of which Quine claims epistemology to be a proper part—is itself a part of our knowledge of the world. Doesn't the appeal to psychology thus involve us in circular reasoning? If psychology is a science known only via sensory stimulation, surely we cannot appeal to it to tell us that information from the senses is reliable. It would be like reading the newspaper to find out whether or not the newspaper is reliable.

The answer is that Quine's claim about what we have to go on does not really indicate acceptance of the first task. We must certainly give up "dreaming of deducing science from sense-data" (*OR* 84). "I am of that large minority or small majority" as he puts it in *Pursuit of Truth,* "who repudiate the Cartesian dream of a foundation for scientific inquiry firmer than scientific method itself" (*PT* 19). Quine rejects "first philosophy" (*TT* 67), urging instead the "recognition that it is within science itself, and not in some prior philosophy, that reality is to be identified and described" (*TT* 21).

Quine's empiricism is not the idea that sensation or sensory experience is all that can ever justify knowledge-claims, and he might well accept that no one can prove that they are not dreaming, or that it is not all a big hallucination. But he rejects the whole enterprise of finding something more secure than science or ordinary knowledge-claims on which they might be based. If such a thing is *impossible,* then it is pointless to try it. There are scattered reasons for thinking it impossible, but perhaps the overriding one is simply that the history of attempts to find such a thing have been uniformly unsuccessful; this in turn shows that if we assume we *do* have more or less the knowledge we think we do, and we *do* want to understand the relation of sensory evidence to theory, then it is *not* going to be: the sensory evidence justifies the theory, in the sense that the theory is somehow logically derivable from it. (Contrast Russell, who, in *The Problems of Philosophy*, assumed that ordinary beliefs about the external world are generally justified—but also accepted at more or less face value the task of justifying them on the basis of the occurrence of sense data.[1]) Note also the connection of this with the thesis that there is no such thing as knowledge that is wholly *a priori,* that is, which in principle could not be upset by anything empirical: If there is a Cartesian foundation which explains why beliefs about the physical world are justified by experience, then presumably it would have to be *a priori*; if nothing is quite *a priori,* then perhaps no such thing is possible.

The distance between traditional and naturalized epistemology is vividly illustrated by what they have to say about Hume's problem of *induction,* the problem of extrapolating the observed to the unobserved (it was touched on in Chapter 1). Kant took it at face value, and sought an *a priori* proof that induction is valid. According to Quine, no such thing is possible. "The Humean predicament," he wrote, "is the human predicament" (*OR* 72). But neither is such a thing needed. The principle of induction—or rather the various principles that underlie good induction—is more general or abstract than particular laws of nature, but they are, all the same, empirical. They are thoroughly interwoven with and assumed by empirical science as a whole, and thus could not be withdrawn without the collapse of empirical science. But according to holism, that is par for the course: holism explains why the most general principles or laws are exceedingly unlikely to be revoked, without thereby counting them *a priori,* categorically distinct from empirical truths generally. Indeed as has emerged from twentieth-century studies of induction by Carl Hempel, Nelson Goodman, and others, the question of what makes for good induction is far more closely interwoven with the question of what the world is like than Hume or Kant realized; all the more reason to deny that natural science depends on a pure *a priori* principle of induction (*OR* 114–38).

What then *is* the status of the claim that sensory stimulation is all we ever have to go on? The claim has two aspects, descriptive and normative. In its descriptive aspect, the claim is based on experience. We find that certain creatures receive sensory stimulation, and are so disposed that, in consequence, they come to express verbally a theory of the world, speaking not only of rabbits and rain but of microscopic animals, sub-atomic particles, quasars and black holes, the spatial and temporal limits of the cosmos, irrational numbers, and infinite sets. There is broadly a causal relation between sensory stimulation and theory, primarily a neurological one. Naturalized epistemology is the study of that exceedingly complex relation. It is philosophical—in the sense that its concern is a highly abstract one about knowledge—but it is still science:

> It is part and parcel of empirical science itself ... The motivation is still philosophical, as motivation in natural science tends to be ... Unlike the old epistemologists, we seek no firmer basis for science than science itself; so we are free to use the very fruits of science in investigating its roots. It is a matter, as always in science, of tackling one problem with the help of our answers to others.
>
> (*SS* 16; see also *OR* 78, *RR* 2–3)

The claim's normative aspect is not *a priori* either; rather it derives from the descriptive empirical aspect. One thing that experience teaches is that hypotheses not based on observation—those of soothsayers, religious sages, perhaps metaphysicians—seldom make for correct predictions (*PT* 19). Of course as we know from the thesis of the underdetermination of theory, *no* theory is based merely on observation. In successful science, rather, we typically begin with theories that do have some record of successful empirical prediction, and alter them with a view to making more and even better predictions. Famously, such alteration or hypothesis-formation is not precisely rule-governed; rather there are general maxims of conservatism, simplicity and familiarity in addition to the imperative to maximize correct prediction of observation (see *WB* for much more). Standards for what count as good science are therefore set by science itself: science shows us what sort of theories work, and also how they might be improved. Normative epistemology, then, is a bit like engineering or medicine, in that its aim is to derive prescriptions for how to do something—in this case how to formulate theories—based on what has been successful in the past and what not. In fact the analogy with medicine is perhaps more than analogy, as both epistemology and medicine are partly struggles pitting knowledge of nature against nature:

> Normative epistemology is the art or technology not only of science, in the austere sense of the word, but of rational belief generally ... Podiatry, appendectomy and the surgical repair of hernias are technological correctives of bad side effects of natural selection, and such also in essence is normative epistemology in its correcting and refining of our innate propensities to expectation by induction. A vest-pocket specimen of this is the exposure and correction of the gambler's fallacy: the insidious notion that a run of bad luck increases the likelihood that the next try will win.
>
> (*FSS* 50; see also Hahn and Schilpp 1986, pp. 664–5)

Unlike norms of so-called abduction—the framing of new hypotheses or theories based upon what best explains the phenomenon—norms of induction— the prediction of events based on observed patterns—do admit of rigorous mathematical treatment (statistics, some forms of probability theory, decision theory, inductive logic), but the point is the same: neither are *a priori*, and both sorts of theory are normative, or have direct normative implications. Of course the same could be said for deductive logic itself, even if the idea that is not *a priori* is more distinctively Quinean, and harder to swallow whole.

All of this may be summed up by Quine's phrase "reciprocal containment" (*OR* 83; see also *WP* 230). Natural science contains epistemology in the sense that epistemology is one of several branches of natural science. Epistemology contains natural science in that its subject-matter is the whole of natural science, in the broadest sense of the word "science," encompassing human knowledge as a whole: it seeks to understand the general dynamics and structure of the whole thing. Normativity, meanwhile, flows both ways: by example, successful science shows epistemology what sort of theory works, and serves as its model; but epistemology, taking the wider view, self-consciously articulates the success of science in its most general patterns, and may thus issue correctives. Similarly, a good tennis coach learns the best way by watching the best players, and may then correct the less accomplished, without thereby claiming to know something that is not already exemplified by what tennis players do.

Evidence and the Connection of Language to the World

According to many positivists or logical empiricists of the 1930s, the meaning of a sentence can be identified with its observational consequences, its *verification conditions*. Some sentences have no observational consequences, in the sense that they are consistent with any observations: those are the analytic sentences. Quine, as we saw, denies that, besides observation sentences themselves, individual sentences have particular sets of observational consequences of their own: the thesis of epistemological holism was that only whole theories have observation consequences. Another way to put the same point is that there is no such thing as evidence for or against a single theoretical statement; only whole theories can be supported or contravened by evidence (even if, in practice, we often single out a single statement of a given theory as the one being tested; for example when checking fingerprints on the murder weapon, we may consider "Jones was the murderer" to be at issue, not the whole theory of fingerprints). In later work—especially in "Two Dogmas in Retrospect" of 1991—he would soften his view somewhat, averring that theoretical sentences have their empirical consequences only as parts of larger "chunks" theory, "clusters of sentences just inclusive enough to have critical semantic mass" (268); but this complication is best set aside for now.

Now Quine does not deny that meaning should in some sense be identified with verification conditions or empirical consequences. He writes, for example:

> Language is socially inculcated and controlled; the inculcation and control turn strictly on the keying of sentences to shared stimulation. Internal factors may vary *ad libitum* without prejudice to communication as long as the keying of language to external stimuli is undisturbed. Surely one has no choice but to be an empiricist so far as one's theory of linguistic meaning is concerned.
>
> (*OR* 81; see also *RR* 33–7)

The point should be familiar from Chapter 3: since meaning is necessarily public, attributions of meaning must be answerable to observable speech behavior. This comes down, as we have seen, to matters of assent and dissent from sentences, especially observation sentences (see *TT* 40, *OR* 84). The verification of theory and the assignment of meaning thus concern the very same thing. The verification theory of meaning, then, went wrong only in being atomistic, assigning verification conditions to sentences independently. Just as the unit of verification should be the whole theory, the unit of meaning, in a sense, is the whole language (though for strict accuracy, more nuance would be required in view of later developments, as noted).

To study observation sentences and their relation to the rest of a creature's language is the same thing as studying the relation of evidence to theory. But, since we are now in the field of naturalized as opposed to classical epistemology, we study this relation naturalistically, as a matter of psychology, or rather psycholinguistics (see *TT* 40).

There is also a point to make as to the kind of thing that evidence is, or rather a point about what it is not. The classical epistemologist was right to single out the relation of evidence to theory as critical for schematizing science, but wrong to think that the relation is that evidence, where conceived as observation, justifies theory. But now that we are taking the naturalistic stance, how exactly should the notion of *evidence* be conceived? The empiricists, following Descartes in this respect, thought that science can and must be seen to be justified by whatever is most certain. And that, for the empiricist, was the occurrence of sensory experience, items of subjective experience: whatever else may be so, one cannot doubt that one is getting a red-sensation, or a tickle. But is the evidence for a scientific theory—that is, science as actually practiced—best conceived as the occurrence of sense data or some such thing? Certainly it is not. Not only is the domain of such experience highly fugitive and variable (see *RR* 33–7); it is not even likely that memory—without which observational data would not be of much use—generally works by retaining sense data, like old photographs (*FSS* 15, *RR* 33). On the contrary, although some memories are like that, memory tends to involve conceptualization of some sort, recall of objects and events rather than patches of color and the like. Furthermore—and this is the crucial point—sense data differ from the evidence relevant to science in being subjective, private, and not shareable: whatever the evidence for science is, it is something available to different scientists working together (*RR* 37–9; *TT* 24–30, 39–40; *PT* 1–3; *CCE* 409–19). Even if different scientists do have different sense-data when agreeing to an observation sentence, that does not matter (*FSS* 5). Observation sentences, then, seem to be exactly the right sort of thing for the naturalized epistemologist to regard as evidence: they are public and easily retained. This is not quite right, but for now it will do.

Let us now say something further as to why Quine places observation *sentences* at the forefront of epistemology, and not, say, linguistic *terms* such as "red." For surely, we might think, it is this sort of thing, the application of a word such as "red" to something red, that is most utterly basic to language. Locke, for example, took such a view, and so did some of the early logical positivists. There is a decisive reason, however, for singling out the sentence. The radical translator was faced with the problem of distilling meaning from linguistic behavior. But the only information he could get relevant to the references of *terms* was via the assent-conditions of *sentences*. The method of query-and-assent delivers fairly direct information about the truth-conditions of sentences, but *reference*—the basic semantical property of names and general terms—has to be worked out indirectly from information about truth-conditions of sentences. For the same reason, the items of evidence needed for the analysis of science, if they are linguistic, must be sentences: only about those things does it make sense to speak of scientists agreeing or disagreeing, hence as using to corroborate or discredit theories, and to confirm their mutual understanding.

Agreed verdicts on observation sentences, then, constitute the "empirical checkpoints" for theory for the same reason that they are what make translation possible (*FSS* 44). This is so important that it's worth emphasizing: For Quine, *the connection between language and the world is not the relation of reference.* Despite the title of his best-known book, language does not attach to the world via the connection between word and object. The attachment consists of the causal relation between stimulations and observation sentences. From a naturalistic point of view, this is a welcome consequence, since the notion of reference has always seemed rather mysterious, as if there were mental rays reaching out to distant galaxies, to numbers and other abstract objects, and so on.

Considered in themselves, observation sentences are simply conditioned responses: upon receiving certain stimulations, the native becomes disposed to assent to "Gavagai!," and perhaps comes out with it outright. Observation sentences are in that regard much like the cries of apes and birds, except that ape and bird cries are mostly innate rather than conditioned responses (*FSS* 20, 22, 89).[2] Obviously, human knowledge is vastly more complex than the possession of assorted animal cries. As we will see, the added complexity requires what Quine calls the *referential* apparatus of language: reference is not relevant to the explanation of observation sentences as such—no more so than it is to the explanation of animal cries—but the referential apparatus is essential to the capacity of language to house the full run of human knowledge. In particular, it is what makes possible the expression of fully fledged theoretical laws and their evidential connections to observation sentences. Thus in order to explain the way in which the superstructure of theory is supported by observation sentences, we have to look at observation sentences a little more closely, explaining the way in which the referential apparatus weaves them into language as a whole.

Focusing on the Individual

A simple rendition of *Word and Object* might have it as defining observation sentences as those for which verdicts depend only on present stimulation, and whose stimulus meanings do not vary between members of the community; then as proposing that the translator should translate observation sentences by matching stimulus meanings: one observation sentence should be translated as another just in case the stimulus meanings of the two coincide. To learn an observation sentence is thus to learn to be disposed to assent to it under a certain range of stimulations. But as we have seen, there are two minor complications, plus a major one. The first minor one is that whether or not sentence is observational is relative to the modulus, that is, to the length of the stimulus: a very long modulus could make virtually any sentence observational, since it could include the learning of a theory. The second minor one is that the observationality of an occasion sentence is a matter of degree, since there is a range of cases between something like "That's cold!" and something like "She's pregnant!," depending on the amount of collateral information or theory that mediates between stimulation and disposition to assent. Observation sentences, the maximally non-theoretical checkpoints of theory, should be minimally sensitive to collateral information. The idea was that whereas collateral information would tend to vary throughout the community, dispositions to assent to something like "Cold!" would not, or at least only to a tiny degree.

Those complications can be set aside for most purposes. Generally by an observation sentence we mean an occasion sentence that is highly insensitive to collateral information, and which remains observational even relative to a very short modulus—a few seconds, say. A major complication that can also be set aside at present—we'll take it up again later—but deserves a bit of commentary at this stage, is this. By the time of *Roots of Reference*, Quine had stated that by a "stimulation" he meant the firing of some subset of one's sensory receptors. The complication arises from the assumption that to translate observation sentences involves matching stimulus meanings: for whether or not to translate "Gavagai!"

as "Rabbit!" certainly does not depend on whether or not the native's sensory-receptors are exactly similar to the translator's—no more than whether or not the native's inner mental events are exactly similar to the translator's (see *PT* 40). For the same reason, the status of a sentence as observational should not depend on whether or not it has the same stimulus meaning throughout the community.

In the 1981 essay "Things and Their Place in Theories," Quine thus swapped invariability of stimulus meaning over the community for invariability for a given speaker over time: a sentence is observational *for a speaker* just in case his disposition to assent to it reliably comes and goes depending on sensory stimulation, *and* the range of stimulation on which the disposition depends remains relatively stable over time. A sentence could be defined as observational outright, then, just in case it is observational for every member of the community. However even this won't do, as he came to see by the time of *Pursuit of Truth* of 1992: it doesn't rule out that "a sentence could be observational for each of various speakers without their being disposed to assent to it in the same situations" (*PT* 41). He therefore settled on an observation sentence being "an occasion sentence on which speakers of the language can agree outright [on a verdict] on witnessing the occasion" (*PT* 3).

There are more complexities arising in connection with observation sentences, but they can be deferred to the final chapter. The point for now is that Naturalized epistemology need not be affected by these points about communication by means of observation sentences, about their translation. Using the definition formulated in *Pursuit of Truth* we can ask, of a given observational sentence, how an *individual* succeeds in learning it, how the transition is made from observation sentences to theory, and so on. All these remain, so far, matters of objectively describable fact concerning the individual.

The Psychology of Learning

When a child learns language, the child acquires a conceptual scheme, embodying a theory of the world. According to it, there are various sorts of physical objects in space, which persist over time, which causally interact; to a greater or lesser extent, these respond to being pushed, kicked, heated, and so on, depending on whether they are mere sticks or stones, artifacts or animals, and if so which particular kind. Eventually the child, if educated, learns about things he or she never directly experiences or couldn't: historically remote events, distant galaxies, sub-atomic particles, curved space-time, irrational numbers.

Quine's interest in how the conceptual scheme is acquired, it should be stressed, is not an undifferentiated interest in how the child learns language. His interest, rather, is epistemology: he is interested in what features of language-acquisition are especially relevant to the acquisition of scientific theory, how they fit together, which features play which roles in theory, and so on. So Quine's linguistic categories, as will see, are often rather orthogonal to the grammatical categories employed in theoretical linguistics or traditional grammar. They will leave out a great deal of what we might for other purposes regard as essential to language, and they otherwise slice up language in different ways. Quine's question is: *given* that such-and-such linguistic abilities are the ones that constitute the possession of theoretical knowledge, what does the child have to do to acquire *those?* So Quine will ignore a great deal of what language is in practice—language used to tell jokes, issue commands, express desires, and so on. Not only is his interest restricted to the domain of *statements*—the domain of truth and knowledge—but to certain characteristic forms of statement of most interest in coming to understand the language in which science is housed (see *RR* 92). This will largely take the form of logical schematization, for logic is by definition interested only in the sheer factual element of statements, that is, in truth and truth-conditions. Quine's task, like Carnap's, remains in one way a task of rational reconstruction rather than sheer description: what Quine is describing is something like an idealized mechanism or system, of interest to epistemology in the same way that a ball released on a smooth frictionless plane is of interest to the theory of gravity: since our interest is restricted to certain features or properties, it is better to discuss the simplified or idealized model than have to cope with the irrelevant complexities involved in actual examples (roughness and lack of perfect straightness in the surface, imperfections in the ball, atmospheric pressure, and so on).

Behaviorism and Empiricism

Of course such models are of little value if they do not connect suitably to reality. So Quine will need to say something about how actual human beings could acquire and possess the range of linguistic abilities relevant to epistemology. Locke along with some early empiricists held that the mind at birth is like a blank slate onto which experience is imprinted. The imprints accumulate, with like ones being somehow grouped together to form concepts, the items of thought in which knowledge is housed. The model of pure classical conditioning, formulated by Hume but proposed in a strictly physicalist guise by behaviorist psychology in the first half of the twentieth century, is similar. The child begins by behaving more-or-less randomly—sometimes in response to stimulation and sometimes not, arms and legs flail about, the mouth babbles. Some of these actions are followed by pleasure, others by pain. The child is innately driven to repeat the pleasurable sequences and avoid the painful ones: neural signals that brought about pleasure are repeated, those that brought pain inhibited. The child thus learns to behave in such a way as to bring about pleasure and avoid pain. The parallel with early philosophical empiricism is that the envisaged learning mechanism is completely general, and what is learned depends entirely on stimulation or experience. In neither scenario is the mind quite like a mass of jelly, that is, completely without any innate propensities relevant to learning—the liking for pleasure and averseness to pain are not learned—but they are minimal: in neither case is the mind equipped prior to experience with any detail as to how reality might be.

Although his name is associated with both empiricism and behaviorism, Quine does not accept either of the above pictures of learning or the acquisition of knowledge. Quine calls himself an empiricist because, as we have seen, he accepts that aside from so-called pragmatic factors such as simplicity and familiarity, nothing corroborates theory in any field but observation and experiment. These are not criteria of *truth*, but they tell us which theories to accept and which not; they are "what decides the game"—the game being the "language game" of science—"like runs and outs in baseball" (*PT* 20). His behaviorism, as pointed out earlier, applies only to the theory of linguistic meaning, and is a consequence of his empiricism as applied to the theory of meaning. Since there is nothing to observe that is relevant to meaning besides linguistic behavior, there is no justification for ascriptions of meaning that are not answerable to observable linguistic behavior. As we saw, Quine accommodates this demand in the most direct way possible, equating the possession of a language with the possession of a set of verbal dispositions.

Similarity Spaces

However, Quine was certainly influenced by behaviorist psychology. A psychology class from his undergraduate days made an impression, and he had as a colleague the behaviorist psychologist B. F. Skinner in the 1950s, who is popularly associated with the idea that pure classical conditioning or "operant conditioning" can explain all learning. And in general, Quine is reluctant to posit complex learning mechanisms when simpler ones, in principle, could explain the learning in question (*TT* 184–6). But Quine, along with everyone else who has thought about the problem sufficiently, accepted that no such completely general or unspecific learning mechanism as pure undifferentiated classical or operant conditioning could suffice for human learning, certainly not that involved in the acquisition of language and knowledge (*RR* 19, *WP* 56–8). The main problem is that of the "similarity space." The child cannot learn by seeking to repeat the *exact* sequence of neural signals that led to pleasure, for the child will hardly if ever get the chance. The mother's breast, for example, undergoes its vicissitudes, and may never be glimpsed from precisely the same angle as last time, or felt in exactly the same way; furthermore each perception of it will be accompanied by miscellaneous other sensations that vary from time to time, of bodily heat and cold, the texture of fabrics, and so on. What the child has to do is to focus on certain features of the overall sensory episode, and regard further episodes as ripe for action just in case they possess those features. But what features? For what sorts of features should the child be on the lookout? If the child were not innately disposed to pick up on some sorts of features of the sensory episode as relevant and worth looking out for, and others not, then clearly the child could never learn: for every sensory episode has *something* in common with every other (and something that distinguishes it from every other). The cat and the stuffed animal, the stuffed animal and the wool sock, the wool sock and the wine glass, the wine glass and the window … there is always some predicate, some "concept" that will join all of any given collection of objects together. Of course we will want to say that in many cases the concept is a complicated or unnatural one; but the child, according to the model of simple conditioning, does not know beforehand whether or not the world is complicated, does not know what is natural and what isn't. And perhaps our sense of what is complicated or natural depends on the concepts we have acquired from our linguistic training; perhaps from some other point of view what we regard as complicated or unnatural would not be. The child is not supposed to know any of this.

What the child needs is an *innate similarity space* (*RR* §5): there must be certain features of sensory episodes such that any two sensory episodes that exemplify them will be classed as similar, in the sense that if one such episode was accompanied by pleasure then the child will seek further episodes with those features, and if accompanied by pain the child will seek to avoid them (presumably by "pleasure" we must mean any positive sort of response—which can be quite subtle, such as simple awareness of desire satisfaction; similarly but the reverse for "pain").

Let us look at how Quine handles this demand. Suppose a chicken is presented with a screen showing seven dots forming a circle. Call this A. Beneath the image is a lever that, when pressed, delivers a food pellet. The chicken perchance learns to press the lever and get the food. The chicken is now shown two screens: screen B is like A but minus three dots, the remaining four forming a semi-circle; screen C has a circle drawn in a solid line, the same diameter as the circle of dots that originally appeared on screen A. If the chicken repeatedly presses the B-lever rather than the C-lever, then we can say that for the chicken, A is more similar to B than to C. This triadic relation, suitably generalized, can serve to order the field of overall sensory episodes, resulting in a similarity space. The whole complex of innate dispositions to order sensory episodes in this way constitutes the creature's innate similarity space. More exactly, we can think of the animal as undergoing, over any given interval, a "global stimulus": this is the set of sensory receptors ordered according to how they fire or are triggered over that interval.

Quine defines "receptual similarity" of global stimuli simply as "physical similarity of impact of the sensory surfaces" (*RR* 16, *FSS* 17). The more interesting concept of "perceptual similarity" may then be understood in terms of collections of global stimuli that are receptually similar: one such collection A is more similar to B than to C if the animal responds to the A-type as it does to the B-type and but not as it does to the C-type (*RR* 16–21, *FSS* 17–21). The similarity space is the ordering of collections of receptually similar global stimulations by perceptual similarity. Receptually similar episodes will usually be perceptually similar (similarity spaces however may change over time; see *RR* 21), but not typically the other way round. A white rabbit spotted only by virtue of a glimpse of the ears emerging from some tall grass may elicit the same response as a black rabbit with it head and ears obscured by leaves (*FSS* 19). The features of global stimuli that perceptually similar ones have in common are defined as the "salient" features: the ones to which the animal tends to respond (*FSS* 18–19).

Innateness

As may be guessed, this sketch ignores various complications relevant to learning theory even from Quine's restricted point of view (*RR* 16–32). But for our purposes this is enough about innate similarity spaces to make three especially important points for epistemology. The first is simply that Quine agrees for example with Chomsky on the very general point that learning is largely pre-programmed (even if they differ radically over the extent and character of the innateness); even the most staunchly behaviorist psychologist must be "up to his neck in innate mechanisms of learning-readiness" (*WP* 57). Second, we can expect from the theory of natural selection that innate similarity spaces will tend to be beneficial (that is, conducive to the creature's chances of successful procreation). Thus as Quine puts it, "innate standards of perceptual similarity show a gratifying tendency to run with the grain of nature" (*RR* 19). In particular, as already noted, receptually dissimilar episodes are often perceptually similar—that is, the organism responds to them similarly—when caused by the same physical objects or same kinds of physical objects. We are, as Quine stresses, "body-minded" (*RR* 54): our sensory-motor systems have evolved largely in order to keep track of medium-sized physical objects such as stones, plants, and animals (which are of course the same for everyone; *CCE* 475, 479, 486–7; *FSS* 19–20). As robotics engineers have appreciated, it is a vast computational task to get a visual system to recognize and keep track of such objects through all their diverse effects upon sensory equipment—all the ways in which they "appear"—but natural selection, by definition exquisitely sensitive to what most benefits the organism, has managed it. Further, things we are innately disposed to treat as similar do tend to have similar causal propensities. Obviously a prehistoric ape wired so as not to expect the same from one leopard as was observed previously would not have lasted long. The survival of the fittest ensures that the inductive inferences we naturally make tend to turn out right, and it does so by rewarding some similarity spaces and punishing others (see *RR* 16–20 and *OR* 114–38).[3]

The third point is one that may be familiar from Wittgenstein's famous discussion of rule-following, which culminates in such pronouncements as:

> If language is to be a means of communication there must be agreement not only in definitions but also (queer as this may sound) in judgements.
>
> (Wittgenstein 1958, p. §242)

Wittgenstein's point was that no one could learn language from such things as ostensive definition—pointing to the ball and saying "ball," etc.—unless we were not already predisposed to "take" the language lesson in a certain way: one takes it as a word for balls, not for things that are presently being pointed at, not for things which are sometimes played with by the dog, not for any object so long as it is not raining, or anything like that. Only if we share such dispositions and they remain stable is language possible. In our terms, this means not only that each creature must have an innate similarity space that accords with nature, our similarity spaces must be socially coordinated: if our innate similarity spaces were not similar, then we would not be able to coordinate our behavior, and certainly would not be able to develop language (in late work—*FSS* 22, Quine 2015b, pp. 33–5—Quine calls this the "Pre-established harmony of standards of perception"; to be returned to in our final chapter). Of course, these requirements are connected: since the physical world we have to deal with does not vary depending on who is dealing with it, social coordination will largely— though of course not entirely—be taken care of by the alignment of our natural expectations with the physical environment. Inherited similarity spaces are a kind of "racial memory" (by "racial" he means of course the species; *RR* 26; see also 29, 54; also *WP* 56–8, *OR* 24–5, 90; *FSS* 16). We will return to this issue in our final chapter.

Language: Observation Sentences to Theory

In one way, we said, observation sentences are like the calls of birds and apes: they are responses to present sensory stimuli. They differ from animal calls in being entirely learned rather than often innate, and also in having a certain higher-order structure. The ape shrieks at the sight of a threatening enemy, and the others take heed. In the case of the typical observation sentence, however, what the stimulus brings about is not an utterance of the observation sentence or otherwise an action, but the disposition to assent to it (see *RR* 15). To master an observation sentence is to acquire a disposition to have a disposition. Such mastery tends to be acquired pretty quickly, thanks to shared innate similarity spaces. The child, we may assume, is in some way rewarded for saying "mama" in the presence of mama, "doggie" in the presence of the dog, "milk" in the presence of milk, "red" in the presence of something red. He or she may exploit their innate sense of similarity to try it again. But of course, Mama does not respond quite so excitedly this time; no special cuddles or treats for yet another utterance of "doggie!" What remains is the association between the stimulus and the observation sentence. With a bit of supplementary coaching in the use of "yes" and "no," the child learns to be disposed to say "yes" to the observation sentence in situations perceptually similar to those in which an earlier utterance of "doggie" was rewarded. The child thus becomes a fully-fledged master of the observation sentence (*RR* 47–8).

We are so far citing one-word observation sentences such as "Mama!" or "Milk!" The word "milk," used as an observation sentence, is short for "That's milk," "Here is some milk," or some such thing. The terms used as one-word observation sentences may be of very different sorts: "Mama" is a singular term, referring to an individual body; "milk" is a mass-term, referring to any portion of the great scattered distribution of milk in the world; "doggie" is a general term, referring like "Mama" to individual objects but to more than one of them; "soft" is a general term, but it is not a name for a stuff or substance like milk, and does not individuate as "dog" does: we can count dogs, but not softs. However, these differences amongst the *terms* do not themselves make for differences amongst the corresponding observation *sentences*: we stressed in the last chapter that as observation sentences mastered by the individual, they are all the same sort of thing, fully explicable in terms of their associated stimulus conditions for that individual (see *RR* 52–3, 82; *TT* 4–5, *FSS* 22–3, *OR* 6–8). From the infant's point of view, "Mama!," "Doggie!," "Soft!," and "Milk!" are just like "It's raining," "It's warm," or "It's windy"—appropriate in some sensory circumstances and not others, but no object is being singled out and talked about (*TT* 6). The child uses the sentence, as Quine puts it, only "holophrastically." Of course, we are not wrong, as mature language-users, to point out the presence of a referring term in our mature use of "There's a rabbit." But it is only by virtue of our mastery of much more sophisticated departments of language that we can rightly regard the sentence as containing such a term (see *OR* 7). For the child, it certainly needn't be described in that way, which is the important point. We will say more about this below.

By virtue of the sheer number of observation sentences, and mastery of the language game of "yes" and "no," the child at this stage may already have outpaced the bird or the ape. But however impressive, this is merely a closed repertoire of what for the child may remain unrelated atoms. As thinkers from Humboldt to Frege to Chomsky have stressed, the miracle of language really begins with linguistic *creativity*: the child's capacity to understand and construct sentences that are wholly new to him or her, by the application of grammar, the rules of dissection and combination. This requires the apprehension of sentences as having parts which may be recombined in ways not yet encountered. Let us look at some aspects of this which Quine singles out as critical in the progression from stimulus-response to theory.

Remember that our concern is with the strictly fact-stating aspects of language, the aspect sensitive only to truth and falsehood. Therefore a big step is the learning of the simplest logical connectives, namely the truth-functional sentence-connectives (or at least, those of English that come closest to being truth-functional). We have been through it in the last chapter in connection with translation, but let us run through it again. The child can get a grip on the sentence-connective "not," simply by learning to assent to *not-S* when and only when he would dissent from S. He can readily learn "and" by learning to assent to S *and* S* when and only when he would assent to both S and S* independently. Individually, these add little, since "not" merely inverts the appropriateness of assent and dissent, and "and" does nothing that merely uttering sentences in sequence would do. Used in combination, however, they in principle deliver the full power of truth-functional logic, since all the truth-functional connectives are equivalent to some combination of "not" and "and." So long as the child can get the hang of grouping—the difference between *Not-S and S** and *Not (S and S*)*—the child is now in possession of truth-functional logic (*RR* 76–8, *FSS* 23; as mentioned in the last chapter, the problem of locating the truth-functions in the subject's disposition to assent and dissent is actually more involved than this).[4]

So far we have been thinking of observation sentences as being learned directly, each being taught individually by ostensive learning: we show the child a dog and say "Doggie," or, more likely beyond the first weeks of learning, the child picks up observation sentences by watching other people speak. Indeed with one-word observation sentences such as "Doggie," the beginning language-learner has no other way to learn them. Once in possession of a few multi-word observation sentences, however, the child can learn them by what Quine calls analogical substitution, another step in the development of linguistic creativity (*FSS* 24, *RR* 59–62). Having learned "Black dog," "Black cat," and "White ball" holophrastically, the child, running along the rails of an innate similarity space, might try their hand at analysis, might try "Black ball" in the presence of a black ball; an encouraging response from Papa may encourage further experiments of the same kind. Furthermore, these sentences are *not* simply conjunctions, like "Wet and dog" as a conjunction of observation sentences: "Wet and dog" could be appropriately uttered in the presence of the dog when the *child* is wet, whereas "Wet dog" requires the dog to be wet. Such is what Quine calls an "observational predication" (*FSS* 24). It does not yet involve reference to objects: it is only a more refined variety of observation sentence, since each such sentence *could* be acquired in response to presently occurring stimulations. The child, we might say, is still dealing only with the specious present.

Observation Categoricals

A dramatic first step beyond the specious present and into theory comes with "observation categoricals." Examples include "Whenever smoke, fire," or "Whenever rain, river rises." Aside from the device "Whenever __.__," such sentences are constructible from devices already learned, but their import goes beyond the here and now (*PT* 9–11, *TT* 27). Unlike observation sentences, they are standing sentences rather than occasion sentences. They involve a primitive form of *generality*, whereby they can be asserted irrespective of present stimulation (*FSS* 25). They express inductive expectations, and thereby afford a means of communicating something recognizably theoretical, something like a law of nature. An observation categorical is a "miniature scientific theory" (*FSS* 26). Psychologically too they represent a more complex kind of achievement. Mastery of an observation sentence, we said, is the acquisition of a second-order disposition: it is a disposition to become disposed to assent to the sentence under certain conditions. The observation categorical indicates a relation between second-order dispositions: one is so disposed that, if one is disposed to assent to "smoke," then one is disposed to assent to "fire." Such are examples of the sentence-to-sentence links that unify the web of knowledge that Quine had more vaguely sketched in "Two Dogmas of Empiricism."

Furthermore, although observation categoricals are the simplest kind of theoretical statement, they are, according to Quine, the statements actually at issue when a more sophisticated theory is up for testing (*FSS* 44, *PT* 9–12, *TT* 27–8). Theories consist of standing sentences—sentences whose truth-values do not vary over time—and do not imply observation sentences directly. A physical theory does not tell us, for example, that the tide is in. What it might tell us, rather, is that if the moon is overhead, then the tide is in. That is the sort of theoretical statement that can be tested, by testing the truth-values of its component observation sentences: wait for the truth of "The moon is overhead," and check that of "The tide is in." If the latter is false then the theory has been disconfirmed; if it is true, then, although the theory has not thereby been proven true, it has passed an empirical test.

The "empirical content" of a theory, accordingly, resides in the collection observation categoricals that it entails (*TT* 28).

Reference

An animal in possession of observation sentences, sentence-connectives and observation categoricals, is thereby minimally a theoretical animal, but it is not thereby a referring animal.[5] Let us see what according to Quine the animal would have to do in order to become one (the ensuing follows *TT* 23–8). Quine illustrates the way in which genuine reference enters in by considering pairs of statements such as these:

(A) If there is a raven, there is a black raven.
(B) All ravens are black.

(A) can be tested by checking the truth-values of the components individually. (B), however, is not like that. To bring this out further, let us rewrite (B) in a different form:

(B*) If something is a raven, then it is black.

White ravens would disconfirm (B) or (B*), but would not disconfirm (A), if every white raven were always for some reason accompanied by a black one. In order to grasp that the white raven accompanied by a black one disconfirms (B*) without disconfirming (A) the child must be able to check that something is a raven, and then check that *it* is black. Concurrently watching out for ravens and watching out for black ones is not enough. This ability, the ability to think or talk about an object as falling under a given general term, but also think or talk about that same object as falling under a different general term, is the essence of referring, if anything is. The child must now *keep track of the same object*, and talk about *it*. The mastery of such language is Quine's criterion for the description of the child as referring to objects and talking about them. Of course, there are perceptual mechanisms involved. Quine is well aware that even very young infants track moving objects across the visual field and so on; but what is in question here is the specifically linguistic phenomenon of reference (see *RR* 54, *CCE* 478). A child might well exercise the psycho-motor capacity for visual tracking, yet be limited to non-referring devices of language. That ability might be a prerequisite for referring, but is not sufficient for it.

Cross-reference

The devices which most conspicuously signify the accomplishment of reference are *cross-referring pronouns* such as "it" as used in (B*), or "she" in "If a woman becomes president, then she will get criticized for what she wears" (see *FSS* 27ff, *RR* 89–101, *TT* 5–6). Such devices are used in such a way as to refer to the same object in repeated occurrences throughout a sentence or longer stretch of discourse. However, as signaled by the evident equivalence of (B) and (B*), the presence of this kind of cross-reference can lay concealed, as there is no pronoun in (B). Furthermore, in English, the ways in which such devices function in concert with such expressions as "every," "a," "some," "any," and the like is exceedingly complicated. All the same, this complexity is largely redundant, and not worth entering into for Quine's purposes. For those purposes, as we pointed out earlier, it is appropriate to consider an idealized and simplified model, so long as the model contains the features that are of interest. Thus consider the following variant on (B*), using parentheses to indicate grouping in an intuitive manner:

(B**) Everything is such that (if it is a raven, then it is black).

We can assert the existence of non-black ravens by negating it:

(C) Not (everything is such that (if it is a raven then it is black)).

That is, to deny that all ravens are black is to say that non-black ravens exist:

(C*) There exists something such that (it is a raven and not (it is black)).

As we will see in more detail in the next chapter, a small handful of devices from English—the relative pronouns, "and" and "not," devices for grouping, plus the quantifier "Everything is such that"—with some small adjustments, are sufficient for the whole of what Quine calls the *referential apparatus* of English. The child, in principle, needs only to master these in order to acquire full-fledged theory, a fount of discourse that is genuinely about objects in the world.

Identity and Difference

Still, reference is not quite complete; it remains "dim" (*TT* 5) until the child masters one more linguistic resource. This is the "apparatus of individuation" embodied in expressions for numerical identity such as "This is the very same cat as that." It would be consistent with the child's facility with such sentences as "All ravens are black," "Some cats have no tails," and so on to suppose that the child regards ravens and cats as momentary things, not the robustly enduring animals that they are (even as short-lived things they would still be black or tail-less as may be). In order to get credit for talking about the enduring spatio-temporal entities that we credit ravens and cats with being, the child must learn when to say "This is the same cat we saw yesterday," "This is Grandma's cat," and such like, where "is" means the "is" of identity. He must be able to *re-identify* a given object over time. The child must learn the expressions for numerical identity, and with them the identity-conditions of different sorts of object—that of *spatio-temporal continuity* in the case of ravens, cats, and other physical objects or bodies. The apparatus of individuation thus includes the logical notion of identity together with the whole commonsense framework of space, time, and enduring objects (*FSS* 36, *PT* 24–5). Reification, as Quine puts it, is theoretical.

We noted a few paragraphs back that observation sentences such as "That's black" can always be learned as wholes, "holophrastically" as Quine often puts it. Considered just as an observation sentence—its mastery consisting in the acquisition of a disposition to assent to it in certain circumstances—the sentence need not be conceived as having any internal structure: in the right circumstances, the child comes out with or assents to the whole thing, end of story. This holds even for more complicated observation sentences, such as "The rain is coming down now up over the hill," even though it would be surprising if it were used without awareness of its internal structure. The observation sentence, however, is "Janus-faced" as Quine puts it (*CCE* 109): though "as a response to neural intake" it is happily conceived as unstructured, we must, when considering it in relation to theoretical language generally, conceive it as compounded out of parts that recur in other sentences in the language. The employment of cross-referring pronouns as in (B**) brings with it the segmentation of a sentence such as "That is black"—learnable as a whole observation sentence—into the demonstrative pronoun "that" and the predicate "_ is black." In English such a predicate is itself compounded out of the general term "black" and the copula "is," but again for our purposes this is not important: as we will see in more detail in the next chapter, it is really the predicate that is essential to theoretical language as such, whether or not predicates always admit of further syntactic disassembly. The predicate "_ is black," meanwhile, will recur in theoretical sentences such as "Every raven is black." It is by virtue of such recurrence that theoretical statements stand in logical relationships, including the entailment of observation categoricals (*TT* 24ft). It is thus by virtue of mastery of cross-referring devices and their accompaniments that the child gets hold of the structure of theory: the relation between observation sentences, observation categoricals, and more complicated theoretical sentences essential to the full factual import of a theory.

Language and the World

All the same—and this is essential to understanding Quine—we are not to understand the emergence of referential language as the emergence of a linkage between language and the world that is additional to the causal link borne by observation sentences to stimulation. It is not as if, with the emergence of referential language, the child sprouts a new but immaterial link between his words and the world, namely the relation of reference. The link between language and the world is the relation of observation sentences to stimulation, nothing more. The capacity to refer just is the capacity to use a certain complex linguistic apparatus in conjunction with observation sentences. The force of calling the acquired apparatus "referential" is to indicate the vast theoretical importance of the resulting gain in structure (see *PT* 29–34). This may sound unpersuasive, as if we were not really acknowledging the existence of reference. But remember, Quine's aim in these inquiries is to determine what it is, from a thoroughly naturalistic standpoint, that constitutes the acquisition and possession of theoretical language. Theories, of course, are *about the world*: no one denies that being "about the world"—referring—is something that theories do. But the ordinary notions "refers" or being "about" things are not terms to rest with in science. In the same way, no physicist denies that gravity pulls objects to the ground. It is the way we speak. But just as the inquisitive physicist wants to know what constitutes this so-called pulling, and may tell us that gravity is not at all the sort of thing that might have been supposed, so Quine wants to know what facts are actually in question when we speak of "reference" or "talking about things," and is certainly prepared to conclude that there is more to it, or less to it, then we might have thought. In his view, a language or proto-language consisting only of observation sentences, sentence-connectives and observation categoricals would lack the kind of structure that would justify calling it referential: it is simply not necessary, in order to explain it, to regard its users as doing anything like those linguistic activities that we speak of as "mentioning an object," "talking about it," and so on. Once a language-user does master those devices, however, that mastery itself, operating atop a foundation of observation sentences, is sufficient for describing the user in those ways. If so, then there is no need to suppose that mastery also brings about an entirely new phenomenon, in the way that rotating a stick inside a hole eventually brings about a flame: once the relevant underlying features of the phenomena we speak of as reference have been identified and described, that is all there is to the story.

The point can be appreciated in another way that indicates an additional point of agreement between Quine and the later Wittgenstein. It is tempting to suppose that the child who says "rabbit" when shown a rabbit is thereby *naming* the thing, referring to it. But if that is what the child is doing, then clearly that activity can be explained in Quine's way, as the utterance of an observation sentence, albeit one that looks and sounds identical to the term "rabbit." If so, then if we want to credit the child with referring to rabbits, clearly the child must be able to do something more than say "rabbit" in front of a rabbit. This further ability is the ability to use the apparatus of pronouns, predicates, and related devices as described by Quine. Only if the child has learned all or at least a significant portion of that, does it fully make sense to say, of a child saying "rabbit," that he is referring to rabbits. Wittgenstein compared the "stage-setting" needed in order for the idea of naming or referring to ways in which we might describe the role of a component in a mechanism:

> "I set the brake by connecting up rod and lever."—Yes, given the whole of the rest of the mechanism. Only in conjunction with that is it a brake-lever, and separated from its support it is not even a lever; it may be anything, or nothing.
>
> (Wittgenstein 1958, p. §6; cf §257)

Sense-data Finessed

Finally, a word about Quine's connection to his empiricist predecessors, with which this chapter began. Quine should very much be seen as contributing to that great conversation—that exquisitely difficult philosophical one about items of supposed direct awareness—that arose roughly with Locke and Berkeley and their "ideas" (of sensation), developed with Hume and his "impressions," through Kant and his "judgements of sensibility," through Russell and his "knowledge by acquaintance," and through Schlick, Carnap, and Neurath's battles over "protocol sentences." Quine was a witness to the tail-end of the protocol debates, was impressed with his teacher C. I. Lewis' emphasis on sense-data as well as that of Russell, and indeed remained undecided over the status of statements reporting one's phenomenal states or states of sensation until the 1950s, *after* his celebrated "Two Dogmas" (and just before *Word and Object*). As part of his progress toward Naturalism, however, he began to see sense-data as being too fragmentary and fleeting for the foundation of knowledge; on the contrary, "[e]xperiment suggests" as he came to see it, "and introspection as well, that what are sensed are not primarily those sensory elements, but significantly structured wholes" (*RR* 1). By "significantly structured wholes" he means roughly bodies, ordinary physical objects extending in time, for example, stones, cities, and rabbits.[6] Quine came to take the "phenomenalist appeal to sensory given as a theory independent starting point for knowledge as a myth," reports Robert Sinclair, "since our descriptions of sense data, empirical givenness or sensory qualia … already presupposes a prior scientific theory or scientific understanding of the phenomena in question" (2022, p. 68). Quine's final scheme with observation sentences finesses his way around the problem because it does not begin with objects of cognition that serve as a foundation for knowledge; *there are no items of direct awareness* in his official scheme. Objects come in only at a later stage of knowledge, and the stimuli responsible for a disposition to assent to an observation sentence need not consist of items of awareness at all (for more see Verhaegh 2018, Sinclair 2022, *RR* 1–3).

There is also a more substantive point of logical theory at work in Quine's having drawn the boundary as he has between referential and non-referential language, language that portends an "ontology" and that which does not. We will take up that point in the next chapter.

Further Reading and Historical Notes

See note 6 for more of Quine's attitude toward "sense-data" or "experience." The latter makes an appearance as late as "Two Dogmas," but it was not long before what he called "the flabby reference" to experience—a weasel word, perhaps—gave way to the frankly physicalist notion of sensory stimulation, as in *CCE* 398. See also Austin 1962 for some contemporaneous and influential thoughts on sense-data. The notion of "observation sentence" of *Word and Object* (1960) culminated a long development which began not only as a graduate student faced with the sense-data doctrines of C. I. Lewis and Russell, but, as mentioned, with the famous "Protocol" dispute amongst members of the Vienna Circle, of which Quine had some second-hand experience during his visit to Carnap in Prague, 1933 (see Quine's brisk, but valuable, account of the road from the British empiricists' emphasis on "ideas" through language to full-fledged naturalism in "Five Milestones of Empiricism," *TT* 67–72). Otto Neurath had raised the flag for Protocol Sentences—the basic evidence for empirical science—pertaining to physical events exterior to the subject; Morris Schlick had raised it for internal events within the subject. It was objectivity versus certainty. Carnap had switched from certainty to objectivity by 1933, the time when he met Quine. The advantage of Quine's observation sentences, you might say, consists in giving up on the idea of the sentence's being explained in terms of the subject's being *aware* of an object or state of affairs. See the articles by Neurath, Schlick, and Carnap in the Protocol section of Ayer 1959. Quine's account of the ontogenesis of reification—or what you might, in a tongue-in-cheek way, call the "essence of reference"—which is the main concern of the *Roots of Reference*, has not received a lot of critical attention, but again see Hylton 2007 chs. 4–7. The idea of naturalized epistemology has received by contrast a mountain of discussion, partly because the idea, roughly understood, goes back at least to Hume; see Stroud 1981, Kim 1988, Roth 1999, the essays in Gibson 2004, Hylton 2013, and Verhaegh 2018.

Ontology I: Truth, Physical Objects, and the Language of Science

The Ontological Question

The problem of ontology, as Quine puts it in his essay "On What There Is," boils down to a simple question: What is there? (*FLVP* 1) The question what *exists*, to Quine's way of thinking, may be a fancier way to put it, but it is the same question.

That this should be a question for *philosophy* might seem strange, if we did not already know that it is one. Stones, vegetables, animals, stars, telephones, hydrogen atoms, four-leaf clovers—all these things exist; fairies, the Loch Ness Monster, the planet Vulcan—those things do not. But it was not philosophers who discovered the existence of those existing things, or who established the nonexistence of those nonexisting things. Of course, the philosopher might doubt these existences and nonexistence claims; he might argue that we don't really know what exists and what doesn't. But we can set that sort of skeptical challenge aside—a variety of the skeptical challenge most famously posed by Descartes—which doubts *all* ordinary knowledge-claims, not only ones about existence. The question of ontology is not an epistemological question; it is not the question whether or how we know what exists and what doesn't. It is simpler: What exists? This is certainly a *question*: beyond mundane and obviously existing things like black dogs, and obviously nonexisting things like flying donkeys, there are disputable ones like life on other planets, or Beethoven's immortal beloved. But again, exactly where is the philosophical question here, and not just questions for astronomers, historians, zoologists?

The traditional answer is that certain sorts of existence questions are not to be settled by empirical means. Philosophers from Plato onwards, for example, have held that in addition to particular existing things which cometh into being and passeth away, there must also exist *universals*—*properties* or *essences* such as triangularity, justice, and so on: these exist necessarily and independently of their being exemplified in particular cases, and our knowledge of them is entirely *a priori*. Plato's theory can sound a little mystical or otherwise farfetched, but we do seem to talk about various sorts of things whose existence cannot be established by using a telescope or any such thing. For example, we say there is a prime number between 12 and 16; it follows trivially that *there is* a number, that is, that numbers exist. We say John and Susan are both fussy about food, and therefore that *there is* something they have in common—an attribute or property. We say that despite all, *there is* something we agree on—a proposition or belief. We even say *there exists* a way that things might have been—a possible world or state of affairs. Thus the brute fact is that many statements that we take to be true seem straightforwardly to be *about* some rather special entities—numbers, attributes, propositions, possible states of affairs or worlds. Such entities, it seems, are non-physical: if they do exist, then certainly they are not physical objects along with turnips and mice, and cannot be discovered by looking. Do they really exist? How do we find out?

Some progress can be made by noticing that some apparent references to comparatively weird entities are only manners of speaking, without genuine ontological import. If we say there is a lack of enthusiasm for the proposal, we could just as well have said that no one is enthusiastic about it; we need not recognize the existence of a queer entity, a *lack*. But in other cases it is much less evident that the apparent entities can be explained away in that manner. In mathematics, reference to numbers seems essential, perhaps not just a convenient manner of speaking. And similar things have been claimed for the other items on our list. In general, whether or not the relevant forms of speech really are indispensable seems to be a philosophical question, a question calling for philosophical analysis and reflection.

Ontological Reduction

Our conviction that certain apparent cases of existential import are really only apparent ones is quite strong—we feel quite sure that there are not really such things as lacks, for example (similarly, as Quine notes, there aren't really such things as "sakes," as in "for her sake"; *WO* 235). The reason, it seems, is that way of speaking is superfluous. But if that is the reason, then surely we should recognize genuine cases of existential import only when it is *not* superfluous—only when it is strictly necessary. We should not, as William of Ockham said, multiply entities beyond necessity.

Thus arise projects of "ontological reduction." Take the question "Do bodies exist?"—where by "bodies" we mean ordinary things such as stones, mice, and turnips. On the one hand, the answer seems trivially yes: turnips exist, they are physical objects, ergo, physical objects exist. But turnips are entirely constituted by various sorts of molecules configured in certain ways, which in turn are constituted by atoms configured in certain ways. Thus: given that such-and-such atoms exist in such-and-such configurations, perhaps there is no *further* question of whether or not turnips exist; "turnip" is just a name for certain atomic configurations. Similarly for stones, mice, and other ordinary bodies. Since the existence of bodies is fully accounted for, explained in terms of, the existence of atoms, atoms are all that really exist. An ontology of atoms is entirely sufficient on this view, in the sense that nothing we say commits us to anything besides configurations of atoms.

With respect to any given domain or subject-matter, however, different reductionisms are conceivable. In the case of bodies, for example, some philosophers have held that it is the unobservable entities of theoretical physics that need reducing to bodies, not the other way round. For it makes no sense to speak of unobservable things that exist. Still others favored the kind of phenomenalistic reduction attempted by Carnap in his early work the *Aufbau*, the reduction of talk about bodies to talk about sense-experience. In psychology, Gilbert Ryle and other so-called analytical behaviorists have been thought to hold that mental states and entities including sense data should be reduced to behavioral dispositions. More recently, functionalists hold that mental states can be reduced to the more complicated yet physicalism-friendly idea of a functional state. In mathematics, not everyone accepts the reduction of numbers to sets, and some others have held that neither sets nor numbers are actually needed for the purposes of science (as argued lately by Hartry Field—Quine himself once seriously considered this latter idea, the thesis of "Nominalism"; it is discussed briefly in the next chapter).

Carnap's Ontological Deflation

But if possibilities of reduction leave some ontological questions undecided, then how are they to be decided? According to Carnap, as we saw in Chapter 2, they needn't be; for there can be no factual disputes over questions of this kind. As we have noted, we can always ask *particular* existence questions, such as whether there are active volcanoes on Mars, whether there is a rational number whose square is 121, and so on. But questions about *whole categories* of things—as the questions typically called "ontological questions" tend to be—are quite different. As Carnap put it in *The Logical Syntax of Language,* certain sorts of expression—"number," "property," "set," "thing," "body"—are "universal words," such that questions about whether such things exist are really questions about whether a given language includes words for those things and, if so, whether or not it is useful to employ such a language (Carnap 1937). If they make any sense at all, supposed metaphysical existence questions—ontological questions—are questions about languages, asked using what Carnap called the formal as opposed to the material mode of speech:

> *Translatability into the formal mode of speech constitutes the touchstone for all philosophical sentences,* or, more generally, for all sentences which do not belong to the language of any one of the empirical sentences.
>
> (Carnap 1937, p. 313)

We can ask whether or not a given language possesses certain sorts of expressions, but this is not a question about what exists. We can also ask *whether to use* a language containing those expressions, but this is a pragmatic question, not a factual question at all. One asks a factual question only within a language, presupposing its framework of analytic truths and rules of reasoning. Insofar as the question of whether to use a language containing certain expressions can be regarded as an ontological question, the question is pragmatic, not theoretical.

Quine agrees with Carnap that there are no peculiarly philosophical existence questions—this is part and parcel of his Naturalism—but rejects Carnap's way of finessing them (*OR* 52–3, 91ff). For Quine's rejection of Carnap's analytic-synthetic distinction rules this out. There is no sharp distinction between factual issues and merely verbal issues, matters of theory and matters of language. If not, then there is no sharp distinction between theoretical questions and pragmatic questions either, since the former were supposed to be internal questions of fact and the latter were supposed to be external questions of language choice. In that case, we cannot dismiss general ontological questions as mere pragmatic questions of language choice. In the sense in which they are, so is all of science, and they are no less theoretical for that. Thus Quine sums up his rejection of Carnap's position on ontology:

> It is only by assuming the cleavage between analytic and synthetic truths that he is able to declare the problem of universals [categories] to be a matter not of theory but of linguistic decision. Now I am as impressed as anyone with the

vastness of what language contributes to science and to one's whole view of the world; and in particular I grant that one's hypothesis as to what there is, e.g., as there being universals is at bottom just as arbitrary or pragmatic a matter as one's adoption of a new brand of set theory or even a new system of bookkeeping. Carnap in turn recognizes that such decisions, however conventional, "will nevertheless usually be influenced by theoretical knowledge." But what impresses me more than it does Carnap is how well this whole attitude is suited to the theoretical hypotheses of natural science itself, and how little basis there is for a distinction.

(*WP* 132)

The Accountant of Science

Having rejected Carnap's way of drawing a boundary, Quine denies that the ontological questions asked by the philosopher are categorically distinct from the sublunary existence questions addressed by empirical science. Instead, the difference between specific existence questions like "Is there life on Mars?" and more general ones like "Do numbers exist?" is just that, the difference in generality or scope (see *OR* 90–100, *WO* 275–6). There is no boundary crossed from the factual to the linguistic as for Carnap, or from the empirical to the *a priori* as perhaps for Plato or Descartes. Nevertheless, the more general questions are distinctive just by virtue of being exceedingly general, wider and more abstract than the questions dealt with by particular sciences such as zoology, chemistry, and so on. Further, the philosopher asks these questions with an eye toward the systematic elimination of superfluous entities, or rather the replacement of language that seems to refer to such entities with language that clearly does not. The aim is an overall reckoning of the ontological commitments of our knowledge as a whole. If the philosopher is not precisely a scientist, then he is at least a kind of *accountant of science*. The accountant does not make or sell widgets himself, but he tells the firm what it is really spending or committed to spending, what it is really earning or likely to earn; he also advises the firm as to when it might cut costs, and when it had better not. Just as it is sometimes necessary to hire an expert in company bookkeeping, so scientists may recruit a philosopher—an ontologicist—as one who has the instruments and training necessary for commanding a clear view of science as a whole.

Thus Quine writes:

The question what there is is a shared concern of philosophy and most other non-fiction genres ... What distinguishes ... the ontological philosopher's concern ... is only breadth of categories ... Here is the task of making explicit what had been tacit, and precise what had been vague; of exposing and resolving paradoxes, smoothing kinks, lopping off vestigial growths, clearing ontological slums ... The philosopher's task differs from the others', then, in detail; but in no such drastic way as those suppose who imagine for the philosopher a vantage point outside the conceptual scheme that he takes in charge. There is no such cosmic exile.

(WO 275)

Quine's exact job description for the ontological accountant, then, is simply this: *Given our present state of knowledge,* we should seek to formulate it in such a way as to *preserve its empirical content,* but *minimize* its ontological commitments. In order to do this, the accountant must formulate a unified and univocal framework for science (the accounting system). Unlike Carnap, with his multiplicity of scientific languages for different purposes, for Quine's purpose the goal is to formulate a *single* language for science, a language in terms of which the interconnections between different branches of knowledge can be identified and explained and which makes possible a single univocal answer to the basic and supremely general ontological question, What is there?

We will describe this framework in a moment—a framework for "regimen-tation" of our knowledge, as termed it (WO 157). Also we shall describe certain limits to this. But first, we should try to get a feel for why Quine holds that the ontological question is to be addressed in terms of a special language for *science.* Are there not more things in heaven and earth than scientists talk about?

Science and Common Sense

Although Quine is often held up as the analytical philosopher *par excellence,* we are touching here on yet another issue that separates Quine from many analytical philosophers today. Let us illustrate the difference by considering a couple of pertinent examples.

John is thinking about the Loch Ness Monster.
Therefore, there is something that John is thinking about: the Loch Ness Monster.
Therefore the Loch Ness Monster exists.

John and Susan are both fastidious.
Therefore, there is something that John and Susan have in common: the attribute of fastidiousness. Therefore, the attribute of fastidiousness exists.

At least as they stand, these seem to be formally valid arguments in English. But if so, then clearly the mere linguistic form of argumentation in English is not to be trusted. Obviously we cannot conclude, from the mere fact that people think about the Loch Ness Monster, that the Loch Ness Monster exists. But if not, then perhaps we should not trust arguments such as the second either; the possibility of such an argument should not lead us to conclude that there are really such things as attributes.

In fact, as Russell remarked in perhaps unfair opposition to Meinong, we can in similar ways "prove" the existence of all sorts of things; of anything, quite literally, we care to name. We have the Loch Ness Monster, attributes such as redness, actions such as lawn-bowling, the nearness of you, the way you hold your knife, the second coming of Jesus, and so on. We learn our language talking about ordinary bodies such as Mama, rabbits, and balls, but with the acquisition of more complex grammar we seem to be able to "nominalize"—employ a name for—an entity corresponding to almost any grammatical category: noun, verb, adjective, even preposition. But we gain no theoretical insight by simply announcing: Yes! All these things exist! Quine's idea is that surely it is possible to ask a serious scientific question of ontology—of existence at its broadest— calling for a disciplined answer. Ordinary language affords no such discipline. For if we want to deny that every noun-phrase, gerund, and so on stand for some entity, then we have to ask exactly which rule is violated by the purported existence-proof in English. And such questions often simply lack clear answers. As Quine puts it:

> The common man's ontology is vague and untidy in two ways. It takes in many purported objects that are vaguely or inadequately defined. But also, and what is more significant, it is vague in its scope; we cannot even tell in general which of these vague things to ascribe to a man's ontology at all, which things to count him as assuming. Should we regard grammar as decisive? Does every noun demand some array of denotata? Surely not; the nominalizing of verbs is often a mere stylistic variation. But where can we draw the line?
>
> It is a wrong question; there is no line to draw. Bodies are assumed, yes; they are the things, first and foremost. Beyond them there is a succession of dwindling analogies … We must recognize this grading off for what it is, and recognize that a fenced ontology is just not implicit in ordinary language. The idea of a boundary between being and non-being is a philosophical idea, an *idea of technical science in a broad sense.*

(*TT* 9; emphasis added. See also *PT* 27)

Some philosophers, by contrast, would hold that ordinary language does herald a definite ontology. But Quine denies that there are exact logical relationships in ordinary language, and as we have seen, denies that there is any fact of the matter as to the real meaning of a sentence. There is no such thing as the true and exact logical form of English, and no such thing as its true and exact semantics. But Quine does deny the existence of the Loch Ness Monster, and also the existence of attributes (except in the sense of *classes*), propositions, and other philosophical esoterica (see next chapter). The reason he can do this, or supposes he can do this, is that the question of ontology, for Quine, is not the question of what entities *ordinary language* is committed to. It is not a question of what exists according to our ordinary ways of talking about the world, or according to our "folk theories." The question is *what exists according to our best theory of the world*, i.e., according to science. The difference is vast. Sir Arthur Eddington, for example, pointed out that according to ordinary ways of speaking, ordinary physical objects like table legs are utterly motionless, without gaps, and intrinsically colored. Physics, however, tells us that they vibrate, are mostly empty space, and have colors only relatively. Common sense tells us that light and radiant heat are completely different things, that the rate of time is always the same, that gravity accelerates heavy things faster than light things. None of these things is true, and we happily defer to the physicist who tells us so (*RR* 6–7). We should do the same when it comes to ontology: many sorts of things may seem to exist according to common sense, but we should be prepared to let science tell us what really does exist.

The deference to science, then, has two aspects. First, it is science rather than common sense that tells us which statements to pay attention to drawing up the ontological accounts. Second, even if we restrict our ontology to what science says there is, we are unlikely to gain sufficient clarity if we conduct the research in terms of that untamed vernacular known as ordinary language. Therefore science itself, according to Quine, needs to be expressed in a special language if its ontological commitments are to be identified precisely—a language, as we'll see presently, that is quasi-artificial or formal, if not completely artificial or formal. "The quest of a simplest, clearest overall pattern of canonical notation," say Quine, "is not to be distinguished from a quest of ultimate categories, a limning of the most general traits of reality" (*WO* 160).

An Austere Language for Science

The language that Quine takes to be adequate for the formulation of science—for its "regimentation"—and which is especially suited for exploring its ontological import as well as its logical relations, incorporates the "first-order predicate calculus" that one learns in a logic class. Indeed the only difference between the bona fide predicate calculus and the language Quine recommends is just that Quine always regards the terms of his language as interpreted terms, not as uninterpreted symbols. (It is another difference between Quine and Carnap, but there is no need to foreground it here.) The following will suffice as a rough characterization of such a language in its most streamlined form (less rough: *FLPV* 80–7, *WP* 221–232, *WO* §§33–39, 157–90). Readers who know their logic can skim, or skip to the next section.

The language contains:

(1) One-place predicates "F_", "G_", … and so on; these take the place of predicates in English such as "_ is red".

(2) Two-place predicates "R_ _", "S_ _", … and so on; these take the place of relational predicates such as "_is greater than_".

(3) Variables "x", "y", "z", … "x'", "x''", as needed.

(4) The truth-functional sentence connectives "~" for negation ("It is not the case that") and "→" for the material conditional ("if-then"). Other useful truth-functional connectives such as "&" for conjunction, "∨" for disjunction and "↔" for biconditionality—"if and only if"—can be defined in terms of "→" and "~".[1]

(5) The universal quantifier "∀" (indicating "For every _").

(6) Parentheses, to indicate grouping (left intuitive here).

The sentences of such a language are formed by:

(1) Attaching n variables to an n-place predicate, resulting in "atomic open sentences" such as "Fx", "Rxy".

(2) Combining sentences by means of the truth-functional connectives to form sentences such as "Fx→Fy".

(3) Attaching a variable to a quantifier and prefixing it to a sentence, as in "∀x(Fx→Gx)" —i.e., "For every x, if x is F then x is G".

A variable that occurs in a sentence that is not prefixed with a quantifier with that same variable attached is said to be "free" in the sentence; otherwise it is "bound." A "closed sentence" is one containing no free variables. Every other sentence is an "open sentence." For example "∀x(Fx→Gx)" and "∀x∀y(Rxy→∀xGx)" are closed sentences; "Fx→∀xGx" is an open sentence with both bound and free "x."

If the function of the predicate of English "is red" is to be borne by the predicate "F_", then we say the predicate is true of each red thing. For two-place predicates, we assign sets of ordered pairs. For example, if the duty of "is greater than" is borne by the two-place predicate "R_ _", then we say the predicate "R" is true of each ordered pair <a, b> such that a is greater than b. A truth-value for each closed sentence is generated in the following way. An "assignment of values to variables" is a pairing of each variable with some object. Each atomic open sentence thereby acquires a truth-value relative to that assignment, depending on whether the predicate is true of the value of the relevant variable, or of the ordered pair comprising their values in the case of a two-place predicate. A sentence prefixed by a universal quantifier "∀" is true on that assignment if it remains true on every reassignment of the relevant variable to some object; otherwise it is false. Finally, for any sentences S and S* and any assignment of values to variables, the truth-value on that assignment of the negation of "~S", and that of the conditional "S→S*", are given by the standard truth-tables.

Finally we can introduce the identity predicate "_=_": this two-place predicate is true of a given pair <a, b> if and only if a is the same object as b. In the fully fledged language of science that includes set theory, this predicate is explicitly definable and hence need not be recognized as part of the basic and irreducible language of science, but it aids comprehension to think of it as always being in play, whether as primitive or as defined.[2]

Two quick remarks. First, such a language is bereft of what Quine called "indicator words," what Russell called "egocentric particulars," what philosophers now call "indexicals" and linguists call "deictic" expressions. Quine acknowledges that such words are probably indispensable as part of acquiring language in the first place and are certainly needed for ordinary communication (*WP* 222–4), but what he is describing is only a language for certain special purposes, especially that of ontology (similarly for tense; *TT* 10–11, *WP* 145–8, 236–7). Second, we are assuming our predicates to be in a cleaned-up form, without the vagueness of ordinary use; for example we assume sharp boundaries, arbitrarily imposed, in the color-vocabulary (if that vocabulary is admitted at all).

"To Be Is to Be the Value of a Variable"

Such is the type of language that Quine recommends for the regimentation of the whole of science. To express *existence* in such a language is straightforward. Suppose we want to say that an F exists, i.e., that something is F (that it's a turnip, a weapon of mass destruction, whatever). To say that something is F is equivalent to saying *it is not the case that nothing is F*; which is the same as saying that it is not the case that everything is not-F. We write it thus:

(1) ~∀x~Fx.

Accordingly, it is customary to introduce the existential quantifier "∃" simply as an abbreviation of "~∀~ ..."; that is, (1) may be written:

(2) ∃xFx.

—where this is read out as "There exists an x such that Fx".

This immediately delivers Quine's "criterion of ontological commitment," as it is often rather solemnly put. To get the clearest possible grip on what exists, formulate the whole of natural science in the most economical way—such is what Quine calls regimentation as we saw—in terms of the first-order logical language as just described; existential commitment is shown forth simply by the existential quantifications—sentences beginning with an existential quantifier "∃x ..." —that the theory counts as true (*OR* 97). This does not mean that there is no sense whatever to the question of the ontological commitments of a theory expressed in ordinary language, but it does mean that a clear answer depends on what turns out to be the best reformulation in terms of a regimented language (see Hahn and Schilpp 1986, pp. 533–4). Given the reformulation, the question of what a theory says there is—*its* ontological commitments—is settled by the existential quantifications it counts as true; the question of *what there is* is settled by which ones really are true. Of course our best theories may be mistaken, but the philosopher's method of identifying ontological commitment is not supposed to be specially authoritative, as if the philosopher had some access to truth not available to science. "There is no such cosmic exile," as the quotation earlier says. The most that can be done is to find, using a regimented, first-order language, the best formulation we can of present science as a "going concern"—science, that is, understood as fallible, and not final (*WP* 206). It is Naturalism again.

This is really all there is to Quine's oft-cited quip "To be is to be the value of a variable" (*WP* 199, *FLPV* 15, 102–3, *PT* 31; cf. *WP* 201). The quip is merely heuristic, certainly not an official definition of the concept of existence or of the English form of words "to be" (or "exists"); Quine is not suggesting that word might be defined rigorously in terms of something more basic (see again *OR* 97). But it does serve to invoke an underlying technical point. We just saw that in the standard semantics of a regimented language, we speak of *assignments* of objects—"values"—to variables. Consider the open sentence formed by removing the existential quantifier from (2):

(3) Fx.

We say that an existential quantification like (2) is true just in case there is some assignment of values to variables whereby the open sentence (3) comes out true. Thus the truth of "Something is such that it is a toad" is the truth of "It is a toad" for some assignment of "it" to an object; likewise for "∃xFx" and "Fx." To be is to be the value of a variable.

In later years Quine would often stress that the slogan should be seen as utterly vapid, a truism (see *TT* 174–5, *PT* 26–7, *OR* 91–8; cf. *WP* 203). Indeed the idea is equivalent to Quine's smart-alecky initial answer to the question "What is there?," *viz.*, "Everything" (*FLPV* 1). The existing things are just those we speak of when speaking of everything. The excursion through the technicalities of the first-order predicate calculus is pedagogically valuable nonetheless: "to be the value of a variable" is the metalinguistic reflection in regimented language of "to be"—existence as ordinarily described (somewhat as identity may be described as the truth of "a=b" for certain referents of "a" and "b").

Singular Terms and Existence

Consider the sentence "Everything exists." Is this really true? One might think not. Pegasus, for example, does not exist. Therefore not everything exists. Surely it is thus true to say: Some things do not exist. Isn't that quite clear? When we say, "Some men are in the drawing room," it certainly follows that there are men in the drawing room. Likewise, then, doesn't it follow from "Some things do not exist" that *there are* things that do not exist? But if *there are* such things, then such things exist; nonexisting things exist!

Of course, that can't be right. Part of the problem—a problem perhaps first noticed by Kant but which Frege and Russell subjected to more definitive scrutiny—is that "exists" seems to function grammatically as a predicate, like "__ is in the drawing room." So does "__ does not exist." On the face of it, "Pegasus does not exist" is of the form "Pegasus does not canter." If so, then in each case, the sentence is true just in case the predicate is true of the subject. But then there must (in some sense) *be* such an object as Pegasus, and "Pegasus does not exist" cannot possibly be true. As Quine puts it, "It would appear, if this reasoning were sound, that in any ontological dispute the proponent of the negative side suffers the disadvantage of not being able to admit that his opponent disagrees with him" (*FLPV* 1).

These sorts of problems arise in ordinary language because it contains meaningful but non-referring names. If it did not, then presumably there would be nothing wrong with the predicate "exists" (as opposed to the quantifier), except that it would be vacuous, that is, true of everything, like "is self-identical." It would also be irrelevant to expressing general denials of existence claims such as

"Leprechauns do not exist," for which "~∃x(x is a leprechaun)" is sufficient. Now it is certainly possible to devise a formal language which mimics the behavior of singular terms and "exists" in English, and which does not allow invalid proofs of existence. Quine's position, however, is that the sorts of complications introduced by non-referring names are much more trouble than they are worth. Indeed the whole problem is avoidable, for scientific language simply does not require the use of names, and loses nothing for not having them.

The key is provided by Russell's theory of definite descriptions. Let the following represent any statement whatsoever containing a definite description:

(4) ... The F ...

We've been through the rudiments of Russell's theory at pp. 17–18 of Chapter 2. Clearly a definite description is logically in order in all the same positions as a name: if we replace the definite description occurring in grammatically well-formed a sentence with a name, or vice versa, the result will be a grammatically well-formed sentence—attributing some possibly complex condition to the ostensible object. Thus for convenience let us represent the context " ... _ ..." with a predicate letter, rewriting (4) as:

(5) The F is G.

Or in the logical style:

(6) G(The F).

(6) can thus serve as a model for any statement containing a definite description. Russell's central ploy was to claim that the truth of the following is necessary and sufficient for the truth of (6):

(7) ∃x(Fx & ∀y(Fx → x = y) & Gx).

This says that there is something that is uniquely F, and which is G. (Perhaps Russell is not really in a position to make this claim about ordinary language—a case which Paul Grice and Peter Strawson famously made in their 1950 piece "On Referring"—but for Quine's purposes, as we're about to see, this potential mismatch will not matter.)

Now suppose the regimenting scientist wishes to get the effect of the proper name "Socrates." He may invent a predicate, say "Socratizes __," stipulating that it is to be true of just one object at most, namely Socrates. He may thus form the definite description: "The Socratizer." Then to get the effect of "The Socratizer is wise," we can just apply the Russellian recipe, yielding:

(8) ∃x(Socratizes x & ∀y(Socratizes y → x = y) & wise x).

This says, in effect, that there is one and only one Socratizer, and he is wise (see *FLPV* 5–8, *WO* 176–86, *PT* 28, *WP* 205, 238).

Obviously this is not the way English works. But Quine is not proposing an "analysis of proper names"; the strategy is not an hypothesis about English or any natural language, and in particular Quine is not suggesting that sentences like (8) show forth the real underlying meaning or form of English sentences containing proper names. Nor does it matter that the scientist might have to use the name "Socrates" to indicate the object "Socratizes" is true of. The point is to offer a *replacement* of proper names for the ontologically minded purposes of the philosopher-scientist; or not a replacement so much as a *way of avoiding them*. Proper names, as we saw, create quandaries as regards existence. But they are clearly not needed for the rigorous formulation of science; wherever we need to get the effect of them, we can use the ploy exemplified by (8). Puzzles surrounding their ordinary use may thus be discounted as arising from the practical needs or indiscipline of ordinary language, not from genuine theoretical issues. The proper names of ordinary language, then, are irrelevant for the task of ontological accounting.

Predicates and Universals

Another kind of expression that some philosophers have thought to be ontologically committing are general terms such as "fish," or predicates themselves, *viz.* "_ is slimy" (*FLPV* 9ff). At least at one stage of his career, Russell, for example, would have said that "All fish are aquatic" is really a statement about two *universals*, the universals *being a fish* and *being aquatic*. Even the statement "That is a fish" would be explained as ascribing the universal referred to by "fish" to an object. What Russell had in mind was what Quine would call the "copy" theory of language (*WP* 232, *OR* 27): that the function of every significant expression is to name some entity, in such a way that the sentence is a kind of map or diagram of the state of affairs that obtains if the sentence is true (Russell, *The Problems of Philosophy*, chapter 12). Thus "Socrates is wise" is true if and only if there is a state of affairs comprising Socrates and the attribute *wisdom* (the story is more complicated in the case of generalizations such as "All fish are aquatic").

In Quine's view, such an invocation of universals (attributes, properties) is spurious. In a typical semantics of a first-order language such as that described above, the truth-conditions of sentences are explained without invoking universals at all. A predicate such as "_ is a fish" is explained as being *true of* an object just in case the object is a fish; if *true of* is the semantical relation relevant to predicates, there is no need to invoke a separate relation of naming for predicates, as if the only difference between names and predicates lay in the sorts of things they named.[3] The general term "fish" is understood as part of such predicates as "_ is a fish." The objects *of which* such predicates are true or false are as the case may be, but these are already in the range of the variables, the ones attached to the quantifiers "∀" and "∃".

Of course, this does not mean that nobody *can* be charged with affirming the existence of a universal. One can certainly do so by means of the existential quantifier (*FLPV* 12–13): one can assert "∃x(x is a universal)"; one who does so is committed to the existence of universals, and the remaining question is whether or not one is right. Quine's point here is not to argue that universals or attributes do not exist, but that the question of whether or not they do is not settled merely by the use of general terms or predicates (Quine does deny the existence of attributes, but for quite different reasons, as we will see in the next chapter).

Posits, Reality, and Reduction

So much for Quine's method of determining what exists: regiment our best theory in terms of a first-order quasi-formal language, implement as many ontological reductions as is consistent with preserving the empirical content of the theory, and pay attention to the existential quantifications it counts as true. So what sorts of results does Quine envisage? What positively exists, according to Quine?

Throughout his career, Quine gave meticulous attention to the broad ontological questions that have exercised philosophers: about numbers, classes, physical objects, attributes, propositions, and so on. About *abstract* objects— everything on this list except physical objects—the issues are interwoven with the question of what is known as the "extensionality" of the language of science. This is a large topic, reserved for Chapter 6. In this section, we will look at Quine's attitude—often misunderstood—toward physical ontology (and the status of mental objects).

Posits and Reality

Perhaps the central misunderstanding arises from the fact that although Quine is a realist—believing in the existence of ordinary bodies along with atoms and the other entities of theoretical physics (*TT* 21, *WP* 246–54; cf. *WO* 22–3)—he sometimes says things that sound like the words of a non-realist. For example:

> As an empiricist I continue to think of the conceptual scheme of science as a tool, ultimately, for predicting future experience in the light of past experience. Physical objects are conceptually imported into the situation as convenient intermediaries—not by definition in terms of experience, but simply as irreducible posits comparable, epistemologically, to the gods of Homer.
>
> (*FLPV* 44)

We are tempted to insert a "nothing but" between "as" and "a" in the first sentence, and the comparison with the gods of Homer certainly makes it sound as if physical objects are not real. But that is certainly not the point. The clue is the word "irreducible." As Quine puts it in *Word and Object*:

> To call a posit a posit is not to patronize it … Everything to which we concede existence is a posit from the standpoint of a description of the theory-building process, and simultaneously real from the standpoint of the theory being built. Nor let us look down on the standpoint of the theory as make-believe; for we can never do better than occupy the standpoint of some theory or other, the best we can muster at the time.
>
> (*WO* 22; see also *TT* 1–2)

What Quine means by "positing" is simply the use of a language containing certain sorts of terms, whether the adoption is by instinctual learning or the self-conscious adoption of refined theory. In this sense *all* objects are "posits"; but this does not mean that they are thereby unreal. All it means is that we do, as a consequence of language-training and internal wiring, acquire the use of certain linguistic terms, the ones for those objects:

> We posit molecules, and eventually electrons, even though these are not given to direct experience, merely because they contribute to an overall system which is simpler as a whole than its known alternatives … Actually I expect that tables and sheep are, in the last analysis, on much the same footing as molecules and electrons …
>
> The notion of macroscopic objects, tables and sheep, differs from that of molecules and electrons mainly, from an epistemological point of view, in point of degree of antiquity … Men have believed in something like our common-sense world of external objects as long, surely, as anything properly describable as language has existed … It would be senseless to speak of a motive for this archaic and unconscious posit, but we can significantly speak of its function and

survival value; and in these respects the hypothesis of common sense external objects is quite like that of molecules and electrons.

(*WP* 223; see also *WP* 229)[4]

Thus we can ask how and why the adoption of certain forms of language—the putatively referential ones—takes place. We can try to explain how and why human beings have adopted certain linguistic terms and thereby posited certain entities—ordinary bodies, sub-atomic particles, the gods of Homer—in terms of what is practical, what helps the organism, what explains a certain phenomenon, and so on. Such is the main part of naturalized epistemology as discussed in Chapter 4. Those are themselves epistemological questions, not ontological questions, not questions of what exists or is real. As indicated in the quotation above from *Word and Object*, and as stressed earlier, there is no "cosmic exile": the only point of view from which reality can be described and catalogued is within our ongoing, overall theory of the world. Our ability to describe how and why we came to adopt our best theory does not call into question the reality of what it says exists. Thus—especially since the project of the *reduction* of theory of physical objects to that of experience or sensation cannot be carried out— there is apparently no room for questioning the reality of physical objects; they exist according to our best theory, and there is no point of view from which we could identify something in comparison with which they are less real.

Conceptual Analysis versus Explication

If we are wondering whether to include a certain kind of thing in our ontology— that is, if we are wondering whether there are entities of a certain kind—then the question of which entities exactly we would be including depends on the precise "definition" of the kind. Some will be found unproblematically to be included by larger kinds already admitted, as for example the inclusion of Panda bears, provided we had already admitted bears in our ontology (or mammals, or animals, or living things, or perhaps just physical objects). In other cases, it is not so easy. If we are contemplating admitting *souls* in the realm of existing things, or *natural numbers*, it isn't obvious that a decision has in effect already been made. For example, if we are physicalists, the inclusion of souls might be problematic if we are thinking of souls as in some way non-physical. If we are nominalists, the inclusion of natural numbers will also be on the face of it problematic. The standard approach is that a crucial first step will be that of "conceptual analysis." We foreground the word—the concept—of for example "the soul," and we subject it to analysis. We want to find out the real meaning of "the soul." This is more or less the same as what Socrates recommends in the Euthyphro, except that instead of a Platonic Universal, we are dealing with a relatively earth-bound entity, a concept of natural language. Once we know more about the concept, it becomes clear exactly what admitting the corresponding kind of entities will involve.

But Quine does not accept that there are such fine-grained facts to be discovered by conceptual analysis. Even Carnap saw the problem and perhaps indeed passed it on to Quine, writing of the futility of asking such semantical questions, for "in the case of an ordinary language ... the words have no clearly defined meaning" (1962, p. 427). Quine for his part said "Ordinary language is only loosely factual" (*CCE* 285). And no wonder: it arose amidst the traffic of ordinary people with ordinary needs, and it would be strange if it had more determinacy than such needs call for. Commenting on the conundrums of personal identity in 1995, Quine writes:

> They are questions about the concept of person, or the word "person", which, like most words, goes vague in contexts where it has not been needed. When need does arise in hitherto unneeded contexts, we adopt a convention, or receive a disguised one from the Supreme Court.
>
> (*FSS* 39)

And earlier he had subsumed the point under a point of ontology in general:

> The common man's ontology is vague and untidy in two ways. It takes in many purported objects that are vaguely or inadequately defined... [And] we cannot even tell in general which of these vague things to ascribe to a man's ontology ... where can we draw the line?
>
> My point is not that ordinary language is slipshod, slipshod though it be. We must recognize this grading off for what it is, and recognize that a fenced ontology is just not implicit in ordinary language. The idea of a boundary between being and nonbeing is a philosophical idea, an idea of technical science in a broad sense. Scientists and philosophers seek a comprehensive system of the world, and one that is oriented to reference even more squarely and utterly than ordinary language. Ontological concern is not a correction of a lay thought and practice; it is foreign to the lay culture, though an outgrowth of it.
>
> (*TT* 9)

Quine and Carnap thus agree that such an activity is not happily characterized as "analysis"—with the implication of finding out what was there in language all along, as suggested by the purported parallel with chemical analysis. Instead, they advocate "explication" in their special sense: the replacement of existing words or phrases with more precise ones, often similar to the old ones but not necessarily so:[5] "[E]xplication is elimination," wrote Quine (*WO* 260); "The task of explication consists in transforming a given more or less inexact concept into an exact one or, rather, in replacing the first by the second", said Carnap (1962, p. 3). Where what is in question is a not-yet-explicated term K, it is often pointless to insist that there is an essence of K to be drawn out, either by "conceptual analysis" of the term for K or inquiry into the "nature" of K. Still, the notion may be judged to be scientifically necessary, perhaps governed by some principle or conjunction of principles—even if the notion is crucially vague, and maybe will invoke unwanted entities or entities one considers superfluous. The task then is to replace the notion with an improved version, validating the principles in terms of entities which already have the seal of scientific approval.

An example from Quine's *Word and Object* will nail the point down. Quine is assuming that all things—as we'll see in more detail presently—are either physical objects or classes (sets). But what is an *ordered pair*? They are rife in mathematics, indeed they seem essential to it. Quine notes that the ordered pair is "a device for treating objects two at a time as if we were treating objects of some sort one at a time" (*WO* 257) and introduces a "typical use" of the device, that of assimilating relations to classes. Consider the relation of *fatherhood*, a suitably assimilated version of which includes the pair comprising Abraham, Isaac (in that order). While order is immaterial in the case of some relations, in this case—the fatherhood relation—it does matter: in the usual notation, the pair <Abraham, Isaac> is a member of our envisaged class whereas the pair <Isaac, Abraham> is not.

So exactly what is an ordered pair? For a foil Quine presents Peirce's answer, that the two individuals constituting the pair is (or is represented by) a "mental Dyad" consisting of two images with symbols attached to them, one meaning "First," the other "Second." Dismissing this as obscure, Quine declares: "We do better to face the fact that 'ordered pair' is (pending added conventions) a defective noun, not at home in all the questions and answers in which we are accustomed to imbed terms at their full-fledged best" (*WO* 258). So we are free to add the missing conventions. He then points out that it is "a special virtue [of the notion] is that mathematicians pretty deliberately introduced it, subject in effect to the single postulate: 'If <x,y> = <z,w>, then x=z and y=w' (*WO* 258), a postulate that can be satisfied in various ways, one due to Norbert Wiener, another to Kazimierz Kuratowski." As easily verified, identifying the ordered pair <x,y> with the unordered pair of sets {{x, ∅}, {y}} as Wiener suggests, or as {{x}, {x,y}}, as Kuratowski suggests, does the trick.[6] Either choice is a satisfactory (and there are others). Thus the notion of ordered pair does not actually require anything more than elementary set theory itself, which Quine is assuming is already accepted.

Any account that satisfies the specified condition of adequacy will serve. This represents a rather profound difference between the orthodox view of philosophical or conceptual analysis—and of ontology—and Quine's view (and Carnap's view). Very roughly, the orthodox philosopher takes ordinary language as expressing tolerably sharp concepts (or denoting tolerably sharp universals, properties, or kinds), whereas Quine does not. Many terms—especially as we will see in the next chapter, ones which you would have thought are of philosophical interest, like "property," "necessity," and "essence"—are not thought worthy of figuring officially in a statement of ontology (Quine famously or notoriously avouched a predilection for "desert landscapes" *FLPV* 4). The philosopher is free to change those that are needed:

> This construction is paradigmatic of what we are most typically up to when in a philosophical spirit we offer an "analysis" or "explication" of some hitherto inadequately formulated "idea" or expression. We do not claim synonymy. We do not claim to make clear and explicit what the users of the unclear expression had unconsciously in mind all along. We do not expose hidden meanings, as the words "analysis" and "explication" would suggest; we supply lacks. We fix on the particular functions of the unclear expression that make it worth troubling about, and then devise a substitute, clear and couched in terms to our liking, that fills those functions. Beyond those conditions of partial agreement, dictated by our interests and purposes, any traits of the explicans come under the head of "don't cares".
>
> (*WO* 257)

For a "don't care" case, one can cite examples such as whether or not {x, y} is a member of <x, y>: if you're following Kuratowski then it is, if you're following Weiner then it is not, but nothing substantive hangs on the answer one gives to the question. Similar, as we'll see in the next chapter, is the question of whether 2 ∈ 3; the truth of this plainly artificial sentence will depend on whether we accept a certain set-theoretic rendition of the natural numbers, but in itself is of no independent interest.

The idea may seem familiar to you under the currently popular name of "conceptual engineering," but that there are (at least) four important differences. (1) It might seem intuitive to speak of "concepts" rather than "words," but to do so is to prejudge the issue of whether, or in what sense, the concept expressed by a word in one language is the same as the one expressed by a word in another. It is less presumptuous to speak simply of words, where by a word we speak not of a mere sound or phoneme-sequence, but of a meaningful word of some particular language. (2) Neither Quine nor Carnap care especially if explicated words fail generally to "catch on" with wider public (the "implementation problem"); their recommendations are directed only at a small coterie of ontologically minded philosophers which they are in communication with. (3) They positively welcome it if philosophical problems lapse—if they cannot be formulated or have easy answers—using the explicated word (the "trivialization problem"); for them, this is what philosophical progress looks like. (4) Finally the new items are formulated and results stated but there need not be any special normative force invoked beyond any "oughts" or "cans" involved in philosophical argument generally.

What There Is

There are three basic types of objects that one might recognize: the physical, the mental, and the abstract. The abstract will be discussed in the next chapter; and as we will see, Quine identifies mental objects—at least the respectable ones—with physical objects. Accordingly we shall take some care in coming to grips with his ontology of physical objects.

As we said, Quine accepts the general motive behind ontological reduction: We should seek, when formulating our definitive account of reality as we know it, to minimize its ontological commitments. Unnecessary existential commitments should be eliminated. Unnecessary, however, for exactly what? Ideally, the point would be this. Suppose that our overall theory of the world is written out as some huge conjunction of sentences T. What we want is a reformulation of T—call this T*—that has the *same net empirical consequences* as T, such that no other reformulation of T with the same empirical consequences is ontologically more economical than T*.

In practice, this ideal will never be realized, and it is too much of an idealization even on its own terms (even setting aside the vagueness of "more economical," not to mention the idealization of "*our* theory"). No one is ever going to produce such an overall reformulation of everything we take ourselves to know, and ontological economy is not the only criterion of "best theory." Theories should strive for explanatory power, maximum concord with observation, conceptual simplicity, and so on (as in *WB*). There will always be trade-offs between these things. We can, however, consider how some key aspects of how the reformulation might go, and focus for illustrative purposes on ontological economy, invoking other considerations only as they crop up.

Bodies such as stones, apples and rabbits, as discussed earlier, are the "primordial posits"; keeping track of them and talking about them is incomparably useful to the human animal. Science certainly deals with all sorts of bodies—biology with animals, astronomy with stars, geology with rocks. Does physics deal with bodies? Here is a lack of clarity in the concept of a body. For example, bodies are supposed to be at least somewhat solid, but it is unclear what it would mean to say, of a single atom, that it is solid. Nor is it clear just how well held together a body must be, how squishy or friable it can be, whether it can be completely discontinuous (as when we speak of the car, despite its temporarily having been taken apart). For these and similar reasons, Quine proposes that the idea of a body should be replaced by the more artificial idea of a "physical object": a physical object is simply the material content of *any* portion of space-time (*TT* 10–13). Thus rabbits will be physical objects, and so will rabbit-stages. But, since physical objects are the material content of *any* portion of space-time, they can be discontinuous, or scattered, or "gerrymandered": the material content of a certain discontinuous region of space-time, for example, would encompass Paris, my left shoe, and the planet Mars. We don't tend to talk about such objects, but they exist. The definition of a physical object is not a notion of common sense, but it yields some direct dividends besides eliminating the vagueness of "body."

First, we can identify *events* and *actions* with physical objects: an event is simply the material content of a continuous portion of space over a relatively short time, in the case where some physical states of that material are changing during that time (an action is the case where the relevant material content is that of an animal or animal-stage). This implies that if you are both walking and chewing gum over a given interval, then the walking and the gum-chewing are the same event; but still it is not the case that all walkings are gum-chewings or vice versa. Nothing that holds in general of gum-chewings holds in general of walkings nor the reverse (*TT* 11–12).[7]

Second, the *criterion of identity* for physical objects—the standard for when we have one and when we have two—is unlike those for most ordinary bodies in being simple and clear: physical objects are identical when and only when their spatial and temporal boundaries are the same. We thus have a principled way out of famous identity puzzles such as the Ship of Theseus. Beginning at time t_1, the planks of Ship A are replaced slowly, one-by-one. The result, later at t_2, is Ship B—comprising different planks from those of ship A—but at t_2 there also emerges Ship C, assembled from the old planks from A. Obviously B ≠ C, as one ship cannot be in two places at the same time. But is A the same ship as B? Is A the same as C? Neither? What is certainly true is that the matter (*qua* physical object) composing Ship A at t_1 is a temporal part of the same *physical object* as the matter composing Ship B at t_2, *and* a temporal part of the same *physical object* as the matter composing Ship C at t_2. These are different physical objects, since they are in different places at t_2, despite the coincidence of their spatial coordinates at t_1. This is just a four-dimensional analogue of a three-dimensional case of the part-whole relation like, say, Hawaii, which is part of the northern hemisphere but also part of Polynesia, which extends into the southern hemisphere; there are three objects involved, but one is part of both the one and of the other. Nothing mysterious about that. Identity puzzles about ships, then, afflict the notion of a "ship"—what are the identity-conditions of ships—not that of "physical object" in Quine's sense (try the puzzle of the sculpture and the clay at home). Presumably, if needed—perhaps for legal purposes—the notion could be sharpened; ships could be defined as those physical objects that satisfy some rather complicated condition, yielding A = B or A = C as seems convenient or more in accord with common sense.

Third, it becomes straightforward to recognize certain entities which are very much like universals or attributes, yet remain physical objects. Begin with *mass-terms*—nouns that are not count-nouns—such as "milk," and "gold": we can think of these as standing for certain highly scattered and changeable physical objects comprising all the world's milk and all its gold, ever and in the future. To speak of "some milk," then, is to speak of a spatio-temporal part of that physical object, and to assert "That is milk" is to say of some small physical object that it is part of milk. We can do something similar with abstract nouns such as "redness." It can stand for the physical object comprising all those physical objects whose surfaces are red, or perhaps all the surfaces themselves. This sort of thing could be made more precise if needed.

It thus appears that wherever we are using nouns to speak of the material world, that talk can be explicated as referring to physical objects, in Quine's technical sense. Such talk could be replaced without significant loss by talk about physical objects.

What then about mental entities? Quine is often portrayed as a physicalist, or materialist, and in one sense that is accurate. But it is a sophisticated sense. For events in consciousness, he maintains, *are* physical, even if they have a "subjective" side: "the dualist ... is bound to agree that for every state of mind there is an exactly concurrent and readily specifiable state of the accompanying body"—even if it is the state of brain itself that would be specified. And then we can "just reinterpret the mentalistic terms as denoting these correlated bodily states, and who is to know the difference?" (*TT* 18–19; also *WO* 264–6). What we are accustomed to call our mental states are really just physical states, even though of course many of them have properties which we cannot explain, notably conscious properties. But that is a fair price, as mentalists cannot explain them either, and the physicalist is quite right to cling on to the laws of conservation until the bitter end.

Some will worry about "reductionism." Does the view "repudiate the mental state of pain or anger in favor of its physical concomitant, or does [the account] identify the mental state with a state of the physical organism (thus a state of the physical organism with the mental state)?" Quine finds only rhetorical reasons between the two, but he grants that "the latter version sounds less drastic" (*WO* 265). Second, one must appreciate how far physics has come from the sixteenth-century idea that causation is mechanical, and that the paradigm physical object is a mid-sized item such as a stone or a billiard-ball. Gravity, relativity theory, quantum entanglement, various sub-atomic "particles" show us that ordinary experience is but a fleeting glimpse of the whole. "The objective is just full coverage of the ultimate ingredients and forces of the world, whatever they may be. The buck stops in physics" (*CCE* 166). If the mind seemed to have unforeseen emerging powers, the physicist will strive to integrate it with the rest of physics.

We shall return to the topic in Chapter 7.

Ontological Relativity

Imagine that the theory of Quinean physical objects is expressed in the first-order predicate calculus. According to a well-known theorem, the "Lowenheim-Skölem theorem," any set of sentences of the first-order predicate calculus that is true in some interpretation is also true in some interpretation *in the domain of natural numbers*. This means that for every predicate in our imagined theory of physical objects, it can be interpreted as true of natural numbers only, in such a way that all the old sentences retain their truth-values in the new interpretation. So much is simply a theorem of mathematical logic, nothing controversial. But does it follow that our whole theory of the material world could be interpreted as concerned only with numbers? One might naturally think not, since surely the change in subject-matter would affect the *empirical content* of the theory; a statement about numbers, surely, could not have the same empirical content as one about rabbits.

It follows from previous definitions, however, that our theory of physical objects, its predicates reinterpreted so as to be true only of numbers, *would* leave its empirical content unchanged. The reason is that the empirical content of a theory is defined as the collection of its observation categoricals, and observation categoricals do not themselves require the use of reference for their explanation. Quine concludes from this not that our theory of nature is "really" about numbers, but there is no fact of the matter as to what a given theory is really about—what its ontological commitments are—except relative to a given interpretation of the theory, that is, a given translation of it into a "background" language. Such is Quine's doctrine of "Ontological Relativity" (*OR* 26–68).[8] In order to understand it, let us backtrack a little.

In fact, we have already considered ontological relativity in Chapter 3, in the guise of the "inscrutability of reference." The idea was that the native term "gavagai" could be translated as either "rabbit," "rabbit-stage," or "undetached rabbit-part," consistently with all empirical evidence for translation, so long as compensating adjustments are made in the translation of the native apparatus of individuation—expressions corresponding to such expressions as "is the same as." Crucially, the stimulus meaning of the observation *sentence* "Gavagai!" is unaffected by the different references ascribed to the "gavagai" as a term: that is what makes them empirically adequate translations.

After *Word and Object*, Quine would streamline, strengthen, and generalize this idea, using the idea of a "proxy function" (*WP* 217, *OR* 55–62, *TT* 19–22, *FSS* 71–3, *PT* 31–3). A function such as the square function connects an object—a so-called "argument"—to another, a "value" (the value of the function for that argument). The arguments for the function comprise the "domain" of the function; the values comprise the "range" of the function (sometimes called the "counter-domain" of the function). Thus the value of the square function for the argument 2 is 4, for 12 it is 144, and so on. A "one-to-one" function is one which "maps" each argument from its domain onto a different value, and never the same argument onto more than one. So "spouse of" is one-to-one if the domain is composed of monogamous married individuals; "square of" is one-to-one (with respect to the natural numbers—0, 1, 2 … —as the domain), for every natural number has a unique square and no number is the square of more than one.

Now suppose we have a theory expressed in a first-order language as discussed, where the universe of the theory is D. A "proxy function" is a one-to-one function which takes *every* element of D as its arguments, and maps them onto other objects, which may lie wholly within, partly within, or wholly without the original universe D. An example of a proxy-function is "spatio-temporal complement of": the spatio-temporal complement of a dog, for example, is the entire universe minus the dog. We can reinterpret each predicate of the theory as true of the proxy of x wherever it was true of x. Thus if the predicate G was true of x, we now interpret it as true of the proxy of x. Similarly for two-place (relational) predicates. If we temporarily re-allow names into our language, it's easy to see how a proxy-reinterpretation preserves the truth-value of every sentence of the original scheme. Suppose a dog is named "Fred," and the (natural language equivalent) sentence is "Fred is spotty." This is true if and only if Fred's proxy is the proxy of a spotty thing (Fred, for example), which is obviously true. One can show that such reinterpretation preserves the truth-value of every interpreted sentence of the original theory.[9] The whole thing is perhaps trivial, but true nonetheless.

Reinterpretation using a proxy function does not disturb the stimulus meanings of observation sentences, *whatever* proxies it connects with the original domain. The proxy-interpretation accords with linguistic dispositions just as well as the old interpretation. Indeed our *own* theory could be reinterpreted so as to be about completely different things without disturbing the truth-values of any of the sentences it comprises, and perfectly consistently with our actual linguistic dispositions, our behavior with respect to all sentences including observation sentences. We could take our word "rabbit" to refer to rabbits, or to numbers, or to various other things, including unit-sets of rabbits, or cosmic complements of rabbits. But there would be no difference in the way we speak, in what passes in our minds, or in which sentences come out true. It would remain as ever that the presence of rabbits would make us disposed to assent to "Rabbit!," and even that the word "rabbit" would bring about a certain mental image in our minds. Quine writes:

> "There's a rabbit" remains keyed to the sensory stimulations by which we learned it ... the term does continue to conjure up visions appropriate to the observation sentence through which the term was learned, but there is no empirical bar to the reinterpretation. The original sensory associations were indispensable genetically in generating the nodes by which we structure our theory of the world. But all that matters by way of evidence for the theory is the stimulatory basis of the observation sentences plus the structure that the neutral nodes serve to implement. The stimulation remains as rabbity as ever, but the corresponding node or object goes neutral and is up for grabs.
>
> (*PT* 34; see also *CCE* 415)

Different schemes of reference would make the same sentences true. They are consistent with all linguistic behavior, in the sense of linguistic dispositions. There is no objective reason to assign one reference scheme to a language rather than another proxy-equivalent alternative. The reason this seems so bizarre, of course, is that it is undoubtedly the presence of rabbits that is causally correlated with our use of "There's a rabbit" and such like, not for example numbers. We think of the idea of reference as having something to do with *that*. The lesson, then, is just to repeat the main lesson Quine's discussion of the empirical study of language discussed in Chapter 4: the real objective language-world connection is a certain causal relation (involving rabbits, etc.), but that is not the relation of reference, not a relation between objects and *terms*; it is a relation between environmental events and dispositions to affirm observation *sentences* (see *CCE* 410–12, *TT* 3). We are misled, no doubt, by superficial similarity between "gavagai" considered as a referring *term* and "Gavagai!" as a one-word observation *sentence* (equivalent to "A rabbit is present!"). In fact, as Quine sees it, *"nothing changes"* (*TT* 20, emphasis added)—and nothing has to change in one's mental life—with such a change of ontological scheme (*TT* 20).

Ontology versus Semantics

Quine explicitly equates ontological relativity with the inscrutability of reference (or better, the *indeterminacy* of reference: *PT* 50–2). Since, according to the lesson of proxy-functions, the possible reference-schemes for a language appear to be quite unconstrained, this seems to mean that just as there is no fact of the matter about reference—the inscrutability of reference—there is none about ontology. But what happens, then, to the whole Quinean project of identifying the actual ontological commitments of our theory? Hasn't the rug been pulled from under it?

The answer is no. The reason, as Quine puts it, is that when answering the sorts of scientific questions of ontology we are interested in when we ask "What is there?," we "acquiesce in the home tongue" (*OR* 49). This means, at bottom, that when answering basic ontological questions such as "Do numbers exist?" or less basic ones such as "Are there tigers on Kamchatka?," we are *using* our language, just as we do when answering any other scientific question. There is nothing peculiarly language-relative about the answer to those questions. When *using* the home language, then of course "'Rabbit' refers to rabbit-complements" is false, as surely false as "Rabbits are rabbit-complements." Indeterminacy arises only when we ask semantical questions *about* a language: to what items do these expressions refer? Does "rabbit" *really* refer to rabbits or rabbit-complements? To *that* sort of question there is no objective answer; there are objective answers only to questions about which overall translation schemes are empirically adequate, and these may assign very different references to "rabbit." As a non-semantical matter concerning what exists, ontology is a well-defined enterprise; as a semantical one concerning the relation between words and the world, it is not. It is an attempt at "transcendental metaphysics," which is thereby revealed to be empty. The only objective and scientifically discoverable word-world relation is the relation between observation sentences and stimulation, which is a causal relation, not a semantical relation.

Quine's own slogan, "To be is to be the value of a variable," may well have misled some readers into supposing that the thesis of the inscrutability of reference—hence ontological relativity—undermines ontology. For "being the value of a variable" is a semantical relation; the slogan thus appears to identify existence with standing in a semantical relation to a linguistic item. As we explained earlier, that is not the point of the slogan. The slogan is merely a tongue-in-cheek way of conveying the idea that it is only when it is presented in a rigorous first-order language, with its existentially quantified variables, that we have a sharp criterion for identifying the existential commitments of a theory.

For all that, however, ontological relativity—in particular the mere fact that changing ontology is so easy—changes the complexion of things to be sure. In later writings Quine agreed that with ontological relativity "ontology has undergone a humiliating demotion" (*CCE* 317), and verged in the end on a "structural" conception of ontology (*CCE* 449–60). But there we must leave it.[10]

Truth

Quine's program for determining what exists—formulate our current theory of nature in a first-order predicate calculus and attend to the resulting existential quantifications—is nothing like a *definition* of existence. It is a sharpening, not a definition. Nor is the basic question of the ontological commitments of our theory of nature—of existence in its most general terms—a semantical question, a question about the relation of our theory to the world. Such a question could be answered only from a position of "cosmic exile," which is impossible. Such, yet again, is the thesis of naturalism. We can catalogue the world, as Quine puts it, only within a theory.

Much the same goes for truth. Truth applies to sentences just as reference applies to predicates—a relation often spoken of as "true-of"—for example "is a dog" is said to be *true of* every dog (Quine himself once used the term "denotation" to cover both; *FSS* 59–67). And certainly truth has an important and thoroughgoing role to play in serious science which deserves examination; indeed it hardly seems conceivable that we could get by without using the phrase "is true" or some equivalent. However it is easy to be misled. Philosophers have often assumed, abetted perhaps by common sense, that truth is a relation between certain entities—sentences, statements, propositions, thoughts, or beliefs—and the world, or parts of the world such as facts or states of affairs. Quine does not think that such a theory of truth is viable. "Truth," he says in keeping with Naturalism, "is immanent," meaning that we can speak of truth only insofar as we work within the very system of statements—or "conceptual scheme" as he often puts it—to which we attribute truth; there is no coherent idea of an external standard in the form of a correspondence relation between statements (or similar entities) and the world (see *WO* 19–25). There are some complex technical issues in play here, but we should be able to gain a sense of Quine's position without going very far into those.

Quine and Tarski

We can start by considering the basics of the famous proof of the indefinability of truth by Alfred Tarski, a friend and ally of Quine. Tarski [1936] proved that truth cannot be defined for a language by using that very same language. He proposed that truth for a language L is "materially correct" only if it consistently ensures that every sentence of the following kind is logically derivable in the language:

"s" is true-in-L if and only if p.

—where "s" is replaced by a sentence of L and "p" by a sentence that translates that sentence (do not worry about the presence of the word "translation").[11] An example would be:

"Schnee ist weiß" is true-in-German if and only if snow is white.

Such are Tarski's "T-sentences" (the form of which is called the "T-schema"). The language for which truth is defined is called the "object language," and the language one uses to give the definition the "metalanguage."

A theory that conforms to the T-schema brings out what is cogent in the idea of correspondence. Quine said "such is the correspondence" (*PT* 80)—meaning merely that the T-schema is all that's left of the idea of correspondence. In particular it does not survive as a proper two-place relation "x corresponds to y." Yet what's left of the idea is partly accurate, in that the truth of a claim depends partly on extralinguistic reality, not merely "coherence" with other sentences.

Now if we were to give a definition of "truth-in-L" using L itself, then the object language is identical to the metalanguage, and the definition will imply all sentences of the following form, special cases of T-sentences:

"s" is true-in-L if and only if s.

—where "s" is replaced by a sentence of the language L—which in this case is English. Quine calls this intra-linguistic form the "disquotation schema." An example in English of a disquotational T-sentence would be "'Socrates is wise' is true-in-English if and only if Socrates is wise."

The reason that a truth-definition cannot successfully be formulated in the very language it pertains to is that, since the language for which truth is defined would contain "true," it would make possible the construction of "Liar Sentences," such as the following:

This sentence is not true.

One can prove, using the T-schema, that this sentence is true if and only if it is not true, a contradiction. Such is the Liar Paradox, made famous by the Cretans and then Russell.[12]

To this negative result Tarski added a very important positive result. This is that a consistent and materially correct definition of truth for a language *can* be given, so long as the definition is formulated in a language that is "mathematically stronger" than the language for which truth is defined (one language is mathematically stronger than another if when using it one can prove all the theorems of the other and then some; note that by a "language" is meant really a theory). The metalanguage may include the object language, or be wholly distinct from it. Furthermore, such definitions do not themselves make essential use of any semantical concepts (such as "reference" and "true-of"), except insofar as they are explicitly defined in non-semantical, hence innocuous terms. The key is that whereas a language of the kind envisaged has infinitely many sentences, it has only finitely many simple predicates. So for example, "F _" might be explained as true of an arbitrary object just in case that object is a dog; if we do this for each predicate, we have a definition of "true of" for a certain portion of the language without using any semantical concepts in the metalanguage. Given some further rules governing the truth-functional connectives and the quantifiers, the T-sentence for each sentence of the object language emerges as a logical consequence of definitions without relying on any semantical concepts including truth. This result is important because it shows that the liar paradox (and related semantical paradoxes) do not entail that the concept of truth cannot be used in serious science.

This positive result does not solve the "general" problem of truth. What Tarski does is to show how to construct truth-definitions for particular languages. Following the recipe, we can define truth for language LI using L2; then we can do it for language L2, then for L3, and so on. But "true-in-LI," "true-in-L2" and so on are different predicates, in which the reappearance of the English word "true" is inessential. These definitions do not tell us what is necessary and sufficient for the truth of an arbitrary sentence of L for *variable* L, that is, irrespective of which language L happens to be.

Such a universal definition would apply to the very language we are using, which is impossible without contradiction.[13] The correct inference to draw from the indefinability of truth-in-general is not that the general notion of truth is inscrutably primitive, as if, in a complete theory of everything, we would nevertheless have to include an irreducible predicate "_is true" (though some philosophers have held this view, or something like it).[14] The reason is that a truth-predicate of universal scope would be inconsistent, as just described. "Truth off the hierarchy," Quine writes, "absolute truth, would indeed be transcendent; bringing it down into scientific theory of the world engenders paradox. So naturalism has no place for that" (*CCE* 472). Tarski's results are very much of a piece with Quine's general attitude toward semantics. Quine argued on other grounds that the relation of language to the world cannot be explained in terms of reference. Tarski's results seem to show that such an explanation would actually be logically inconsistent; for the general theoretical availability of the concept reference would make it easy to define truth for English in English, for example as:

For any s, s is true-in-English if and only if "is such that s" refers to everything.[15]

This might seem a little artificial, but a little reflection should show that it counts each true sentence as true, and each untrue one as not true. But then it must generate inconsistency.

Generality and Semantic Ascent

So Tarski's results add to the case against a general semantical theory of the relation between language and the world. Nevertheless, the concept of truth has an important function. This function is indicated by the very triviality of disquotational T-sentences, such as

"Snow is white" is true if and only if snow is white.

For every sentence of English, there is a T-sentence that states a condition necessary and sufficient for the truth of that sentence. We cannot consistently accept *every instance* of the disquotational T-schema:

"p" is true if and only if p.

—for that would generate inconsistency. But this does not stop us from accepting every instance of the schema wherein the quoted sentence does not include the word "true" (or any cognate notions); for only ones that do, or sets of those, can generate paradox. Thus although in one sense the concept of truth is obscure—it is paradoxical—in another sense it is crystal clear: suitably restricted, it seems trivial and transparent. To say that a sentence is true is equivalent to affirming the sentence itself. Thus at bottom, the notion of truth is quite pedestrian and does not involve anything so exotic as a language-world relation. To call something "true" is not to invoke a theory, in the way it is to call something an "organic molecule." In particular, nothing substantive is thereby assumed about semantics or syntactical structure: all that is assumed is that the thing is a sentence of one's language.

Why then can't our theory of truth just be: accept all instances of the disquotational T-schema "'p' is true if and only if p," so long as the sentence put for "p" lacks the word "true" (or any cognate notions)? Quine is often held to propose something like this, that he is a "deflationist" about truth. But that cannot be quite right. Suppose we have a whole class of sentences which do not themselves contain "true." Suppose this class is infinite, such as the class of all sentences of the form "If p then p." We cannot *assert* every such sentence, since there are too many. What we want is to assert that every such sentence is *true*. This goes beyond the trivial use of "true" attached to a single sentence, and cannot be achieved by simply invoking a single T-sentence (or conjunction of them). A sentence of the form "For all sentences s, if s satisfies such-and-such condition, then s is true" is not itself a T-sentence. But Tarski's positive results show how such sentences can be proven—again, so long as the proofs are conducted in a language that is stronger than the language being discussed. So in particular, one can prove a sentence which says that every instance of "If p then p" is true, and also more interesting things such as that every sentence logically derivable from a set of true sentences—such as a set of axioms for arithmetic—is true.

For Quine, what Tarski's positive results show is that we can get the effect of *generalizing* using a truth-predicate, yet in such a way that the theoretical import of the truth-predicate is explained by the idea of disquotation. As Quine puts it, what "true" does is to make available another "dimension of generalization" (called "oblique generalization" at *PL* 97). We can generalize on "Socrates is mortal" by writing "Every man is mortal." Similarly we can generalize on "If time flies then time flies" by writing "Every sentence of the form 'If p then p' is true," or on "'p' is provable in the theory T and p" by writing "Every sentence provable in the theory T is true" (*PT* 80–1). We do not have to regard it as strictly speaking nonsense to speak generally of "mathematical truth," "logical truth," or indeed "truth."

Such, in general, is the role of what Quine calls "semantic ascent" (*WO* 270–6, *PL* 10–13, *PT* 80–2). Despite the limits of semantical notions, it is essential and internal to science that we should be able to talk *about* languages and theories, especially for the purpose of comparing them. It happens not only in logic and mathematics, according to Quine, but in physics and other empirical sciences, when a theory as a whole is compared with another (*WO* 272). This may indeed have encouraged the idea that a certain irreducible semantical perspective—a metaphysics of the word-world relation—is essential to science, that science presupposes a certain metaphysical picture.[16] What Tarski showed was that no such thing is implied by the utility and even indispensability of semantic ascent: so long as we do not try to transcend the *whole* of science at one go, we gain the effect of semantical notions without assuming them as ultimate or wholly general in their application. The lack of cosmic exile is not a real impediment to knowledge.

In this chapter we have been commenting on Quine's account of truth, reference, and ontology. His position is that those concepts play theoretically important roles—they may enter legitimately into our best theory—but our account of those roles must not involve the incoherent idea of cosmic exile, a vantage point somehow external to the sum of knowledge. The exact reasons for the impossibility of cosmic exile are rather different as between truth and ontology, but still the parallel is striking. This is the final paragraph of Quine's "Ontological Relativity":

> Regress in ontology is reminiscent of the now familiar regress in the semantics of truth and kindred notions—satisfaction [*true of,* roughly], naming. We know from Tarski's work how the semantics ... of a theory regularly demands an in some way more inclusive theory. This similarity should perhaps not surprise us, since both ontology and satisfaction are matters of reference. In their elusiveness, at any rate—in their *emptiness now and again except relative to a broader background*—both truth and ontology may in a suddenly rather clear and even tolerant sense be said to belong to transcendental metaphysics. (*OR* 68; emphasis added)

What is to be tolerated of course is not the empty use of such concepts, but the use of the phrase "transcendental metaphysics" to indicate procedures which stay within the proper limits, going step by step. Tarski's work shows how to gain truth-predicates which do this; they provide "better and better truth predicates but no best" (*PT* 89).

Further Reading and Historical Notes

That the general ideas that ontology, what exists, is more or less given by the true existential quantifications of language, and that what *we* take to exist, "our ontology," is given by the true existential quantifications of our language, are not notably controversial even if not universally accepted. No wonder, as Quine points out; it is well-nigh a truism, or so it seems. If one has doubts, Quine can reply that such doubts may well be the product of the vagaries of ordinary language; what he advances can be looked upon as a streamlined improvement. But the further questions of what those true sentences are, and Quine's insistence on regimentation—not on ordinary language as the court of ontological appeal—have been more controversial, and it has to be said understood less well. A good survey of alternative approaches is by Philip Bricker 2014, "Ontological Commitment," in the *Stanford Encyclopedia of Philosophy*. For doubts about the inference for the Inscrutability of Reference to Ontological Relativity, my Kemp 2020. On the connection of Quine's account of explication to projects of conceptual engineering, see Nado 2021. On the question of truth, again Quine's view is not genuinely appreciated for what it is; he is commonly held to espouse the view that acceptance of the T-schema is all that is required, a "deflationist" or "redundancy" view; I have tried to emphasize that is not so. Quine knew Tarski very early in his career and got to know him well in the period immediately subsequent to the Second World War; for details—not least the philosophical angles—see Frost-Arnold 2013. He more or less accepted Tarski's conception of truth (Tarski first presented his approach to truth in his [1936]; an informal presentation of the main ideas is in Tarski [1955]). See my Kemp 2020, and for an interesting discussion—although I do not agree with it in the end—see Bergström 2000.

Ontology II: Extensionality and Abstract Objects

Quine in 1995:

> Extensionality is much of the glory of predicate logic, and it is much of the glory
> of any science that can be grammatically embedded in predicate logic. I find
> extensionality necessary, though indeed not sufficient, for my full understanding
> of a theory. In particular it is an affront to common sense to see a true sentence
> go false when a singular term in it is supplanted by another that names the same
> thing. What is true of a thing is true of it, surely under any name.
>
> (*FSS* 90–1)

The notion of "extensionality" has three aspects, appertaining respectively to
sentences, predicates, and singular terms (that is, names as well as definite
descriptions; otherwise I am assuming the austere syntax of a regimented
language outlined in Chapter 5):

(i)   If two sentences have the same truth-value (they are either both true or
      both false), then wherever one of them occurs as part of a longer sentence,
      replacing it by the other will not change the truth-value of the longer
      sentence.

(ii) If two predicates are *co-extensive* (they are true of all and only the same
      things), then in any sentence containing one of them, replacing it by the
      other will not change the truth-value of the sentence.

(iii) If the language contains singular terms (names or definite descriptions),
      then if two of them are *co-referential* (refer to the same object), then for
      any sentence containing the one, replacing it by the other will not change
      the truth-value of the sentence.

In some discussions (for example in Carnap's), sentences, singular terms, and predicates are all spoken of as having an "extension"—a truth-value in the case of a sentence, a referent in the case of a singular term, an extension (set of things it is true of) in the case of a predicate (a set of ordered pairs in the case of a two-place predicate). Hence the name. The idea of extensionality is often summed up by saying: co-extensive expressions are intersubstitutable "salva veritate"— that is, the truth-value the containing sentence will not change so long as the extension of what is substituted does not change.

It is because of extensionality that the truth-value of any sentence of a regimented language—one based on the predicate calculus—is a "function" of the extensions of its parts: once extensions are assigned to all singular terms and simple predicates of the first-order predicate calculus, the truth-value of every sentence of the language is determined (though there may not be a way of computing what it is). Such was one of the results that Tarski established in his pioneering work on truth and semantics. This clarity of structure, as Quine urged in the quotation above, is vital, and can be brought to bear on all genuinely scientific discourse.

Ordinary language, however, is full of idioms that create *non-extensional* contexts, or "intensional" contexts (we could further distinguish these from what are known as "hyperintensional contexts," but we will not discuss them by that name). Through much of this chapter, we will consider intensional contexts that are smaller than a sentence—cases where the interchange of co-extensional singular terms or predicates may alter the truth-value of the enclosing sentence. Among these are the cases of propositional attitude and modality, topics which have received such an enormous amount of attention in the analytic philosophy of the past seventy years, with Quine's writings serving as a point of common reference.

Dispositions and Causality

First, however, let us consider what Quine has to say about certain extensionality failures that occur only with respect to *sentential* contexts. An example is that of the "counterfactual conditional":

(1) If the doorbell *had* rung, the dog *would have* barked.

We would normally assert (1) only when both "the doorbell rang" and "the dog barked" are false, but these truth-values leave open the truth-value of (1).

The counterfactual form "If p had been the case, then q would have been the case" is thus not truth-functional; it is non-extensional.

We shall set aside the counterfactual conditional itself,[1] but two closely connected and scientifically important notions are those of *disposition* and *causality.* We'll take them in order.

What exactly is a disposition? Suppose we say that a certain substance is *soluble* in water. This means that if a bit of that substance is placed in water, then it dissolves—in the sense that if it *isn't* placed in water, it *would* dissolve if it *were* placed in water. Thus suppose it isn't placed in water, and it isn't dissolving. Clearly, this in itself does not settle whether or not it is soluble in water. In Quine's view, the dispositional idiom is indispensable to science, but this fact does not actually call into question the idea that extensionality is necessary for "full understanding." The reason is that they represent areas of immaturity or ignorance in our knowledge of a given subject-matter. In particular, to speak of a "disposition" is to speak, in relative ignorance, of its underlying physical mechanism:

> Each disposition, in my view, is a physical state or mechanism ... Where the general dispositional idiom has its use is as follows. By means of it we refer to a hypothetical state or mechanism that we do not yet understand, or to any of various such states or mechanisms, while merely specifying one of its characteristic effects, such as dissolution upon immersion in water.
>
> (*RR* 10)

Consider, to take another example, the property of *being flammable.* It is the disposition to burn upon the application of something like a flame or spark. The underlying states or mechanisms are certain chemical properties which ultimately consist in configurations of molecules. If we restrict the discussion to the combustion of hydrocarbons—propane, for example—there are laws of chemistry to the effect that whenever certain hydrocarbons, in the presence of free oxygen, are subjected to a certain amount of energy, combustion takes place: heat, carbon dioxide, and water result. The law itself, however, does not state a disposition, and it is not a counterfactual conditional: it can be expressed in fully extensional language (such are the chemical equations one learns in school chemistry). In a particular case of a flammable substance, then, what explains the observed effect of applying the flame or spark is its molecular constitution. Such is the underlying "physical state or mechanism." The particular underlying reality that would figure in the explanation of flammability will differ from case to case, sometimes known and other times not, but once we have the relevant information, there is no longer any need to speak in terms of dispositions: we can explain the observed phenomena directly in terms of underlying chemical properties and general laws.

Quine's position is that all dispositional concepts in science play the same role: they give us a certain kind of sketch of phenomena to be explained by an underlying mechanism, and thereby point to the mechanism in terms of its causes and effects. But once the mechanism is discovered, the sketch is not needed, and we can revert to fully extensional language. Quine writes:

> So, if I were trying to devise an ideal language for a finished theory of reality, or any part of it, I would make no place in it for the general dispositional idiom. In developing a theory, on the other hand, the idiom is indispensable. Just as in writing an essay one commonly sketches various ulterior paragraphs before completing the front ones, so in developing a theory one sketches in a few key traits of what is meant ultimately to emerge as a satisfactory explanatory mechanism. Such is the role of the general dispositional idiom. And since scientific theory is always changing, the idiom is here to stay.
>
> (*RR* 11–12; see also *WO* 222–6)

The topic of dispositions—along with related ones such as causality, the lawfulness of natural law, and counterfactual conditionals more generally—is a huge one that has spawned an enormous technical literature. Quine's treatment of dispositions is suggestive but not worked out in much detail. We have stopped over it, however, for two reasons. First, Quine's position on dispositions casts his discussions of language and meaning in a new light. If having a language is having linguistic dispositions, and talk of a disposition is really only a promissory note for a structural description of an assumed underlying mechanism, then, since in the language case the relevant mechanism is presumably neurological, it follows that to have a language is really to be in certain sorts of neurological states. We will return to this topic in our final chapter. The second reason is that Quine's account of disposition displays so clearly his general policy with respect to apparent failures of extensionality: non-extensional language is simply not to figure in any definitive account of reality, and can be recognized as essential to science only *heuristically*, as instrumental toward purely extensional accounts of reality. As we will see, this will lead Quine to reject some areas of philosophy, and even would-be science, as so many castles in the air.

The treatment of causation in terms of counterfactual conditionals is very popular, but Quine's treatment of "a caused b," where a and b are events, is equally deflationary, and can be anticipated. Causation is obviously not extensional: the truth of "The dog barked" and "The cat meowed," even if we add information about the times and places of the two events, does not tell us whether one caused the other. Yet Quine writes "[t]he disappearance of causal terminology from the jargon of one branch of science and another has seemed to mark the progress in understanding of the branches concerned" (*WP* 242). The notion is absent from the laws of chemistry, an example of a relatively mature science. Quine regards the predicate "a caused b" as a place-holder for an ordinary first-order generalization, that is, one that gets filled in with something more specialized as a theory matures toward greater clarity, explicitness, and objectivity.

One could be forgiven for complaining this goes too far, that causal relations are the very stuff of which science is made. But Quine is not saying that science has no need of the notion of causality; like the notion of a disposition, the notion of causality, even if incapable of being analyzed with exact precision, is essential to the progress of science—especially for pointing to what needs to be explained, as when we say that smoking causes cancer. Still Quine's picture is that it tends to fall away when we know more, when we find out the underlying mechanism, and it would play no part in a fully regimented theory.

"No Entity without Identity": Abstract Objects, Good, and Bad

A question deferred from our discussion of ontology in the previous chapter concerns the existence of *abstract objects*: numbers, functions, classes, attributes, propositions, possible worlds, and so on. Quine accepts the existence of some items on this list, and not others. In particular, he accepts the existence of the first three, and rejects the rest. In this section we examine Quine's reasons for accepting those first three. The reasons are twofold: first, those entities are needed for science; second, they admit of satisfactory criteria of "individuation"—criteria of identity. In subsequent sections we will examine Quine's reasons for rejecting the other items: that they are not needed in science, and admit of no satisfactory criterion of individuation.

The Epistemology of Mathematics Again

The gradual realization that mathematics is essential to natural science is what, more than anything, characterized the great awakening of natural science in the sixteenth and seventeenth centuries. If it was Galileo who famously said the secrets of nature are "written in the language of mathematics," then it was

Newton who made the definitive early breakthroughs in deciphering them. The basic idea behind Galileo's claim is simple enough: scientific understanding of nature consists in formulating quantitative laws that describe the behavior of material objects in space. This means that all the basic terms of the description are terms for *measurable quantities*: they can be assigned numbers as their measures. Thus when Newton writes $F = ma$, the cash value is that the force acting on an object, even it not itself independently measurable, is always proportional to the object's *mass* and *degree of acceleration*, both of which are measurable. The idea of "force," formerly an occult idea connected with vague ideas of effort, purpose, and necessity, becomes straightforwardly measurable, an empirical concept. Such laws make it possible to predict things such as the orbit of an unseen planet, the flight of a cannonball, the strength needed in a bridge, and so on.

Our ability to discover laws such as $F = ma$ does not seem mysterious: we might simply try various candidates, test their empirical consequences, and accept the ones that always pass the tests. Although such laws are not themselves truths of pure mathematics, our ability to use them, and indeed our understanding of what they mean, seems to be grounded in an understanding of pure mathematics, which has its own truths. Mathematics is entangled with empirical science in one way, independent in another. We saw how Carnap sought to explain the a prioricity of mathematics in terms of the notion of analytic truth, and its entanglement with empirical knowledge by the idea that for any given scientific language, some set of analytic truths is intrinsic to it. Quine rejected that strategy, replacing it with holism. This was the idea that the empirical content of a given theory cannot be explained in terms of the empirical content of particular statements. In principle, the testing of a single observation categorical is really the testing of a much larger block of theory, including all those statements involved in logically implying the observation categorical. If the latter proves false, then in principle, there are indefinitely many adjustments to the set of statements held true that would restore consistency with observation.

Mathematical ideas permeate the whole of science (mathematical truths are those true statements which contain only mathematical and logical expressions— or rather which contain only those *essentially*). Even in the case of something as simple as $F = ma$, the symbols stand for quantities, and acceleration is defined as the derivative of the function describing the object's velocity at given points in time. Clearly the empirical import of a law such as $F = ma$ depends partly on pure mathematics: if the laws for derivatives were somehow different, then the implications $F = ma$ would be different. As it might be put, mathematical laws determine exactly what concept is indicated by "a," and thereby figure in determining the meaning of "F = ma" (see *PL* 95–102, Hahn and Schilpp 1986, pp. 399–400).

In that sense, even the truths of pure mathematics may be said to have empirical content. Yet this also does something to explain why, alongside logic itself, mathematical truth has been felt to be necessary and indeed a realm of a priori truth. For if we tried to change the laws for derivatives—the differential calculus—or the laws of arithmetic, then the changes would be felt all round the university, not just in the mathematics department: the empirical content of every statement involving, however indirectly, the relevant mathematics, would be altered. The changes would send shock waves throughout science. Surely no such wholesale revision of science is conceivable except under the most extreme theoretical pressure; our whole way of thinking, it seems, would be affected. Still, it could happen, at least on some scale. Indeed it may actually be happening: some physicists and philosophers have suggested that some of the weirder features of quantum theory call for changes in logic (the law of bivalence or excluded middle, for example; see *CCE* 394, *PT* 90–3).

Mathematical Objects

So Quine is more impressed by the entanglement of mathematics with empirical science than its appearance of autonomy; the appearance, indeed, can be explained by pointing out how *thorough* the entanglement is.

Mathematics (in its classical form) unavoidably involves quantification over numbers.[2] Arithmetic tells us that for every natural number *there is* a greater one, and so on. And of course for Quine, that is ultimately all there is to say, and all that needs to be said, as regards existence: to be is to be the value of a bound variable, i.e., to be quantified over. Therefore according to our best overall theory, numbers exist.

Since Frege, Dedekind, Russell, and Zermelo, it is evident that numbers of all kinds can be explained in various ways as classes. For example where $\emptyset$ is the empty set, we can (inductively) define:

$$0 = \emptyset, \ 1 = \{\emptyset\}, \ 2 = \{\{\emptyset\}, \emptyset\}, \ \ldots \ S(n) = n \cup \{n\}.$$

—where "n" is an arbitrary natural number, "S" indicates "the successor of," i.e., the number immediately after n, and "∪" indicates the operation of taking the union of two classes, i.e., pooling their members into one class. Then "There are n things that are F" can be explained as "There is one-to-one correlation between the set of things F and n" (which is defined using only logic and classes). Thus the natural numbers have their essential role in counting, and the construction yields the natural numbers as forming an infinite sequence of finite classes ordered by the relation "is a subset of," corresponding to the notion "less than." Such is one way of reducing the natural numbers to classes. Similar if more complicated things can be done for the other sorts of numbers—negative integers, the rationals, the reals, and complex numbers.

Functions and relations can be reduced to classes using the notion of an *ordered pair*. An ordered pair <x, y> as we have seen in the previous chapter can be identified with the set {{x}, {0, y}}. This definition satisfies the condition that

$$< x., y > = < w, z > \text{ if and only if } x = w \text{ and } y = z.$$

That is to say, the definition ensures that we can keep track of which is the first member and which is the second, which is all that we care about when distinguishing the ordered pair from the simple pair set {x, y}, which has no order, i.e. {x, y} = {y, x}. A (two-place, or binary) relation can now be identified with a set of ordered pairs. For example the relation "greater than" can be identified with the set of ordered pairs <x, y> such that x is greater than y. Finally, functions can be identified with certain relations, and the notation "f(x)" explained as "The y such that R(x, y)," where R is a relation, and using Russell's theory of descriptions.

A good question is why this reduction of numbers to sets is progress. Quine used to say—in the 1930s and 1940s, following more or less Frege and Russell—that it was to make out the thesis of logicism, the reduction of mathematics to logic. Afterwards he went with a now more standard way of speaking, that whereas (first-order) logic was complete and indifferent to what objects are being reasoned about, mathematics begins with the introduction of the (interpreted) term "∈" by means of axioms, making its objects sets (mathematics is by contrast with logic incomplete, as proven by Gödel). Still, there is no more economical stance is known than privileging sets—which are very useful in various domains, and in a way are so manifestly simple that at least the basics are taught to children.

Finally, although it would be too much to go in any detail into Quine's role in the development of set theory (the theory of classes), a quick word is in order. Set theory had its serious beginnings only in the latter half of the nineteenth century with Georg Cantor, and then with Frege and Russell and their explicitly philosophical angle. It was formulated in the twentieth century from a more strictly mathematical point of view by Zermelo (added to by Fraenkel), with a significant alternative by von Neumann (added to by Bernays and Gödel). Quine published his own system in "New Foundations of Mathematical Logic" in 1937, and a revised system in *Mathematical Logic* of 1940 (which unlike New Foundations itself is seldom studied for its set theory, but remains of interest for its investigations into "metalogic" or "metalinguistics"). All of these—from Cantor onward—had significant differences, and Quine's has not been studied nearly as much as Zermelo-Frankel's system or von Neumann-Bernays-Gödel's (the differences are analyzed in Quine's *Set Theory and Its Logic* of 1963). But Quine's system, as it appears in "New Foundations," does have the considerable advantage that it has just two axioms other than plain logical axioms, as well as other features that might well be further advantages. For more, see the book by Sean Morris *Quine, New Foundations and the Philosophy of Set Theory* (Morris 2018).

Individuation

The only objects needed for mathematics, then, are classes, sets. The truths of mathematics can all be interpreted as truths about classes. Now we emphasized back in Chapter 4 that for Quine, strictly speaking, language goes referential only insofar as it involves a sharply delineated apparatus of individuation. In particular, it only makes sense to say that the use of a given term is fully referential, a term for certain *objects*, insofar as means are in play to answer questions of identity and difference amongst the purported objects. Only then, as we may put it, do objects "come into focus." This requirement finds expression in another familiar Quinean quip: *No entity without identity* (*TT* 102, *OR* 23). This means that wherever science is to recognize a kind of object, it must provide a criterion of identity for objects of that kind, a general statement that tells us, for any objects x and y of that kind, what determines whether or not x = y. The idea goes back to Frege, and is really quite intuitive. For example, suppose someone claims that during a certain interval he heard exactly 3,498 *sounds*. We ask him: how are you counting them? Where does one leave off and another begin? Can they change? Can they be simultaneous? He answers these questions only very vaguely or not at all. But then, how can he possibly say that *there are exactly 3,498* of them? And if he cannot mean anything definite by that, then what does he mean when he says, *There is exactly one sound,* or even *There is a sound?* It seems gratuitous to say that *there are* certain objects, and he is definitely talking about *them.* He is not really using the term "sound" referentially, as a noun that picks out a kind of thing as opposed to an adjective (adapted from Quine's fat man in the doorway, *FLPV* 4).

That is why, although Quine welcomes classes into the ontology of pure science, he does not allow *attributes, properties* such as *being green, energetic,* or *made of bricks:* granted the objects are well-defined, it is clear what distinguishes the class of green objects from the class of objects made of bricks, and we saw in Chapter 5 that certain scattered physical objects could play some of the roles of certain attributes such as greenness. But what is the criterion of identity for attributes themselves? Obviously membership in classes comes and goes in a way that would be irrelevant to the individuation of attributes, which do not change identity depending on what objects bear them. Nor are attributes the same just in case the same objects bear them, as attested by Quine's pair-wise example "creature with a heart" and "creature with a kidney," which are presumably co-extensive but would not indicate the same attribute. The natural thought is that attributes are identical when the corresponding predicates are *necessarily* true of all and only the same things, or that their co-extensiveness is a matter of analytic truth (*OR* 19–23, *FLPV* 156–7, *TT* 100–12). But this appeals either to analyticity, which has long since been out of the picture, or to the idea of necessity which, as we will see presently, Quine also excludes from the factual content of science. The question of when we have one attribute and when we have two does not seem to have a precise answer. "[A]ttributes, I have often complained, have no clear principle of individuation," says Quine (*TT* 100).

Quine's notion of a *physical object*, as we saw in Chapter 5, has a sharp criterion of identity: x and y are the same physical object if and only if their spatio-temporal boundaries coincide. In the case of classes, the criterion is equally sharp: x and y are the same class if and only if they have the same members (that is: for every object z, z is a member of x if and only if z is a member of y). Thus with both physical objects and classes, we have sharp criteria of identity. Our best theory of nature, then, should proceed with just those entities and nothing else (and anything that can be reduced to them); our language for those things satisfies all the demands of sharply referential scientific language. It is an elite club, and aspiring members will certainly have to prove themselves.

Nominalism?

Historically, what is meant by "Nominalism" is the doctrine that no abstract entities exist, that only physical entities exist and only as tokens, not types (or that only physical and mental entities exist, or that only mental entities exist, the last famously advocated by Bishop Berkeley). The bugbear was the queerness of universals, properties, or relations. For reasons which should by now be evident, Quine does not go for universals; it is not necessary to use predicates or general terms that we should accept them as naming universals or otherwise entities that can be "instantiated" by objects in the subject-predicate relation. In that sense, Quine definitely is a nominalist.

More recently, the Nominalist position tends to focus on mathematical entities, especially on the numbers themselves conceived as abstract *objects*, the instantatiors rather than the instantiated in the subject-predicate relation. For the Nominalist, to speak of them as "existing"—even if one is thinking of their set-theoretic surrogates—is only a *façon de parler*: such talk can be construed or re-construed as referring at most to physical objects. The possibility of nominalism in this more focused and more recent sense was, for a time, of enormous interest to Quine. In 1947 Nelson Goodman and Quine jointly published "Steps towards a Constructive Nominalism," and in *Word and Object* (§55) of 1960 Quine devoted not a little effort toward a nominalistic construal of parts of physical theory, even if it was ultimately rejected. The appeal of it seems obvious: besides the premium on ontological economy, on Occam's razor, there is the appeal of the thought that only that which is part of the sensible world is properly called "real."

Nevertheless Quine lost interest in these attempts. There are two broad reasons.

First, although he and Goodman said at the beginning of their 1947 piece that they do not believe in abstract objects, that is not the same as saying that they believe that there are no abstract objects. As befits a rational individual, Quine himself maintained an agnosticism, not an atheism, throughout the early period. It was only *steps towards* nominalism that were announced; he was never in a position to claim that nominalism could in fact be achieved, could be "executed" (*CCE* 23). And all the while he was batting from other side, so to speak: *Mathematical Logic* of 1940, *Set Theory and Its Logic* of 1963, and various papers, including "New Foundations for Mathematical Logic" of 1937, are all major contributions to abstract set theory, which construed numbers as abstract objects, namely sets.

Second, his attitude toward questions of existence gradually changed. In the 1930s and 1940s, still influenced by Russell and his teacher C. I. Lewis, he tended to take an "internalist" epistemological perspective, placing importance on "experience" and "sense-data." But the 1950s he became persuaded that sort of thing could not work for reasons we have been through. He developed instead his scheme of observation sentences and their causal interface with the physical stimulus, and with it the thesis of the inscrutability of reference—which explicitly became the program of Naturalized Epistemology and the thesis of Ontological Relativity. From this point of view, all "reification is theoretical" (*PT* 25), by which he means that all "positing" is done, if partly pragmatically, for reasons of theory. Indeed in later years he avowed that the "question of existence, or what there is" is not so important as he thought as a youth, when it was "the most basic question of philosophy and science." In "the fullness of time the scales fell from my eyes" (*CCE* 189); what matters is the structure of a proposed ontology, not so much the particular nature of the ontology. "Ontology has suffered a humiliating demotion" (*CCE* 317); it is "indifferent" (*PT* 31), "defused" (*PT* 33), he confesses.

So the distinction between physical or sensible objects and abstract objects fades to comparative insignificance (it furthers the case that the entities of modern physics such as quarks and photons are not at all like the standard examples of physical things, such as apples or rabbits). In fact at certain points he was tempted by "Pythagoreanism," the thesis that the only objects are numbers, or sets (*WPO?*). This is perhaps why Quine showed little interest in later attempts at nominalism, such as Hartry Field's (1980), even if they are arguably more successful that Quine's earlier attempt with Goodman.

Propositional Attitudes

The cases of extensionality failure we considered in the first section of this chapter concerned non-truth-functional sentence-connectives. These engender contexts where replacing a sentence with another with the same truth-value may fail to preserve the truth-value of the larger sentence which contains the first. A simple and easily explicable example of substitution failure at the *sub*-sentential level is that of quotation. Consider:

(2) "Venus" has five letters.

It so happens that "Venus" and "the morning star" refer to the same object, the planet Venus. But of course we cannot infer:

(3) "The morning star" has five letters.

It is not hard to find an explanation. The expression "'Venus,'" as it occurs in (2), is not the name of Venus; it is the name of "Venus"—a name of a name, not of a planet. As Quine put it, the expression "Venus" does occur in (2), but the position in which it occurs is "referentially opaque": inserted into that position, the name "Venus" does not do its customary job of referring to Venus. That explains why the context

(4) "__" has five letters

is not open to substitution of co-extensive expressions. Instead, what happens when we insert an expression into the blank of (4) is that the quotation marks together with the expression form a name of that expression, and the sentence says something about that (though Quine shows how to define quotation strictly so that it does not in fact violate extensionality; *ML* 23–6, 33–7, 281–7).

Frege held that something similar goes for indirect quotation, and for the related expressions of propositional attitude such as belief. Consider:

(5) John believes that the morning star is a planet.

As we know:

(6) The morning star = the evening star.

The very bright celestial body visible in the eastern sky just before dawn is also the one visible in the western sky just after sunset. But we cannot infer:

(7) John believes that the evening star is a planet.

John, ignorant of (6), might even think that the evening star is *not* a planet. It thus appears that the context

(8) John believes that _ is a planet

is referentially opaque. But unlike the case of quotation, it is much trickier to explain why, less straightforward to understand what the words are doing if not referring in their usual way. According to Frege, the expression

(9) _ believes _

is simply a two-place predicate, standing for a certain relation: belief. What sorts of things does it relate? Obviously one side of the relation is taken by persons, the believers. But what of the other side? Frege held, in effect, that an expression such as

(10) that the morning star is a planet

is a special kind of singular term that stands for what we now call a "proposition." Propositions are not sentences, but the meanings of sentences. They are abstract objects.³ Thus for example "Snow is white" and "Le neige est blanche" express the same proposition, as do, presumably, "Monday comes immediately before Tuesday" and "Monday is immediately followed by Tuesday." Thus for Frege, a sentence formed by filling the blank of (4) with a referring term does not thereby yield a sentence about the referent of that referring term, but about the term itself. Likewise in the case of (8), except that instead of getting a sentence about the *term* inserted there, we get a sentence about John and a *proposition*.

Such considerations are indeed amongst the most powerful in favor of the postulation of propositions, or *thoughts* as Frege himself called them (see *PL* 1–13). Quine's refusal to accept the existence of propositions can be guessed from what has gone before. The problem is not that they are abstract entities; we have just seen that Quine is no enemy of abstract entities. The problem is that they lack a workable criterion of identity. There is no problem *formulating* such a criterion. We can say, for any two sentences S1 and S2:

(11) The proposition expressed by S1 = the proposition expressed by S2 if and only if Sl and S2 are synonymous.

The problem, as Quine devoted a chapter of *Word and Object* to arguing, is that there is no general and objectively applicable criterion of synonymy (also see *TT* 43–54). Synonymy is a perfectly good practical concept of ordinary life, but not one to welcome into "austere science," i.e., our best theory.⁴

If not, then what is to be made of the situation represented by (5), (6), and the (let us assume) falsity of (7)? Quine's solution, in effect, is to assimilate the case to (4). That is to say, we can record belief as a relation between believers and *sentences*, items of language. For example, we can paraphrase (5) as

(12) John *believes-true* "The morning star is a planet."

(12) is to be understood in such a way that it could be true even though John does not speak English. If we are prepared to grant that animals have beliefs, then even a cat, says Quine, might be regarded as believing-true "A mouse is there." The job of sentences such as (12) is simply to classify believers in the way that we do with our ordinary belief-sentences, but in a way that does not violate extensionality, and does not invoke any insupportable abstract entities (see *PT* 71–2).⁵ Thus if we thought that the idiom of belief were needed for science, then we could make do with sentences like (12). (12), is not meant as an *analysis* of (5)—an explanation of what it *really means*—but as a *replacement* for it (an explication of it, in the sense described in the previous chapter).

"Quantifying-in"

Set aside Quine's quotational gambit for the remainder. Another issue arises from belief-sentences' appearing to be open to *quantification*. To illustrate, let us consider Quine's famous example (the following is based on *WP* 185–91, *TT* 119-20, *PT* 70–1). Ralph has seen a certain man in a brown hat behaving suspiciously. Symbolizing "the man in the brown hat" as "MBH," we write:

(13) Ralph believes that MBH is a spy.

It thus seems to be true that

(14) ∃x(Ralph believes that x is a spy).

The move to (14) is that of "quantifying into" a propositional attitude: the quantifier sitting *outside* the verb "believes" governs the second occurrence of "x" *inside* the verb. Since MBH is not a figment of Ralph's imagination, *there is* someone whom Ralph believes to be a spy. This is a much more interesting state for Ralph than simply: Ralph believes that ∃x(x is a spy). Ralph believes there are spies, but so does everyone; the point of (14) is that he is unlike most of us in that he suspects someone.

Now a certain Bernard J. Ortcutt is known to Ralph as an upstanding member of society, certainly no spy. Hence

(15) Ralph believes that Ortcutt is not a spy.

But unknown to Ralph,

(16) MBH = Ortcutt.

Now if we infer (14) from (13) granted that MBH exists, then by exactly parallel reasoning we can from (15) infer:

(17) ∃x(Ralph believes that x is not a spy).

Ralph is in a peculiar but not unheard of situation. (14) says that there is a certain someone whom Ralph believes to be a spy. (17) says that there is a certain someone whom Ralph believes not to be a spy. The peculiarity stems from this man's being in fact MBH, otherwise known as Ortcutt; but note that neither (14) nor (17) contain that information.

To bring this out further, contrast the singular cases:

(13) Ralph believes that MBH is a spy. (*de dicto*)

(18) MBH is such that Ralph believes that he is a spy. (*de re*)

As indicated, the distinction between (13) and (18) is the distinction between belief *de dicto* and belief *de re* (such is the terminology that has taken over; Quine originally spoke of *notional* and *relational* belief). (14) is also *de re* but the contrast of (13) with (18) presents the nub of the matter. The difference is which expression is within the scope of which. Together with the existence of MBH, (13) seems logically to imply (18)—Quine calls the move "exportation"—but it seems that (18) does *not* logically imply (13). The idea is that in (13), the term we employ inside the scope of "believes" must not only refer to Ortcutt but must reflect Ralph's way of thinking of Ortcutt. In (13), the position occupied by "MBH" is referentially opaque, not open to substitution by co-referentials. In (18), by contrast, "MBH" is referentially transparent: the position occupied by "MBH" in (18) is open to substitution by co-referring singular terms (such as "Ortcutt").

In earlier work—(1953) *FLVP* 139–42, (1955) *WP* 183–94—Quine began by casting doubt on the very intelligibility of sentences like (14) in view of (13) and (15): (14) says that there is an object which Ralph believes to be a spy, yet (13) and (15) disagree concerning that very object whether Ralph has that belief. But to cut a long story short, Quine came to accept the situation like that represented by (13)–(18)—or rather more acutely by the conjunction of (18) with:

(19) MBH is such that Ralph believes that he is not a spy.

—which seems to be inferable from (15) and (16) so long as (18) is inferable from (13).

Not only (14) and (17), but (18) and (19) are logically consistent: Of MBH, Ralph believes him to be a spy, and also believes him not to be a spy. That happens. Nor does it ascribe inconsistency to *Ralph* in the sense of a failure of reason: it does not entail that there is some sentence such that Ralph accepts both it and its negation, There is no contradiction in Ralph's *de dicto* beliefs.

Quine's later position, however, is that the *de re* constructions should not be retained in serious science. The reason is a further wrinkle that emerged after Quine first told the story of Ralph, one pointed out by Robert Sleigh. Ralph believes like everyone that there are spies, and suppose he also believes, as everyone naturally does, that it is most unlikely that the contest should be a draw for who is the shortest spy. So Ralph believes that there is a shortest spy, and also, of course, that the shortest spy is a spy. Assuming that Ralph is right, and accepting exportation, we have that the shortest spy is such that Ralph believes that he or she is a spy. But that seems, to the innocent ear, not to be the case. It seems that for Ralph to have that belief *about* this person, he must know who that person is, which he does not. And Quine is skeptical that the question of whether one knows who the relevant object is can be anything but a context-dependent matter, a pragmatic matter. Sometimes one knows the face but not the name, other times one knows the name but not the face (*TT* 121). The expression "knows who" does not track a clearly definable epistemic state.

This does not erase the vague idea that somehow (18) or (14) reports a genuine relation between Ralph and a certain man, but Quine is willing to dismiss this as illusory:

> Propositional attitudes *de re* presuppose a relation of *intention* between thoughts and things intended, for which I can conceive of no adequate guidelines. To garner empirical content for [(14), (17)] we would have to interrogate Ralph and compile some of his pertinent beliefs *de dicto*. I conclude that the propositional attitudes *de re* resist annexation to scientific language, as propositional attitudes *de dicto* do not. At best the ascriptions *de re* are signals pointing a direction in which to look for informative ascriptions *de dicto*.
>
> (*PT* 70–1; see also *PT* 72, Hahn and Schilpp 1986, p. 187)

The idea behind this last remark is that the legitimate point of such a sentence as (14)—or rather its English counterpart "There is someone whom Ralph believes to be a spy"—is not actually to indicate a distinctive relation between Ralph and an object. Instead, it indicates that for some singular term N, there is a true *de dicto* belief-sentence formed by connecting "Ralph believes that" to the result of inserting N into the blank of the predicate "_ is a spy." Such sentences are often indispensable when we ourselves do not know what singular term this is—or, as we would more naturally put it, we don't know who it is that Ralph believes to be a spy. They are also useful when we do know, but for one reason or another do not care to specify it.

So far, then, Quine's attitude in this case is much like his attitude toward the dispositional idiom: it is a sometimes inescapable heuristic, but not to enter into the ideal language for a finished theory of reality. It is not true, however, that all *de re* belief-constructions can be explained in this way, as promissory notes for *de dicto* ones. Russell once suggested the example "I thought your yacht was longer than it is." Let A be the yacht in question. What Russell is saying about his own past beliefs cannot be represented like this:

(20) Bertrand believed that A is longer than A.

Russell was not saying that at a certain time, he had a contradictory belief. To get the effect of Russell's sentence, we have to quantify over lengths (officially these can be identified with numbers, values of the function "the length of," in some preferred unit of measure). What we want to say is not that Bertrand thought that the length of A is longer than the length of A, but rather:

(21) ∃x ∃y (x = the length of A and y is greater than x and Bertrand believed that
        y = the length of A).

That is, there are lengths x and y such that x is the length of A, and y is greater than x, and Bertrand thought that y is the length of A. In order to describe Bertrand's mistake, we have to quantify into the scope of "believes"; the *de re* approach appears mandatory.

However, we should bear in mind the wider picture. What is true, according to Quine, is that ascriptions of *de re* propositional attitude may be very useful not only the social sciences and psychology, but also in rigorously physicalistic psychology, in something of the way that the dispositional idiom is useful, for classifying underlying neurological realities. But a theory of those, of course, would not employ relations to yachts or spies. Thus even if there are some striking cases such as that of Bertrand and the yacht, the idea that there *must be* a general science of the relation between neurological states and external objects, of *de re* belief, may not seem so prepossessing; hence Quine's remark that he can foresee "no adequate guidelines": what makes sense and seems thoroughly familiar in one kind of case may not admit of the kind of generalization demanded by science.

Modality

Extensionality failures crop up also in the context of *modal* sentences (as the term is used in philosophy), those that state what is possibly true or necessarily true. It seems to be not only true but necessarily true, for example, that 8 is greater than 7; it *couldn't* have been otherwise. Hence:

(22) Necessarily (8 > 7).

It is also true that:[6]

(23) The number of planets = 8.

But it seems we cannot infer:

(24) Necessarily (The number of planets > 7).

For of course it is only contingently true—not necessarily true but true all the same—that there are more than seven planets; there could have been fewer. Substitution of co-referring singular terms, in such cases, seems to fail.

Quine inferred that we cannot quantify into a modal context. That is, we cannot place a quantified variable inside the scope of "Necessarily" or "Possibly" where the quantifier sits outside. Thus we cannot from (22) infer:

(25) ∃x [Necessarily (x > 7)].

The objection parallels the one about Ralph: What is this thing that is necessarily greater than 7? Eight, the number of planets? So the number of planets is necessarily greater than 7? Surely not.

There is a large philosophical industry which holds that there really are facts about what is necessarily as opposed to contingently true, possibly true though not actually true, and thus that modal logic—the logic of "Necessarily" and "Possibly"—is demanded in serious science. Others remain agnostic about that, but maintain that Quine's objections do not themselves pose problems for modal language. We cannot begin to survey the field here. But we can describe the most influential style of defense against Quine's objections in just enough detail to understand his response.

To begin, consider the *de re* analogues of (22) and (24):

(26) 8 is such that necessarily it is greater than 7.

(27) The number of planets is such that necessarily it is greater than 7.

The idea is that although (24) is false, (27) is true. For consider the number of planets, *viz.*, 8; is *that number* necessarily greater than 7? Yes it is. For here we are not asking whether a certain statement or proposition is necessarily true, but asking, of a certain *object*, whether *it* is necessarily greater than 7.

Furthermore, on this view, there is no puzzle whatever concerning quantification or the transition back and forth between the *de dicto* and the *de re*. The key concept is that of a *rigid designator* as introduced by Kripke (prefigured by Ruth Barcan Marcus, who spoke of "tags" of objects, and Dagfinn Føllesdal, who spoke of 'genuine singular terms'). Although it is not strictly necessary to make the point, it will simplify the discussion to speak in terms of "possible worlds." A statement is said to be necessarily true if it is true in every possible world, and possibly true if it is true in at least one. And just as the truth-values of some sentences vary from world to world, so does the designations of some singular terms. The expression "The number of planets," for example, designates 8 *with respect to the actual world,* but with respect to other possible worlds, where there are more or fewer planets, it designates 5, or 23, or whatever. Hence the falsity of (24). By contrast, (22) is true because when we talk about a given possible world using the expression "8," we always talk about the same object, namely the number eight. "8" is thus a rigid designator: what it designates does not shift depending on what possible situation we are talking about. That object is greater than 7 in every possible world; "8 > 7" is a necessary truth, and (25) is true.

The reason that (24) is false, then, is not that somehow 8 fails to be greater than 7 depending on how we refer to it. The reason is that with respect to some worlds, the non-rigid designator "the number of planets" picks out a number that is not greater than 7. But if all that is so, then it seems we can make sense of substitution within modal contexts. The orthodox criterion of inter-substitution was that substitution of one singular term by another preserves the truth-value of sentences so long as the two singular terms are co-referential. We simply have to strengthen this requirement: within the scope of a modal operator ("Necessarily" or "Possibly"), substitution of singular terms preserves truth-value so long as the two singular terms are co-referential at every possible world. That is, co-referential singular terms are inter-substitutable in modal contexts so long as they are rigid designators. Thus a *de dicto* modal statement is logically equivalent to its *de re* analogue if the relevant singular term is rigid.

As may be guessed, Quine did not accept this solution. Earlier in his career he had assumed, as most people did in modal logic until perhaps the late 1950s or even after, that necessity and possibility are not features of the world, but products of our descriptions of it (*WP* 158–76, *FLPV* 139–59; *NEN*; cf. Carnap 1947, p. 173f). Thus the necessity of 8's being greater than 7 would be explained by the analyticity of "8 > 7" or by its being a logical truth, or some other feature of the sentence. Contra Quine, however, the *de re* constructions (26) and (27) locate the modality in the world, in the things. To take another example, "being human" would be a necessary property of Aristotle, of the man himself, and remains so irrespective of how we refer to that man—whether as "the teacher of Alexander," as "Aristotle," or whatever. Having taught Alexander, on the other hand, is a contingent property; Aristotle might have refused the job. Thus for any object, there are its contingent properties but also its necessary properties. The necessary properties are said to be "essential" to it, in the sense that it could not exist without them.[7]

Since the landmark work of Kripke and Putnam in the 1960s and 1970s, philosophy has grown well accustomed to the idea that things have essences, discovered not by analyzing the meanings of words but also empirically, as in the case of water being essentially H_2O. As before, however, the seeming intelligibility of certain cases does not imply the acceptability across the board of the notions in question. To accept the idea of rigid designation into the language of science is to accept that there are facts of the matter about which properties of a given object or substance are essential to it and which not: if we can speak of the same object in all possible worlds, then the question arises exactly which if any of its properties it has in all possible worlds. If none, then what does it mean to say that it is "the same object"? If some, which? (*TT* 118–22, 173–4; Hahn and Schilpp 1986, pp. 94, 292; *FLPV* 154–8).

Might Aristotle have failed to be rational? Could he have been a monkey? A hamster? Can there be an objective science of such things? Quine's answer, as expected, is that there is little reason to think there could be. The main consideration, surely, is just that science itself does not provide any encouragement: the modal adverbs "necessarily" and "possibly" simply do not figure in the theoretical language of physics or natural science generally. It remains a peculiarly philosophical idea that there should be facts about what is necessary and what isn't, a metaphysics of essence. And perhaps irreducibly so. As Hume observed, necessity cannot be *observed*; it has to be imposed on or read into what we observe in some other way (see *Q* 139–42). Of course mathematical truth can't be observed either, but we've been through that: mathematical language is thoroughly interwoven with natural science, thereby securing a complex and indirect but nonetheless real and incorrigible connection with observation. No such status can be claimed for idioms of modality, leaving the question of their objective application up in the air.[8]

As with other non-extensional notions, Quine explains the disputed idioms in terms of their heuristics and pragmatics:

> In respect of utility there is less to be said for necessity than for the propositional attitudes. The expression does serve a purpose in daily discourse, but of a shallow sort … In its every day use … "necessarily" is a second-order annotation to the effect that its sentence is deemed true by all concerned, at least for the sake and space of the argument. A similar second-order role is cut out, then, for "possibly." Since it means "not necessarily not," "possibly" marks its sentence as one that the beliefs or working assumptions of concerned parties do not exclude as false. Such utility is local, transitory, and unproblematic … the sublimity of necessary truth thus turns not quite to dust, but to pretty common clay. (*PT* 13–4, order altered; see also *WP* 48–56, *FSS* 98–9)

The sort of use Quine has in mind is quite humdrum. You say that if Dorothy comes to the party she'll drink too much, I express doubt by saying "not necessarily." Needless to say, this is not supposed to be an analysis of what it is for a statement to be necessarily or possibly true; it is only a sketch of what the usefulness of the words "necessarily" and "possibly" actually consists in.

Further Reading and Historical Notes

In the early days—in 1920 to 1960—non-extensional phenomena, hence "Modal" logic, was often held to be explicable logically or linguistically, by "individual concepts," or "Fregean senses," not by properties of the objects themselves (see Carnap's *Meaning and Necessity* 1947 and *Introduction to Semantics* 1942). This was the original focus of Quine's worry; as noted the shift to the "object-oriented" or metaphysical conception of modality from 1960 only made things worse, in Quine's view. Much of the discussion of Quine's extensionalism—pre-1960 and after—centers on the fact that Quine's arguments for it are strictly speaking invalid, that one can resist them. However Quine's reason for sticking to extensional language—when presented in a regimented theory in canonical notation—to put it at its most elementary level, is just that the alternative is not scientifically rigorous. Non-extensional notions always take some special insight, some intuition, on the part of the human theorist to apply. There is no question that in ordinary life such notions are familiar and perhaps indispensable, but qualifying them as science is another matter. There is of course some formidable work pushing against Quine's extensional policy. Kripke's 1980 *Naming and Necessity* adds considerable substance and cogent philosophical speculation to the notions of necessity and essence, but perhaps the first appearance of the key idea—though without Kripke's metaphysical interpretation and application—is in Ruth Barcan Marcus 1961, replied to in Quine (*WP* 175–82). See also the essays in Linsky 1971; in particular it features prescient essays on the aspects of the topic by Føllesdal, Smullyan, and others, as well containing Kaplan's masterful "Quantifying In." D. Lewis—student of Quine—proposes in his 1968 and 1986 an extensional modal logic, as the price of recognizing the reality of possible worlds. For an excellent short anti-Quine parley on metaphysics, see Rosen 2013. For Quine's further ruminations on Nominalism, see Chapter IV (of Quine 2018 [1942] 105-138)—when he was close to accepting it—and 233-238 of Quine 1960, for the exact reasons against.

Science, Philosophy, and Empiricism

We have now completed our survey of the claims and arguments for which Quine is best known (with the exception of ones in pure logic and set-theory). In this final chapter, we attempt to do three things. First, we will try to see more of the motivation for Quine's naturalism—his denial of "first philosophy" and his idea of reciprocal containment—and to appreciate more deeply the relation of Quine's philosophy to analytic philosophy in general. Second, we will consider a few less well-known claims and arguments. Third, we address a few specific sources of unease with Quine's overall position, concerning Quine's versions of both naturalism and empiricism.

The Rejection of First Philosophy

Let us begin by saying a bit more than we have about how Quine's critical activities—of the theory of meaning, modality, and so on—are supposed to sit with his rejection of first philosophy. Quine's naturalism does not lead him to deny that there is really any such legitimate enterprise as philosophy. Philosophy, as we have seen, has its critical and legitimate role at the margins of science, plus its uniquely central and abstract role in it role in clarification and as ontological accountant. It also underwrites a certain sort of critical argument against certain areas of philosophical activity: if a certain philosophical project or family of concepts cannot be shown to integrate with scientific knowledge, then that strongly indicates that the project has no real theoretical value, the concepts no real application. That is one way to put it, but what does "integrate" mean here, and what exactly is "scientific knowledge"?

There may not be clear-cut answers here. The term "knowledge," for one, is not one that Quine can regard as marking out a definite domain or phenomenon: knowledge, alongside concepts like belief and meaning, is exactly the sort of concept that Quine sees as problematic. Not only does it inherit the perplexities and indeterminacies of those concepts, it adds further ones due primarily to its normative implications. These ramify in manifold ways, as outlined in the vast literature on Gettier cases, the lottery paradox and so on. The moral that Quine draws is that the word "knowledge" should not be used in our best scientific descriptions of the world, and that it should be seen, like the concept of meaning, as a practical device, in good order for its normal purposes which it has served well from time immemorial, but not admitting of a precise clarification that would serve any valuable theoretical purpose. Nor does Quine suppose it a candidate for explication (as in Chapter 5). We should, as he puts it, "give up the notion of knowledge as a bad job" (*Q* 109).

What then of "science"? Quine intends it in a loose sense that includes most if not all of those true statements imparted to students in universities, but not all knowledge. For example one knows where one's neck is or normally where one's keys are; but that is not scientific knowledge in any sense of "science" however inclusive. One will have to look rather to the more systematic kinds of knowledge that aim at generality, explanation, and theory, in the broadest sense (again, words like "theory" and "explanation" can show us where to look, without our having to assume that they admit just as they stand of exact definition). If we survey the departments of human knowledge of this kind—not just the hard physical sciences but meteorology, psychology, economics, history—confidence will not be encouraged that there exists a univocal and universal method for generating theoretical explanation, a fully inclusive scientific method (see *FSS* 48–50, *WO* 19–25). As Quine together with Joseph Ullian put it, describing the general problem of discriminating reasonable belief from unreasonable belief:

> Not only are the criteria not foolproof; they do not always even point in a unique direction. When we meet the Virtues for assessing hypotheses we will find that they require us to look at candidates for belief in multiple ways, to weigh together a variety of considerations. Decisions in science, as in life, can be difficult. There is no simple touchstone for responsible belief.
>
> (*WB* 8)

Nevertheless, two general themes emerge. One is extensionality, as we saw in the last chapter. When we are "limning the true and ultimate structure of reality," as Quine once rather intemperately put it (*WO* 221), the language must be extensional, as discussed in the last chapter. Sciences that are incapable of achieving this, or least have so far not been able to achieve it, Quine relegates to "Grade B" or "second-grade" status (*OR* 146, *CCE* 442) at best—sciences that trade in dispositions, causation explicitly so-called, the propositional attitudes, and so on go here (but they must have other scientific virtues even to make second-grade status; otherwise it's presumably third-grade or lower). The other theme is simply the general idea of empiricism itself, the idea that theories make objective claims on reality only insofar as they admit of empirical corroboration—only insofar, at least, as they admit of being *disconfirmed by* observation. Thus Quine:

> when I cite predictions as the checkpoints of science, I do not see that as normative. I see it as defining a particular language game, in Wittgenstein's phrase: the game of science, in contrast to other good language games such as fiction and poetry. A sentence's claim to scientific status rests on what it contributes to a theory whose checkpoints are in prediction.
>
> (*PT* 20)

Quine is quick to warn that this sort of claim is not intended as a claim about knowledge issued from a transcendental standpoint, a standpoint superior to the claims of natural science itself:

> Even telepathy and clairvoyance are scientific options, however moribund. It would take some extraordinary evidence to enliven them, but, if that were to happen, then empiricism itself—the crowning norm, we saw, of naturalized epistemology—would go by the board. For remember that that norm, and naturalized epistemology itself, are integral to science, and science is fallible and corrigible ...
>
> In that extremity it might indeed be well to modify the game itself, and take on as further checkpoints the predicting of telepathic and divine input as well as of sensory input. It is idle to bulwark definitions against implausible contingencies.
>
> (*PT* 20–1)

What validates science at its best is its formulation in extensional language with suitable empirical checkpoints, yet the claim that is what validates science is itself validated by science. The feeling that there is a circle here is a measure of our perhaps incorrigible belief that there must be a first philosophy, a way of validating scientific method (or other knowledge-generating methods) that does not depend on what science tells us. Quine rejects this. But he does not, like Wittgenstein perhaps, or like more recent philosophers of science such as Feyerabend, conclude that prevailing scientific method cannot profitably be schematized in such a way as to formulate norms that can in turn be brought to bear on the more questionable departments of knowledge. Such is the idea behind Quine's extraction of his two principal norms, extensionality and empirical checkpoints (see *FSS* 49–50).

The only possible argument in favor of these two norms, indeed the only possible argument that does not violate the stricture against first philosophy, is that they prevail in the most successful regions of science. Those are not merely the regions of science that have the highest strike rate so far as *truth* is concerned. Both chemistry and theoretical physics would for Quine be amongst the most successful, but the main propositions of the former are much more certainly true, and much less likely to be overturned by later discoveries, than those of the latter. The point rather is diachronic rather than merely synchronic: it is characteristic of the development of the most deeply explanatory sciences—the ones that admit of precise and maximally general quantitative laws and hence prediction—that they are extensional and admit of empirical corroboration. Those things are not *sufficient* for something's being science in the honorific sense, but they seem to be necessary, in the sense that there are no counterexamples. As Quine stresses, that we don't acquire knowledge by clairvoyance or divine revelation are things we know from experience, not on *a priori* grounds. Methodological norms come from reflecting on the progress of science, not from an independent and prior philosophy; "knowledge," as Quine puts it, "outpaces knowledge of knowledge" (*FSS* 2).

Quine's criticisms of the vernaculars of modality and *de re* propositional attitudes, then, largely boil down to the claim that they cannot be made to fit the mold of the most rigorous science: unlike uncontroversial central cases of science, they are non-extensional and lack enough empirical checkpoints. As we saw in Chapter 6, Quine takes care to introduce an extensional surrogate for propositional attitude sentences—in the form of sentences affirming a relation between an agent and a *sentence*, as in "Alan believes-true 'Snow is white'"—presumably because he wants to preserve the cognitive standing of the relevant parts of such disciplines as Psychology and History. For modality he describes a strictly pragmatic use of the relevant idioms—"It is possible that" and similar (*TT* 113–23)—but there is little to be gained in such a maneuver; "[i]n thus writing off modal logic," he says, "I find little to regret" (*TT* 121).

Quine and Analytic Philosophy

Quine was analytic philosophy's dominant figure after the Second World War, the standard-bearer after the eclipse of Russell and then Carnap if anyone was. But his relationship to much of the philosophy that goes under that name is complex, and often contentious. Take the case of modality. The topic has filled the pages of the professional journals, and spawned enough books to fill a small domestic library. Superficially, a slice of Quine's work contributes to that. Yet Quine's conclusion is that the topic is not worth pursuing; there is little or no genuine knowledge to be gained by doing so. If such activities are understood to be *analyses of concepts*—as befits the name "Analytic Philosophy," and as some mid-century analytic philosophers took them to be—then Quine denies there are objectively determinate concepts to be discovered (see *PT* 55–6, *WO* 157–61).

On the other hand, not many contemporary analytical philosophers would accept that what they do is conceptual analysis, where by that we mean simply the revelation of the meaning of a word. Encouraged, perhaps, by the Kripke-Putnam idea that there are necessary but non-analytic truths (such as the statement "Water = H_2O"), most would say simply that the target is a certain phenomenon about which the aim is to generate a theory. To many philosophers working in these fields, Quine's negative conclusions about these topics look like mere prejudice, or based on arguments from ignorance. Quine, it seems, merely deems unintelligible what other philosophers find acceptably clear, or concludes that a problem cannot be solved because he cannot solve it. We have already surveyed Quine's official reasons for excluding the idioms of modality and propositional attitude from the "austere language of science," but there is more to say about the point of view from which those reasons issue, more to say about what Quine is doing when he presumes to exclude something from science.

Appeals to Intuition

We know that Quine rejects the idea of *a priori* knowledge. He argues in painstaking detail that the notions of convention and meaning cannot explain it, and then sketches a picture of knowledge whereby no statements are wholly *a priori*, but have features that explain why they should seem so. Such is Quine's epistemological holism, the famous web of belief. All this is well known and very explicit in Quine's writings (though it is qualified in his later work). There is, however, another strain of Quinean opposition to the *a priori* that is less well known and far less conspicuous in his writings. It is less conspicuous because during his formative years, Quine assumed it went without saying. The philosophical community he knew, and to which his published papers were primarily aimed, included the Vienna Circle and its sphere of influence (that is, the various species of "Logical Positivists" or "Logical Empiricists" including Carnap), and philosophical logicians such as Church, Tarski, and others working in those fields and their students. With a few exceptions—including that of perhaps the greatest logician of all, Kurt Gödel—all of these people rejected the synthetic *a priori*. This was primarily because developments in logic, mathematics, and natural science itself seemed to have shown that there was no longer any need to invoke it. Such was a central platform of Carnap's work, who for Quine remained the "towering figure" (*WP* 40).

This opposition can be sharpened by saying that Quine was suspicious of the role of "intuition" or "insight" in science or philosophy. Consider what is going on when a philosopher undertakes to give a definition or theory of knowledge. Although by now it takes place is a more sophisticated context, the technique employed—and here for brevity we will have to engage in a certain degree of caricature—is very much the procedure that philosophers have always followed since Socrates for answering questions of the "What is X?" variety, whether or not it is called "conceptual analysis." The goal is a theory that entails as much as possible of what we *already* take to be true regarding the phenomenon and which, in conjunction with conceivable empirical facts—examples—determines the empirical application that we intuitively expect. Success in this area is never more than partial, but there is no lack of disconfirmed theories. The cases that Gettier and others have described, for example, show that not all justified true belief is knowledge.

How do we know that such judgments—our "intuitions" as we say—are correct? What makes them authoritative? For Plato, encouragement came from mathematics: since intuition surely is authoritative with respect to mathematical truth, and since the sorts of questions being asked are like mathematical ones in not being empirical, it is very tempting to suppose that there really is a kind of philosopher's paradise, a realm of *a priori* knowledge of such things as *knowledge, necessity*, and so on, where the knowledge would not concern mere facts about the meanings of words. Such, perhaps, is the spell of philosophy, the "bewitchment" that Wittgenstein spoke of as its chief danger.

If we look back, as best we can, over the history of human knowledge, we can begin to break the spell. The reason is the sheer fact that what seems clear and obvious does not remain static. It changes, changes with the advance of knowledge. At each stage of our knowledge, we may well be subject to the illusion that our questions (expressing curiosity about what we don't know) are clear and have definite answers, and that the concepts in terms of which they are asked will be retained in the statements that answer them. Studying the history of science, it is not long before we realize that this is not so. Some very early Greeks or Egyptians, or cave-dwellers perhaps, may have asked questions like, "What makes things move?"; a little later, "What are material things?"; later still, "What is force?." Such questions would be enough, perhaps, to incite some thought and investigation, which inform some partial answers, which incite new questions, new hypotheses, and so on. But it is a mistake to assume that at every stage, the question-asker already knows exactly what would answer the question, what sorts of investigations to pursue, how to conduct them. The concepts involved in modern physics were scarcely dreamed of early on. Every stage along the royal road to knowledge is to some degree a stage of confusion from the point of view of subsequent ones. The progress of science is partly progress of recognizing that mere familiarity and fluency with certain concepts is not well correlated with actual clarity and explanatory value, together with acquiring sharper standards for what clarity and explanatory value are (see *TT* 46, 184; Hahn and Schilpp 1986, p. 228). The progress of science partly is a matter of learning what rigorous knowledge is and how to get it.

Quine is not normally regarded as an historically minded philosopher, but it is characteristic of him, early and late, to doubt that we really know what we are asking when asking certain philosophical questions, and to argue that human knowledge is better off without some of the concepts in terms of which many signature philosophical questions have been asked. It is better off rejecting certain questions as confused, misdirected, hopeless or pointless, and thus giving up certain theoretical ambitions as incoherent or otherwise not worthwhile. This comes not because Quine is a thorough historian of science, but because he has thought carefully about certain key episodes with which his studies of the foundations of mathematics made him thoroughly familiar (*WP* 3–20), especially the paradox of the liar and that of the set of all sets that are not members of themselves: the intuitions themselves are contradictory. He took those lessons to heart. And the lesson that seems to have impressed him most is that theoretical progress is very often achieved not by the "analysis" of some notably perplexing phenomenon or concept—an answer to the question What is X?—but *replacement* or *expulsion* of the relevant bits of language, as discussed in Chapter 6. The idea was famously advanced by late-nineteenth-century physicist Heinrich Hertz. Noting that the question "What is force?" seems to summon up an ill-behaved assortment of ideas, mental pictures, and so on, Hertz suggested that the term should simply be removed from formulations of physics. For in that case:

> When these painful contradictions are removed, the question as to the nature of force will not have been answered, but our minds, no longer vexed, will cease to ask illegitimate questions.

> (Hertz 1899, p. 186)

Let us consider a clear example that seems, from early in Quine's career, to have impressed him deeply (see *WP* 145, *WO* 248–51), as showing that the actual progress of human knowledge is very different from the sort of thing so often seemingly assumed by philosophers. This is the case of the *infinitesimal.*

Case Study

Suppose we fire a rocket. From being stationary, it *accelerates*—goes faster and faster—eventually reaches a peak velocity, then *decelerates,* is momentarily motionless, then falls back to earth. Its velocity is always changing. Velocity (speed in a given direction) is defined as a ratio of units of distance travelled to units of time—*miles per hour*, for example. So, in order to measure the rocket's velocity on the way up, we need to measure the distance travelled during a certain time interval. Doing so, however, does not tell us the whole story. For the velocity of the rocket is always changing. If we measure the rocket's velocity in the usual way—say between two instants t_1 and t_2—we learn its *average velocity* during that time interval. But what if we want to know its exact speed at *one exact moment?* How do we measure that?

Suppose we want to know the rocket's velocity at an exact instant *I* which lies inside the time interval $<t_1, t_2>$. We can of course measure the average velocity during that time interval. However, the rocket may have changed speeds a great deal during that time interval (even though its speed must, at *some* point during the interval, have been equal to the average velocity over the course of the interval). We know that the rocket does not change speeds instantaneously; it accelerates smoothly, then decelerates smoothly. We can get a more accurate result if we measure average velocity over a smaller interval around *I*. In fact, the smaller the interval we take, the less the speed will vary during that interval, and the closer we get to the instantaneous velocity at *I*. It stands to reason, then, that the instantaneous velocity of the rocket at *I* is equal to the average velocity during an *infinitely small* interval around *I*. The size of the relevant interval, as it is put, is *infinitesimal.*

The problem generalized is that of finding the "steepness" of a curve at a given point: the relation of time to the rocket's height can be illustrated with a graph in the Cartesian plane: the curve will first rise slowly, then faster and faster, then slower and slower until the top, then falling back as the rocket falls to earth. The velocity at a given point is the slope of the tangent of the curve at that point (the tangent of a point on a curve is a line that passes through the point without passing through the curve). The curve can be represented as some function $y = f(x)$ indicating height as a function of time. The *derivative* of this function is the function that yields the velocity at any given moment—i.e., the slope of the tangent. Thus if a and b are two points on the curve with y between them, then in general the smaller the distance between a and b, the closer the slope of the line between a and b will be to the slope of the tangent line passing through y; if the gap between a and b is infinitesimal, it will be equal to it.

Newton, famously, showed how to systematize these and related methods for solving problems of mathematics and mathematical physics. Not long after, the Irish philosopher Berkeley criticized the apparent reliance of the "calculus" on the seemingly paradoxical notion of the infinitesimal. What in the world is that? How can something be infinitely small without being nothing? Needless to say, the philosopher did not put a stop to the activities of mathematicians; the mathematics "worked," as did its application to physics and engineering.

In the nineteenth century, however, momentous progress was made in clarifying the foundations of this area of mathematics. In particular, Karl Weierstrass (1815–97) formulated a perfectly clear and rigorous definition of the notion of the *limit* of a function.

Consider the following infinite series:

$$1/2, 1/4, 1/8, 1/16...$$

We can symbolize an arbitrary term of this series as:

$$f(n) = \frac{1}{2^n}$$

For example, the third term of the series, where $n = 3$, is 1 divided by 2^3 (2 x 2 x 2), that is 1/8. f, as defined above, is a *function*: plug in a number (as an "argument"), and it yields a unique number as output (the "value" of the function for that argument). Now consider what happens when we take the values of this function for the first three arguments 1, 2, 3, and add them together. We then get

$$1/2 + 1/4 + 1/8 = 7/8$$

Doing this is what is called taking the "bounded sum" of our function, symbolized:

$$\sum_{n=1}^{3} \frac{1}{2^n}$$

More generally, we can consider the function

$$G(i) = \sum_{n=i}^{i} \frac{1}{2^n}$$

It is easy to see that if we add together the first i terms of our sequence, the result gets closer to 1 as i increases. At no point in the series does it quite reach 1; but the sum of *all* the terms of our infinite series:

$$1/2 + 1/4 + 1/8 + 1/16 + ...$$

is exactly equal to 1. Thus we say: the *limit* of the function G as i increases without bound is 1.

Thus consider our rocket, and consider the operation of taking smaller and smaller intervals around the instant I, and computing the average velocity over those intervals. If we represent this as an infinite sequence—the first term is the average velocity over the largest interval, the second is the average velocity over an interval wholly inside the first one, the next inside the previous, and so on— then clearly the limit of this series must be equal to the instantaneous velocity at I. We can thus explain the concept of instantaneous velocity in terms of the concept of limit.

But what exactly is a limit, and how do we know that the notion of a limit does not presuppose that of the infinitesimal? Weierstrass's key contribution in this area was to give a *precise* non-metaphorical definition of the limit of a function that shows that it makes no such presupposition. ($|x|$ is the absolute value of what is put for x, e.g. $|-2| = |2| = 2$). The limit of a function $f(x)$ as x approaches a is c, symbolized –

$$\lim_{x \to a} f(x) = c$$

– just in case for all ε greater than 0, there exists a real number δ such that:

$$\text{if } 0 < |x - a| < \delta, \text{ then } |f(x) - c| < \varepsilon.$$

This is a little hard to understand at first glance, but the idea is straightforward. Suppose the value of a function is "tending towards" a certain number c as we feed into it numbers that get closer and closer to a. Think of ε as a *standard of approximation*. The idea is that no matter how small the standard of approximation, there is a number close enough to *a* such that the value of the function, for all arguments that are at least as close as that number to *a*, is always within that standard of approximation. The crucial point for our purposes is that this definition *makes no reference to any objects except numbers* (real numbers). Otherwise, it employs only arithmetical symbols and logical operations, including "if-then" and the quantifiers "for all" and "there exists." There are no funny objects or strange concepts whatsoever.

The philosophical payoff for our purposes is simple. Weierstrass did not analyze or explain the concept of infinitesimal. He showed that the calculus could be formulated in such a way as to involve no such concept at all. If someone nowadays insisted on asking, "But still, what *is* the infinitesimal?," complaining that *that* question hasn't been answered, we would tell him he simply hasn't understood the theory of limits, that perhaps he'd better re-read the first chapter of his calculus book. And even *before* Weierstrass, the question would have been futile, despite what would have been the familiarity of the concept to the practicing mathematician. More generally, what this shows is that one cannot always isolate a given concept—not even one that does figure in present science—and profitably ask, "What is it?," or try to analyze it or give a theory about it (think of cause, of belief). One has to take a wider view of the role of the concept in science as a whole, and one must allow that clarification or progress may be best served by replacing or dropping the concept. Furthermore, this attitude may be appropriate *even when we do not yet know how to avoid or replace it.*

Such is exactly Quine's attitude toward, for example, truth: Tarski showed how to define truth-predicates for restricted purposes without invoking the paradoxical general concept of truth. Also proper names: Russell's contextual definition of sentences of the form "The F is G," along with the conversion of proper names to definite descriptions, should be looked upon as showing that there is no theoretical function fulfilled by proper names that cannot be fulfilled without them (*WO* 260–1). What especially strikes Quine in these sorts of cases is that, whatever quandaries attend the notion in question, it is possible to clarify the legitimate theoretical *role* for which the notion has hitherto been invoked. Once the role is identified, the task is to devise something unobjectionable to play it. It's worth it to revisit Quine's comments on Kuratowski's definition in set theory of the ordered pair (first quoted in Chapter 5, p. 110):

> This definition is paradigmatic of what we are most typically up to when in a philosophical spirit we offer an "analysis" or "explication" of some hitherto inadequately formulated "idea" or expression. We do not claim synonymy. We do

not claim to make clear and explicit what the users of the unclear expression had unconsciously in mind all along. We do not expose hidden meanings, as the words "analysis" and "explication" would suggest; we supply lacks. We fix on the particular functions of the unclear expression that make it worth troubling about, and then devise a substitute, clear and couched in terms to our liking, that fulfils those functions.

(*WO* 258–9; also *FSS* 7–8)

Nor does Quine restrict the idea of replacement to seemingly local disturbances like that of the ordered pair or the infinitesimal. Even the very concept of existence could conceivably prove inadequate. The reason is simply that if paraphrase into quantificational logic is our standard of ontology, then if ineluctable scientific developments prove incapable of this style of paraphrase, the question of existential commitment could dissolve:

quantum mechanics invites logical deviations whose reduction to the old standard [the predicate calculus] is by no means evident. On one rendering these deviations take the form of probabilistic predications. On an alternative rendering they call for basic departures from the logic of truth functions. When the dust has settled, we may find that the very notion of existence, the old one, has had its day. A kindred notion may stand forth that seems sufficiently akin to warrant application of the same word; such is the way of terminology. Whether to say at that point that we have gained new insight into existence, or that we have outgrown the notion and reapplied the term, is a question of terminology as well.

(*PT* 36; see also Hahn and Schilpp 1986, pp. 401–2)

Either the concept of existence would have to be modified, or it would be time to dispense with the concept altogether. Quine's distance from the opposite tendency in analytical philosophy, then, might be put like this. Both tendencies may be regarded as mandating the "clarification of our conceptual scheme" in Quine's phrase, but the metaphor of clarification is understood differently. According to the opposite tendency, the idioms of ordinary language already stand for certain phenomena—belief, necessity, and so on—such that we can always profitably ask for more information about those things, often to be revealed by regimentation in terms of artificial logical languages guided by intuition. The answers so revealed will tell us how things really stand with the very things we were talking about all along. The *analysis* involved in analytic philosophy is clarification like the cleaning of the lens of a microscope, or the removal of distortions in it, and such like; the objects seen in the eyepiece, or presented by the conceptual scheme, remain as they were, but come more sharply into view.[1] By contrast, according to Quine, much of our language, many of our ways of speaking, simply do not map onto anything that would be described in rigorous scientific language. The pressures of practical life engender ways of speaking that may be indispensable to human life, but which may also turn out to be logically inconsistent—for example the paradoxical use of the word "true," or sorites-inducing words like "heap" or "large"—or irremediably interest-relative, or in some other way unfit for retention in rigorous science. The genuine clarification achieved by analysis, what Quine calls regimentation, is not simply the sharpening of blurred images in the microscope, but also the revelation that some of what we thought we were looking at was mere dirt on the lens.

Lingering Questions, Late Adjustments

It will not surprise the reader to hear that many of Quine's particular conclusions have been strenuously and cogently challenged. I have largely suppressed these challenges. Aside from considerations of space, a central reason is that Quine and his critics are often talking past each other, assuming different things about what philosophy is and what it might achieve. Indeed Quine's actual responses to critics have struck many readers as mere telescopic reiterations of the Quinean picture, as if he could not see why the considerations raised qualify as an objection. As should be evident from what we have already said, the real opposition often lies at a very general level that Quine himself rarely makes explicit. For example, if someone objects that Quine's treatment of belief-sentences in terms of "believes-true" fails to reproduce the exact truth-conditions of sentences in English involving "believes that," then the Quinean answer is that it was never meant to, that the aim was *replacement*, not *analysis*; and then in order to explain why such a thing is to be preferred, and why the demand for analysis relinquished, we have to tell the whole Quinean story. Not everyone has heard it. Still, there are some questions or concerns that arise very much within Quine's framework—in particular some that I think it will be most profitable to raise here if briefly, as a way of ending the book, and as stimulating further study.

Pre-established Harmony

Observation sentences are at the center of Quine's empiricist epistemology, comparable to the Protocol Sentences of the Logical Empiricists or to Knowledge by Acquaintance of Russell. If A and B are observation sentences, then the

"Empirical Content" of a theory is the sum total of accepted sentences of the form "Whenever A, B"—the "observation categoricals" implied by the theory (Chapter 4, pp. 82–3). Observation sentences are simultaneously the "entering wedge" of translation; accordingly they more than anything are what make language a "social art" (Chapter 3, pp. 39–44). However—as we saw in passing in Chapter 4—after *Word and Object,* because of a recognition of a certain evident fact about observation sentences, Quine's conception of what objectively constrains translation would change. In *Word and Object* he had supposed that observation sentences could be translated by matching stimulus meanings: when S is observational, S is translated as S* just in case the stimulus meaning of S matches that of S*. Remember that the (positive) stimulus meaning of a sentence (with respect to a given modulus) is that set of sensory receptors that are fired when the subject is subjected to a certain stimulus (over the modulus), which correlate with the subject's being disposed to assent to the sentence. ("Stimulus meaning" is openly a technical notion, bearing only passing resemblance to "meaning" in the ordinary sense; later, in order to ward off irrelevant objections, Quine would change its name to "neural intakes"; *CCE* 349). In practice, the translator would not bother with exact microscopic examinations of the native's sensory receptors or their own. They would simply assume that, if they were in the same situation as the native—sitting like that, facing that way, etc.—then they would receive the same stimulations. So they can ask themselves what they would be disposed to assent to if they were sitting like that, facing that way. Still, the assumption being made when translating observation sentences is that translator and native would undergo the same stimuli in a given orientation.

The problem is that "receiving a stimulus" is defined for the individual as the firing of a certain array of sensory receptors. But requiring *matches* in stimulus meaning is far too demanding, for different human beings cannot be expected to have exactly similar sensory receptors lined up exactly the same way. Clearly, we learn to speak in the same way as our community irrespective of whether we do. The objective data for translation, then, need not include matches of stimulus meaning.

Even in *Word and Object* Quine was aware of the crucial consideration:

> Different persons growing up in the same language are like different bushes trimmed and trained to take the shape of identical elephants. The anatomical details of twigs and branches will fulfill the elephantine form differently from bush to bush, but the overall outward results are alike.

> (*WO* 8)

Retrospectively—thirty-five years later, in 1995—he wrote:

> Stimulus meaning was what, theoretically speaking, correct translation of an observation sentence preserved. This is uncomfortable theory, however. It calls for sameness of stimulus meaning of the native sentence for the native and the English sentence for the translator, and hence a sharing of stimulations by native and translator. Well, they cannot share neuroceptors, so we must settle rather for homology of receptors. Such homology is by no means to be expected, and anyway surely should not matter, as I remarked in a lecture five years later.
>
> (*FSS* 159)

From his first acknowledgment of the difficulty in 1965, until 1995, Quine gradually adjusted the picture. We'll attend to two important points of inflection.

(1) In 1992 he characterized an observation sentence as "an occasion sentence on which speakers of the language can agree outright on witnessing the occasion" (*PT* 3). This makes their social nature conspicuous, but it doesn't quite scratch the itch as is does not afford any explanation of *why* they agree.

As he went on in the retrospective vein:

> Let me pinpoint the problem. A rabbit appears, the native says "Gavagai," and the translator conjectures "Rabbit." On a later occasion they espy another rabbit, the translator says "Gavagai," and the native concurs. The two occasions were perceptually similar for the native, by his subjective standards of perceptual similarity, and likewise for the translator by his independently testable subjective standards of perceptual similarity. Anatomic likeness of the native's receptors and those of the translator could have helped to account for this agreement, but that is out. What then does?
>
> (*FSS* 160)

Davidson (1993) saw this as supporting his own scheme, which posits a certain triangle whose vertices are the translator, the person being translated, and some external object or event such as a rabbit or something resembling a rabbit. Rather than sticking with the proximate neural events, the stimulus meaning, Davidson goes with the distal cause, namely the rabbit itself, the referent that figures in such a sentence as "It's a rabbit."

Quine did not accept this. He wrote:

> Davidson proposed providing for intersubjective likeness of stimulation by locating the stimulus not at the bodily surface but farther out, in the nearest shared cause of the pertinent behavior of the two subjects. Failing a rabbit or other body to the purpose, perhaps the stimulus could be a shared situation,

if ontological sense can be made of situations. But I remain unswerved in locating stimulation at the neural input, for my interest is epistemological, however naturalized. I am interested in the flow of evidence from the triggering of the senses to the pronouncements of science. My naturalism does allow *me* free reference to nerve endings, rabbits, and other physical objects, so I could place the stimulus out where Davidson does without finessing any reification on the subject's part. But I am put off by the vagueness of shared situations.

(PT 41–2)

This reply contains three strands. First, a general definition of the stimulus meaning of an observation sentence should not appeal simply to the object that bears some sort of causal relation to both translator and subject, for not all observation sentences are straightforwardly keyed in that way to *objects*. "It's warm," for example, is not. Nor is an appeal to *events* satisfactory, for it is unclear what event is relevant to "Red!" Something more general would be needed, such as *situations* or *states of affairs* (furthermore, some measure would have to be formulated for when a situation is "shared," that is, related, in the relevant way, to both translator and subject). The last sentence of the above quotation sounds rather off-hand, but Quine is gesturing at what, from his point of view, would be an extremely complex and problematic idea. The notion of a state of affairs is getting very close to such notions as *proposition* and *possible world* which, as he sees it, tend to get invoked only because we are already assuming the unexplained reality and determinacy of sophisticated semantical or modal notions. The tail, as he sees it, would be wagging the dog.

Second, the invocation of situations would be a mistake from the point of view of naturalized epistemology. Its aim is to describe how a certain kind of structure of verbal dispositions—that embodying referential language—arises in the animal in response to sensory stimulation. From that point of view, it does not matter in the slightest what causes the sensory stimulation. Indeed the very fact that we can fool the subject—give him a fleeting glimpse of a stuffed toy Peter Rabbit, or appropriately stimulate his senses in some more technically sophisticated way—shows that rabbits and such like are irrelevant to naturalized epistemology: the epistemologist wants to know what in point of fact causes the subject to become disposed to assent to "Rabbit!" The answer that gets to the point, and cuts across the various rabbits, stuffed animals and other external causes, is sensory stimulation.

Third—and this is perhaps the most important consideration—Quine saw Davidson's scheme as assuming what needs explaining, certainly what needs explaining from Quine's naturalized epistemological point of view. To *assume* the object of perception, the object of reference, does not explain how people manage to overcome their individual neurological idiosyncrasies to achieve reliable discourse "about" the public, external objects. It just assumes that we do overcome it. Quine aims at an account of language which does not rest on what, in his view, are such unfocused and unexplanatory assumptions.

(2) The second inflection point is Quine's eventual positive response to the problem, which is quite different from Davidson's. In "Progress on Two Fronts" Quine writes:

> What we have is a preestablished harmony of standards of perceptual similarity, independent of intersubjective likeness of receptors or sensations. Shades of G. W. Leibniz, thus, but without appeal to divine intervention. The harmony is explained by a yet deeper, but more faltering preestablished harmony between perceptual similarity and the environment.
>
> (*CCE* 474–5; see also *FSS* 20–1)

He mentions Leibniz because Leibniz propounded a like named doctrine that God sees to it that each "monad"—therefore each of us—has perceptions that dovetail with those of others. Quine goes on:

> This, in turn, is accounted for by natural selection, as follows. We have, to begin with, an inductive instinct: we tend to expect perceptually similar stimulations to have sequels that are similar to each other. This is the basis of expectation, habit formation, and learning. Successful expectation has always had survival value, notably in the elusion of predators and the capture of prey. Natural selection has accordingly favored innate standards of perceptual similarity which have tended to harmonize with trends in the environment … Derivatively, then, through our sharing of an ancestral gene pool, our innate standards of perceptual similarity harmonize also intersubjectively. Natural selection is Darwin's solvent of metaphysics … Harmony without interaction: that was the subtlety. We take its ubiquitous effects for granted, not thinking them through.
>
> (*CCE* 475)

Those who failed to be in perceptual lock-step with others tended not to procreate as successfully as those who did. We gain advantage directly by the broad harmonization of our inductive dispositions with nature; and we gain indirectly by sharing them with one another, especially since the sharing makes language possible. Thus Quine saw fit not to *change* the approach of 1992, but to add some Darwinian explanation pertaining to the wider context.

Five Challenges to Empiricism

I. The "theory-ladenness" of observation sentences. In *Word and Object* of 1960, as we saw in Chapter 3, Quine took notice that a typical observation sentence will be subject to "collateral information," such as the presence of rabbit-fly, which serves, for the wily native, as a sign of the presence of a rabbit. On the one hand, a native might assent to "Gavagai?" without being stimulated by a rabbit, in the case of a rabbit-fly's appearance accompanied by a rabbit but without the rabbit's being visible. On the other hand, a verdict for a single instance of an observation sentence might change: it looked for all the world as if there were a rabbit there, but one sees now that it was only a patch of wildflowers, or the family cat. As a result, as Quine would put in 1975, "[o]bservation sentences are not incorrigible. A witness who has assented to an observation sentence on the spot is permitted to reconsider his verdict later in the face of conflicting theory" (*CCE* 231)—or in the face of superseding information, one might say.

Followers of Thomas Kuhn or Paul Feyerabend will say that observation is "theory-laden." Far from being a neutral means of arbitrating between theories, observational data is always infected by the theories of the observer. Is this a threat to empiricism, or at least to Quine's particular version of it?

Quine considered the question important, as observation sentences are at the center of not only his philosophy of language, but of his epistemology. And he went back and forth on the question of whether observationality should be reckoned a matter of degree, or whether it should be reckoned as absolute despite all. In *Word and Object*, it was a matter of degree, ranging from cases highly infected with theory to the purest cases—from "There is copper sulfide in it," to "There's a rabbit," to "That's blue," to "That looks blue," to perhaps "I'm having a blue sensation," if that counts as observational. (Interestingly, sentences of the tail end of this spectrum are the most incorrigible, are the best candidates for reporting immediate experience, yet normally are not suitable as data for scientific theory.) Then, later, Quine thought of observationality as all-or-nothing when sentences are regarded "holophrastically"—as unstructured like ape cries—but as subject to theory when regarded "analytically"—as semantically complex and therefore as standing in logical relationships to the rest of the subject's language. Then in 1993 he was back again with degrees, emphasizing the temporal priority of a certain holophrastic stage in their acquisition:

> We must recognize degrees of observationality. Assertion of the sentence or assent to it may be more or less delayed or hesitant. There may even be afterthoughts: "Oh, it isn't a dog after all". This sort of self-correction intrudes at the sophisticated

stage where the child has come to appreciate component terms of observation sentences in their referential capacity. It is infection of observation by theory; the anti-epistemologists have a point here. But there are pure cases, and they prevail at the early stages of language acquisition. Observation sentences in this pristine purity are the child's port of entry to cognitive language, for it is just these which he can acquire without the aid of previously acquired language.

(CCE 411)

And then in 1996 he was back yet again with discreteness, off-on. He now subscribes to an "absolute notion of an observation sentence as simply an occasion sentence that commands the subject's immediate assent, however fallible and revisable. Fallibility is then accommodated in a separate dimension, *theoreticity*, which invests observation sentences in varying degrees" (CCE 477). By "immediate assent" he means to invoke the near-causal relationship between the sensory receptors and the subject's assent, which is absent in the case of non-observation occasion sentences as well as standing sentences. Then what he here calls "theoreticity"—theory ladenness—can be recognized as a separate dimension. Well and good, but why exactly this apparent nit-picking? Quine worried that theory-ladenness was a problem, and needs definitively to sort the matter out. If observation is always infected with theory, then not only is the answerability of theory to observational data threatened, different sound theories in science might well be "incommensurable," in Kuhn's terms; since theoretical terms owe their meanings to theories, as a Kuhnian might put it, they might fail to remain suitably constant in meaning for the purpose of comparing the theories. If no sentences are fully observation sentences, then strictly speaking, empiricism paints a false picture of science, with its pretense of checkpoints that are fully observational. One could make the point by saying that there are no observation sentences, strictly speaking.

Whether a sentence is an observation sentence is a separate question from its theoreticity; this enables Quine to refrain from saying that Kuhn and Feyerabend were simply wrong. Whereas he had previously said that they had "overreacted, neglecting significant distinctions" (CCE 409), his latest scheme enabled him to better conceptualize the situation, to the point where he was "won over to Thomas Kuhn and others who have insisted that observation is inseparable from theory" (CCE 477). The reason he could make this concession without giving up the game is just that the status of a sentence as observational is not impugned by such theoreticity as it has. This in turn allows for a straightforward re-avowal a certain regulative maxim in epistemology, that there is a "strong presumption in favour of observation statements"—a "bias that makes science empirical" (*CCE* 229). It is a bias that won through in the sixteenth and seventeenth centuries with Bacon and Galileo, but it has always registered a delicate balance in point of fact. Too much bias results in stasis and sterility, too little in bad science or irrationality, as in astrology or witchcraft.

II. The purported third dogma. Davidson once accused Quine of having within his philosophy an untenable dualism between "empirical content" and "conceptual schemes," which amounts to a "Third Dogma of Empiricism":

> The idea is then that something is a language, and associated with a conceptual scheme, whether we can translate it or not, if it stands in a certain relation (predicting, organizing, facing or fitting) to experience (nature, reality, sensory promptings). The problem is to say what the relation is, and to be clearer about the entities related.
>
> (Davidson 1984, p. 189)

But no account can coherently specify the epistemic relation between scheme and content; the two must engage somehow for knowledge to be possible, yet it is unintelligible how something conceptual can engage with something non-conceptual. "Only a belief can be evidence for a belief," writes Davidson.

Quine's response deals with the matter at a basic level. The "proper role of experience or surface irritation," writes Quine, "is as a basis not for truth but for warranted belief" (*TT* 39). At more length:

> If empiricism is construed as a theory of truth, then what Davidson imputes to it as a third dogma is rightly imputed and rightly renounced. Empiricism as a theory of truth thereupon goes by the board, and good riddance. As a theory of evidence, however, empiricism remains with us, minus indeed the two old dogmas. The third purported dogma, understood now in relation not to truth but to warranted belief, remains intact. It has both a descriptive and a normative aspect, and in neither aspect do I think of it as a dogma. It is what makes scientific method partly empirical rather than solely a quest for internal coherence. It has indeed wanted some tidying up, and has had it.
>
> (*TT* 39)

The empiricist claim—familiar from Chapter 4—is that the empirical content of a theory is its collection of observation categoricals; there is no violation here of the principle that only belief can be evidence for belief. Nor is there any awareness of "surface irritations" in Quine's mature story. The relation between such irritations and dispositions to assent, at least in the purest cases, is causal only.

The two aspects—normative and descriptive—are studied within the narrow confines of naturalized epistemology, taking the truth of one's overall world-view for granted. Truth is indeed a separate question. Of this there is little to say at the general level, other than "'S' is true iff S." A doctrine of "empiricist truth," committed to something like "'S' is true iff it is entailed by a empirically supported theory," would perhaps go against the naturalist credo of "No first philosophy," but in any case is certainly not accepted by Quine, at least not as a criterion of truth (see the section on truth at the end of Chapter 5).

Davidson equates the relation of scheme and content to language and surface irritations, which is not far from the relation of theoretical sentences to observation sentences. If that were what's at issue, then on the surface it would be a relativistic picture: the truth or intelligibility of a theoretical sentence would seem to depend on which scheme—which set of theoretical sentences—was being assumed. Thus our next topic.

III. Underdetermination of theory. This is the thesis, subscribed to by many philosophers of science, that an alternative system of nature could predict and account for experience—past, present, and future—exactly as well as our actual system. It made an appearance in Chapter 3, in connection with the Indeterminacy of Translation. More exactly (and speaking of regimented versions of theories rather than "systems of nature"): Any sufficiently ambitious theory, including our own, implies a vast collection of observation categoricals, which are sentences of the form "Whenever o_1, o_2," with o_1 and o_2 being observation sentences. The sum total of these is the theory's Empirical Content, which we can label "EC." If the entirety of our theory of nature is T, then T implies EC (though not the reverse; EC does not imply T). The underdetermination thesis is that some unknown theory T*, different from T, also implies EC (and implies no observation categorical that is not already in EC; T and T* are "empirically equivalent").[2]

But Quine came to say in 1975 that "[t]he doctrine is plausible insofar as it is intelligible, but it is less readily intelligible than it may seem" (*CCE* 228). This might come as a surprise, since just five years before he had enunciated in some detail what seemed to be an important argument for the Indeterminacy of Translation, the argument for it from Underdetermination of Theory (*CCE* 209–14, "On the Reasons for the Indeterminacy of Translation"). The force of that argument requires the intelligibility of its main premise, the Underdetermination of Theory. Although as pointed out in Chapter 3, the force of the Indeterminacy Thesis does not actually depend on its being demonstrated by actual examples. It is the conceivability of the thesis that is doing the work, as showing that a hard-headed and satisfactory science of language does not assume or entail that translation is determinate; indeterminacy remains an open possibility. The indeterminacy thesis might have to remain a "conjecture," but it is a "reasonable one" (*CCE* 447–8; Orenstein and Kotatko 2000, p. 409). The positive argument for it is ultimately just the lack of a sound procedure that guarantees determinacy (*CCE* 341–6).

In any case, our interest now is with the Underdetermination thesis itself, irrespective of any connection with the Indeterminacy of Translation. As just indicated, underdetermination was found wanting in 1975 (with "On Empirically Equivalent Systems of the World"), but the situation received further clarification in 1992, in *Pursuit of Truth*. What exactly is the difference being envisaged between T and T*? It cannot just be a difference of language; we can assume they are both stated in English. Nor can it just be logical incompatibility. As Davidson pointed out, if T implies a sentence S and T* implies not-S, we can simply rewrite T* so as to eliminate the predicates involved in the clash between S and not-S—say rewrite the predicate "is an electron" to "is a schmelectron"; similarly for others as needed (*PT* 97–8). Now T* does not imply not-S; easy. So the incompatibility needn't be thought of as logical. Suppose then, for simplicity, that T and T* are not appreciably different on the score of simplicity, naturalness and so on. So the only apparent thing left is that the difference is psychological or practical: it is just that we cannot see how theoretical sentences of the one can be reduced to or explained in terms of theoretical sentences of the other.

Quine went on to distinguish an "ecumenical" response from a "sectarian" one (*PT* 99–100). The ecumenist accepts both theories, extending the epithet "true" indifferently to sentences of T and to sentences of T*. A stout empiricist will be gratified, precisely because T and T* enjoy the same empirical support in the form of EC. The sectarian however insists that when one works within T, one is obliged to call T true and T* false, and when one works within T*, one is obliged to call T* true and T false. This will gratify the naturalist, for whom one is always obliged to work within a theory of nature—there being no "first philosophy"—as well as enjoying a leaner theory, of avoiding the excess theoretical baggage of entertaining both T and T* at once.

Quine plumps for sectarianism, the main reason being the bloated ontology endemic to the ecumenical line. EC, it will be recalled, does not itself have any objects; they come in only with theory—quantifiers, criteria of identity, in general the "apparatus of reference" (see Chapter 4). Since T and T* will not agree on what objects there are, it's best to think of them as having separate quantifiers and variables. It will be a bit of an unedifying mess to run both. Yet the sectarian can still enjoy the advantages of each—"shifting from one foot to the other," and even gaining new insights via the "triangulation" afforded by the different perspectives (*PT* 100).

If you are feeling the whole issue being discussed is rather rarefied, unreal—not the style of the hard-headed flesh and bones naturalist—then Quine agrees. "The fantasy of irresolubly rival systems of the world," he says, "is a thought experiment out beyond where linguistic usage has been crystallized by use." One thinks of other philosophical fantasies, like "Maybe I'm a brain in vat," or "Maybe I'm in the Matrix"; perhaps one can't prove that these things are not so, but they are powerless to shake one from one's natural beliefs, indeed those prescribed by naturalism. "No wonder," Quine carries on, "the cosmic question whether to call two such world systems true should simmer down, bathetically, to a question of words. Hence also, meanwhile, my vacillation" (*PT* 101).

For all that, however, one might think that something is amiss. As a naturalist, one thinks that what is described by physics and so on is as real as it gets. Yet by naturalism's own lights—as developed by Quine—we are to think that our conception of reality is potentially optional. And then, right on the heels of the last quotation, we get this:

> Fare these conventions as they may, the rival theories describe one and the same world. Limited to our human terms and devices, we grasp the world variously. I think of the disparate ways of getting at the diameter of an impenetrable sphere: we may pinion the sphere in calipers or we may girdle it with a tape measure and divide by pi, but there is no getting inside.
>
> (*PT* 101)

This is exciting but it is hard not think that Quine is here letting the cat, or rather the Kant, out of the bag. We have what seems to be a picture not unlike Kant's if we read "the world" as "[the sum of] things in themselves," something intrinsically unknowable beyond science which remains the selfsame thing despite its being grasped variously. Is this not naturalism threatening to refute itself? Is this not in tension with Quine's proclaimed realism? Is what is real perspective-dependent? Whatever the best response may be, remember that according to Quine, one's grasp of "real" is immanent, a basic grasp of which is won through ordinary language-training (see "Posits and Reality," Chapter 5, pp. 142–4). The virtues of the competing theories come from those theories themselves; there is no hint of an independent, not say fanciful, perspective on reality.[3]

It is perhaps of some interest that there is not a word concerning underdetermination in *From Stimulus to Science*, a book that Quine published in

1995, three years after the second edition of *Pursuit of Truth*, site of the quotation above.

IV. Chomsky: the status of rules. Chapter 3 mentioned Chomsky, who—along with promoting his own picture—has criticized with some stridency Quine's picture of what it is to have language. He agrees with Quine in discounting semantical notions such as reference as explanatorily unsatisfactory, as not being suitable for use at anything like the basic level, and can be said roughly to share Quine's naturalistic outlook. But what that comes to differs violently at the level of brass tacks. He fundamentally condemns the general behaviorism to which he takes Quine to be committed, and criticizes the thesis of the Indeterminacy of Translation. The issues are fascinating but complicated. In this sub-section we shall just say enough to gain a feel for Quine's response. In the next and final sub-section, we shall consider further aspects of Chomsky's position, and will suggest that his position and Quine's are not fundamentally opposed.

As outlined earlier, Chomsky's picture is that the neurological mechanisms that embody human language are genetically constrained to develop as they do in response to sensory stimulation.[4] It is much like a growing plant: it grows toward the light, and grows longer stems or denser foliage depending on the soil conditions, the intensity of the light, and so on, but many structural aspects of both the juvenile and mature plant, and instructions about how to respond to particular lighting, etc. are genetically wired in. To a very large extent, the human's development of the linguistic capacity is not so much to respond to stimulation as to calibrate an internally developing system, filling in certain blanks such as the details of how language—the deep grammatical structure of which is innate—happens to be spoken locally. Chomsky sees this as the only plausible inference from the "poverty of the stimulus"—a huge gap between the evidence the child has to go on in acquiring language and the rich facility so rapidly acquired (see Hahn and Schilpp 1986, pp. 186–7; Chomsky 1975, pp. 3–35).

What is innate and universal is what Chomsky calls "Universal Grammar" or "UG"; UG is common to Japanese-only speakers, to Swahili-only speakers, and Czech-only speakers, and generally to all biologically human speakers. What constitutes the actually developing system is the "I-language"—the "I" standing for three 'I's: individual, internal, and intensional (meaning it is individuated more finely than extensionally). The subject's development of it depends on UG plus the particulars of linguistic experience. The "E-Language"—"external language"—by contrast, is more or less what is commonly and comparatively vaguely known as a person's language: Japanese, Swahili, Czech (or dialect of same), and is by comparison of limited interest for the theoretical linguist. The Chomskyean program of "Generative Linguistics"—involving (1) formulating the specific principles of UG, and (2), giving procedures for mapping the various I-languages onto it—are gigantic tasks but, Chomksyeans would say, have been accomplished well enough to confirm the general Chomskyean hypothesis.

In "Quine's Empirical Assumptions" (Chomsky 1968), Chomsky voices several objections to Quine's project. I will focus on one which was visited briefly in Chapter 3, now pressed further and somewhat differently.[5]

The objection is that Quine's central argument for the indeterminacy of translation begs a basic methodological question. Suppose A and B are two complete, extensionally equivalent in the sense of predicting the same behavioral outcomes, but in some clear sense incompatible translation schemes for a native language. Suppose the grammars of A and B differ substantially, but each embodies a finite set of grammatical principles which, idealizing, churn out respectively all and only the sentences (or grammatical strings) of the language. Quine concludes that there is no factual difference between the two schemes, on the grounds that there is no empirical difference in the claims between the two—that is, that there is no difference from the point of view of our overall naturalistic theory of the world. Chomsky resolutely disagrees, finding Quine guilty of an unjustified prejudice against psychology or "mentalism." Chomsky freely grants that grammar in his sense is a mentalistic or psychological theory, but *not* in the mysterious Dualistic sense of a separate substance from the physical (1968, pp. 61–2, 66; 2000, pp. 46–63). It is mentalistic only as is commonplace in psychology generally (in for example the science of vision, or the science of hearing). There is no reason to suppose that the only possible evidence is the coarse-grained behavioral evidence of the kind Quine favors. Furthermore, if A and B are alternative naturalistic theories that are underdetermined not just by behavioral evidence but by all possible evidence (past and future), then that is so of any naturalistic theory. The same goes for Universal Grammar itself: it is a substantive naturalistic theory, to be evaluated in the same general way as others.

Quine stuck to his guns. "From experiences with axiom systems in mathematics … we can easily believe in the existence of such alternatives" (*CCE* 216–17), Quine remarks when considering alternative, extensionally equivalent grammars. If there were such alternative grammars, their status would be like that of alternative, equivalent sets of axioms for mathematics. No such axiomatization of mathematics is uniquely correct (for all such axiomatizations are equally correct). It is as if we were confronted with an alien calculator: We can learn thoroughly to operate it, and we can formulate various equivalent sets of axioms which describe the externals of that operation—various equivalent "functional" descriptions—but we have not yet looked inside to see how it works, yielding an "engineering" description.[6] But even if we are able to look inside, and are able to formulate an engineering description of its internal structure, still it remains the case that various functional descriptions are adequate to its external operation. It is a mistake to hold up one alternative axiom-set as being exclusively the right one.

The analogy of the alien calculator might be thought inapt because unlike a language-user, the calculator is in no sense a mental entity. It is certainly not a person or language-user. Isn't the question of the right grammar settled by which is actually being followed by the language-user? Although Chomsky no longer thinks precisely this, it will do here to assume that for Chomsky, a grammar can be thought of as a system of *rules* (in later incarcerations of the view, rules are replaced by a system of "Principles and Parameters"). Quine points to a distinction between "fitting" a rule versus being "guided" by the rule:

> Fitting is a matter of true description; guiding is a matter of cause and effect. Behavior *fits* a rule whenever it conforms to it; whenever the rule truly describes the behavior. But the behavior is not *guided* by the rule unless the behaver knows the rule and can state it. This behaver *observes* the rule.
>
> (*CCE* 215)

According to Quine, Chomsky's grammar is not merely a matter of fitting rules—as in the alien calculator—but is not a matter of being guided by them either (few, at most, can state such rules). It lies somewhere between, in a no-man's land: "[Chomsky's] doctrine … imputes to the natives an unconscious preference for one system of rules over another, equally unconscious, which is extensionally equivalent to it" (*CCE* 216). For Quine, to speak of an "unconscious preference," of an "intermediate notion of rules as heeded inarticulately" (*CCE* 217)—or for that matter to speak of "implicit" rather than "explicit" guiding, of "tacit" rather than "overt" rule following—is just to name the gap, not to make any progress toward closing it.

Quine speaks of "the crying need … for explicitness of criteria and awareness of method," and asks us to consider the problem of verifying the existence of a linguistic universal—which for simplicity we can think of as a grammatical property which is found in all languages (hence its being part of Universal Grammar is its best explanation). Suppose our candidate universal is the subject-predicate structure of sentences. Suppose we find it in some language. How do we know that its presence in this language is not the presence of the purported universal, but a mere artifact of our theorizing in English? Perhaps all we can really say is that English has the subject-predicate structure, and that the foreign tongue has been successfully translated into it. "We are moving in an oddly warped circle" (*CCE* 221), muses Quine. The trouble is not the reliance on the speaker's intuitive judgments, but on ones that involve the theoretical vocabulary itself, the vocabulary one is attempting to fit on to the phenomena.

It is better to think of a grammar, Quine declares, as a notation on a level with symbolic logic, or algebra, or the notation of chemistry. When paraphrasing the essentials of a story problem about rowing up a river in algebraic terms, one does so in order to facilitate calculation. No one thinks that the algebra is somehow uniquely present in any other sense in the story itself. Likewise for the paraphrase of an argument in English into symbolic logic, for the purpose of evaluating the reasoning. For grammar, for Quine, "deep structure is similar in a way to logical structure. Both are paraphrases of sentences of ordinary language; both are paraphrases that we resort to for certain purposes of technical convenience" (*CCE* 225).

So much for Quine's take on the underdetermination of grammar. So far as Chomsky is concerned, there is a great deal more to say, and I have disregarded the many changes that Chomsky's program of universal grammar has undergone over sixty years as well as glossed over details of its substance to say the least. Large topics that I have ignored—this is a book about Quine, not Chomsky—is the latter's aim not merely to generate all and only the grammatical strings of an arbitrary language, but (1) to explain the user's "competence" rather than the user's "performance"; (2) to show why the speaker's judgments of grammaticalness do not necessarily track actual grammaticalness; (3) to demonstrate the necessity of structural analysis rather than linear analysis. And others. The permissible evidence, again, goes far beyond the overt behavior of the speaker (see Chomsky 1975, pp. 179–95; 2000, pp. 52–61).[7] But more generally, Quine's position leaves us back in the maw of the Poverty of the Stimulus: without thinking of UG as something innate and actually realized in the human brain, we should have no explanation of the reality of human linguistic competence, of how the human achieves it so rapidly and based upon such limited and highly imperfect data to which he or she is exposed. Some considerations in the closing sub-section bring this out further.

V. Chomsky: Behaviorism, Galileo, and innate structure. I close with some remarks from a more abstract methodological point view critical of empiricism, both Quine's and generally—by way of additional points concerning his dispute with Chomsky—and briefly linking Quine up with the historical considerations with which this book began.

Quine is an empiricist, as we say and as he says. What exactly does that come to? As noted, for Quine empiricism is on the one hand a regulative if in some sense defeasible maxim in the philosophy of science. It is a normative matter demanding sufficient empirical relevance to would-be knowledge, thereby disqualifying mystics and soothsayers (if not Leibniz and Descartes just like that). On the other hand, it is a straightforward descriptive claim: all real science is in fact empirical (including mathematics, as we have seen). And—aside from the circularity worry, which was dealt with under "The Rejection of First Philosophy" above as well as the opening of Chapter 4—this immediately poses a more straightforward problem, one that is well known to Quine. His writings are full of such remarks as that "the stimulation of his sensory receptors is all the evidence anybody has had to go on, ultimately, in arriving at his picture of the world" (*OR* 75–6); "How, on the strength of the mere sporadic triggering of our sensory receptors, is it possible to fabricate our elaborate theory of other minds and the external world?"(Quine 2019, p. 19); and "Given only the evidence of our senses, how do we arrive at our theory of the world?" (*RR* 1).

This puts pressure on empiricism. As noted further in Chapter 4, he is persuaded that learning requires an "innate similarity space": all other things being equal, if the child were not innately predisposed, say, to treat one rabbit-presentation as more similar to another than to that of a tree, then it is most unlikely that he would ever learn the word "rabbit." An echo is plain with Chomsky's "Poverty of the Stimulus" argument, but in a more schematic sense. Substantial neurological mechanisms that come to embody the subject's knowledge must already be prepared, in a way acceptable to the naturalized epistemologist, with what, in broad outline, is to be done with sensory presentations. In fully naturalistic terms, the more general neurological structures necessary for a human being's basic theory of the world must be genetically determined to develop as they do, as long as sensory input is of a suitable kind.

One trouble concerns "similarity." Anything, as wise philosophers are quick to point out, is similar to anything else; the standards of "similarity" depend on your purpose. Quine of course is well-aware of this, and sketches a behavioral test for the three-way relation "x is for y similar to z." Yet having a test for the presence a property says little about what the property is, how it works, or how it is implemented; a test for the presence of a certain gene, for comparison, need not tell us much about the function of the gene. Another trouble is that most of the interesting properties of the human language capacity have little to do with similarity of perceptions but with grammar itself, in all its wondrous if occasionally baffling complexity (see Rey on "WhyNots," 2020, pp. 21–44). And Chomsky has indeed made a formidable case that innate perceptual structures of the kind Quine describes fall far short of what is needed to account for human knowledge of language. He has written a good deal on the methodology and history of the relevant aspects of science—*Cartesian Linguistics* (1966), *Language and Mind* (1972), *Reflections on Language* (1975), *Knowledge of Language* (1986), *New Horizons in the Study of Language and Mind* (2000), and *Why Only Us?* (2016). He affirms rather an avowedly anti-empiricist, rationalist orientation, in a modern form, both specifically with his notion of Universal Grammar as described above and indirectly and more generally with modern Cognitive Science, of which Linguistics, in Chomsky's sense, is a part.

The books include some illuminating and extensive scholarly detail on the historical articulation of the idea of linguistic competence and of compositionality, plus pointed criticisms of behaviorism as a research strategy in both psychology—Watson, Skinner—and linguistics—Saussure, Bloomfield, Harris—the idea that language can profitably be theorized about as a disembodied corpus of public, interconnected utterances. For the behaviorist, or least a caricature of one, the creature is to be conceived only in terms of stimulus-response, reinforcement, and association, with the mind itself regarded only as a black-box of no intrinsic interest, at most as the locus of stimulus-response relations to be determined experimentally (with stimulus-response patterns expanded to include "operant conditioning," i.e., acquired spontaneous behaviors through conditioning, with food-pellet rewards, etc.). As was made compelling long ago in his scathing review of Skinner's *Verbal Behavior* (Chomsky 1959), it is hopeless to remain in this way at the surface, making no essential reference to internal structure—of the mind or brain—in accounting for human linguistic competence. It is mere word-making to say that anything but the simplest aspects of human language-capacity can be conceived by "extrapolation" or "association," as exemplified by rats pressing levers to gain food. The ability to process newly encountered sentences in all their intricacy cannot be explained as the mere generalization from simple items about which one has previously learned to respond.

One might protest that there is a vast empirically intractable gulf between Quine's similarity spaces and Chomsky's Universal Grammar, in that the former is straightforwardly behaviorally detectable, whereas the latter is certainly not, at least not in any direct sense. That is perhaps true, but if Chomsky is right that one cannot hope to explain language using only Quine's methods, then the point is largely immaterial. Although the theory of Universal Grammar is indeed further removed from the realities it describes, it is still, despite its rationalist elements, a scientific theory, indeed an empirical theory; it is fate rests on its explanatory capacity, its predictive power, and more generally on how well it jibes with data.

Chomsky's review of Quine discussed early in the last sub-section originally appeared in 1968. Yet Quine seems to have persisted unabashed, asking us in 1975 to "consider the case where we teach the infant a word by reinforcing his random babbling on some appropriate occasion. His chance utterance bears a chance resemblance to a word appropriate to the occasion, and we reward him" (*CCE* 244–5; also *RR* 27–32). His opposition in the same article to mentalistic explanation was plain: "Let us then recognize that the semantical study of language is worth pursuing with all the scruples of the natural scientist," he writes. "We must study language as a system of dispositions to verbal behaviour, and not just surface listlessly to the Sargasso Sea of mentalism" (*CCE* 252). And later, writing with seeming defiance in 1990:

> I hold further that the behaviorist approach is mandatory. In psychology one may or may not be a behaviorist, but in linguistics one has no choice. Each of us learns his language by observing other people's verbal behavior and having his own faltering verbal behavior observed and reinforced or corrected by others. We depend strictly on overt behavior in observable situations.
>
> (*PT* 37–8)

That a child relies on "observing other people's verbal behavior and having his own faltering verbal behavior observed and reinforced or corrected by others" does indeed suggest that Quine continued to subscribe to a simpleminded Skinnerian model of learning language, or even worse, a picture of the infant as emitting random behavior, progressing via training as Skinner claimed his rats did, via punishment and reward. Quine also seems to fall into the tempting trap of an empty or ritualistic invocation of the idea of "reinforcement" if not of "generalization" or "association."

But that cannot be quite all that is going on. There are two further angles. First, immediately after the above quotation, Quine goes on:

> As long as our command of our language fits all external checkpoints, where our utterance or our reaction to someone's utterance can be appraised in the light of some shared situation, so long all is well. Our mental life between checkpoints is indifferent to our rating as a master of the language. There is nothing in linguistic meaning beyond what is to be gleaned from overt behavior in observable circumstances.
>
> (*PT* 38)

The last sentence, now with emphasis added, tells us that there "is *nothing* in linguistic *meaning* beyond what is to be gleaned from overt behavior in observable circumstances." If the learner's use of language comports with that of his or her fellows—not only their observed behavior but their hypothetical or potential behavior, their behavioral dispositions as in a generous reading of "what *would be gleaned*"—then there is nothing more to be demanded so far as the learner's grasp of *meaning* is concerned. This was emphasized when Chomsky's opposition to Quine first came up in Chapter 3. But further, not only is this passage consistent with the learner's reliance on an innate similarity space, as also briefly mentioned in Chapter 3 it is consistent with their reliance on more detailed innate grammatical structure, indeed with the neural reality of Chomsky's Universal Grammar. I take it that this point about meaning is central to Quine's philosophy as expressed by the saying 'Language is a social art' of *Word and Object*, something for communication; we can let him slide when he speaks of random babbling.

Second, Quine does not of course propose a grammar in anything like Chomsky's sense, not in *Word and Object* and not later. He describes at most the apparatus of reference—the very spare and sometimes near-artificial resources necessary for precise reification and regimentation, which are his main concerns as in the book *Roots of Reference*—along with a certain reluctance to advance, as an attempt at real explanation, the account sketched of how a human might acquire them:

> I am not bent even upon a factual account of the learning of English, welcome thought it would be. My concern with the essential psychogenesis of reference would be fulfilled in fair measure with a plausible account of how one might proceed from infancy step by step to a logically regimented language of science, even bypassing English.
>
> (*RR* 92; for yet greater artificiality, see *FSS* 33–5, 101–6)

He even calls the project "imaginary" (*RR* 124). So perhaps there is room for a version of Quine's story of regimented science—crucial for his account of the epistemological and truth-theoretic aspects of science—to co-exist with Chomsky's Universal Grammar, construed as real psychological explanation. In this sense, Quine is more a philosopher of science, not so much a philosopher of language. Chomsky himself remarks that Quine's holism is "fair enough" for "the sciences" (2000, p. 186).

Not that Chomsky has been persuaded to back off from his anti-Quine position with respect to natural language, not one iota. From a yet more detached perspective, Chomsky extolls the virtues of the "Galilean" perspective for the theory of generative grammar (Chomsky 1980, pp. 8–10, 218–19). Galileo could not conclusively verify his perhaps counterintuitive hypothesis that the rate at which a thing falls is independent of its weight—and thus that Aristotle's assumption was incorrect that the heavier a thing is, the faster it falls—because practically being unable to eliminate intervening but theoretically irrelevant factors such as air friction, he could not adequately confirm his hypotheses experimentally. The same hindered the verification of his equally anti-Aristotelian Law of Inertia (Aristotle held that objects in motion did not remain in motion without a force being applied to them). But his general hunch was on the mark. Galileo's profound revelation was that, in general, in theorizing about deep aspects of complex phenomena, we should not prioritize at all events exact coverage of actual data, of evidence or experience, at the price of being unable to develop mathematical or formal models of the underlying reality. Only the latter generates real explanation instead of superficial description.

With respect to language, Chomsky underlines the importance of idealization thus:

> Linguistic theory is concerned primarily with an ideal speaker-listener, in a completely homogenous speech-community, who knows its language perfectly and is unaffected by such grammatically irrelevant conditions as memory limitations, distractions, shifts of attention and interest, and error (random or characteristic) in applying his knowledge of the language in actual performance … I this respect, study of language is no different from empirical investigation of other complex phenomena.
>
> (1965, pp. 3–4)

In a more recent work, *Why Only Us?* (2016), armed with changes to Universal Grammar involving the "Minimalist Program" and the operation "Merge," plus various advances in biology and genetics, Chomsky and Berwick have worked at bringing Universal Grammar closer to a biological description of the human brain—the analogue for bringing together the computational or functional description of the alien calculator with its engineering description as above. The resulting picture yields a plausible story of how human language might have evolved; it is what would be wanted by any naturalist worth their salt.

Still, as far as I can see, one can maintain both Quine's abstract picture of the apparatus of reference and Chomsky's picture of natural language and its actual evolution. Which suggests one final remark about the relation between evolution and naturalized epistemology in Quine's philosophy. In a frequently quoted passage, Quine characterizes naturalized epistemology as follows:

> Epistemology … studies a natural phenomenon, viz., a physical human subject. The human subject is accorded a certain experimentally controlled input—certain patterns of irradiation in assorted frequencies, for instance—and in the fullness of time the subject delivers as output a description of the three-dimensional external world and its history. The relation between the meager input and the torrential output is a relation that we are prompted to study for somewhat the same reasons that always prompted epistemology; namely, in order to see how evidence relates to theory, and in what ways one's theory of nature transcends any available evidence.
>
> (OR 82–3)

It is the poverty of the stimulus again. It seems to tell us not only that the gap between the meager input and the torrential output is vast, but that what fills the gap, *for the individual,* is so substantial that the idea of empiricism, as a perspective in naturalized epistemology, is correct only with significant qualifications.[8] Not dissimilar problems confronted Plato, Descartes and Leibniz, but they solved them in different ways—a doctrine of reminiscence in Plato's case, theological underpinnings for the others (Chomsky calls it "Plato's problem"). For the naturalized epistemologicist, what fills the gap, at least vaguely and in large measure, is not anything to do with the individual, but with the species. Which is a product of evolution: that normally painfully slow, but sometimes by random fits and starts rapid process which nevertheless has produced not only ants, flowers, and platypuses, but Gödel and Einstein. Yet it is open in principle to suppose that empiricism—in something not unlike its original form—might profitably characterize in a rough sort of way the generation of innate mechanisms, of needed components of knowledge, in the species rather than the individual. For natural selection is itself a kind of induction: mutations are like random hypotheses, and procreative advantage is like confirmation of the hypotheses. Thus if we think of our ultimate ancestors as some kind of replicating but otherwise nearly featureless protoplasm—here is the analogue of the Lockean *tabula rasa*—then virtually everything that arises in the species, whether by evolution of the species or the fortunes of the individual, is in a certain broad sense a response to the environment. Plausibly this was Quine's view. In his final book, he wrote—we can forgive him for writing "race" when now we'd write "species"—that the project of naturalized epistemology is the "rational reconstruction of the individual's and/or the race's actual acquisition of a responsible theory of the external world" (FSS 16).

Further Reading and Historical Notes

For a wide-angle discussion of empirical method including Quine, see Ebbs 2017. The puzzle of underdetermination crops up here and there in philosophy since at least Descartes—especially when it concerns not all possible evidence but the evidence one happens to have. Restricted to Quine's context, see Bergström 2004, Severo 2008, and myself 2016 and 2019. For an overview of the problem of theory-ladenness, see the *Stanford Encyclopedia of Philosophy* 2017 entry "Theory and Observation in Science," section 3. Davidson's in addition to Quine's is a big name, their long-standing mutual influence acknowledged by both; see the essays in Davidson 1984 and 2001. Differences between the two became sharper as time went on; see my Kemp 2012. For material on Pre-established harmony, see Ebbs 2015, Quine 2015a, 2015b, and myself 2017b. See also Quine's essay "I, You and It: An Epistemological Triangle" (*CCE* 485–92; it is easy to read this as Quine's agreeing on all counts with Davidson, but of course that cannot be quite right). For Davidson's charge of a "Third Dogma," see Sinclair 2014, pp. 362–9. The Chomsky-Quine debate has not received anything like the attention that it might, but see George 1986, Smith 2014, myself (forthcoming), and Chomsky himself 1975, pp. 179–95 and 2000, pp. 46–63, 94–6. For an intriguing style of philosophical behaviorism of the period, see Ryle 1949.

Notes

Chapter 1

1 The matter is more complicated for Leibniz, however, as he held space not to be a feature of reality as it is in itself, but a mode of perception, albeit a "well-founded" one that does afford access to truths.

Chapter 2

1 I am following Verhaegh 2023, for when Quine read the *Aufbau*. A famous, and Quine-approved, philosophical defense of convention is D. Lewis 1969.

2 See Quine's 1934 lectures on Carnap, especially Lecture One (in Creath 1990). Its generally sympathetic tone is belied by Quine's obvious tendency to regard the supposed boundary between the *a priori* and the empirical—the conventional and the substantive—as merely pragmatic. Still, at this very early stage Quine does not challenge the very meaning of the idea that some truths are stipulated as a matter of convention and others are not. Creath argues that Quine's "Truth by Convention"— written the following year—retains this general acceptance of Carnap's position, and that it is not as critical of Carnap as I suggest (Creath 1990, pp. 28–9).

3 There are other kinds of definitions—"recursive" (or "inductive") definitions and "implicit" definitions. A recursive definition of "+" for example tells us that n + 0 = n and that n + s(m) = s(m + n), where s(x) means the immediate successor of x. This determines the truth-value of every sum but does not enable us to eliminate + in favor of another notation (using "higher-order" logic, Frege showed how to convert recursive definitions into explicit definitions using the notion of the ancestral of a relation; the same can be done with first-order logic if set theory is assumed). Implicit definition is the idea that a set of axioms, in some sense, characterizes the objects they are about or the concepts they contain, and is both hazier and more controversial. Quine discusses this in the essay "Implicit Definition Sustained" (*WP* 195–8).

4 *WP* 103, rewritten to suit styles used here.

5 Similar arguments can be constructed with respect to other non-extensional devices such as "John believes that _"; Quine will trace the connections between these devices and the issues in "Two Dogmas" later, especially in *Word and Object*; we will consider these connections in Chapter 6.

6   Quine's discussion at *FLPV* 40 ("Two Dogmas") is very condensed; the discussion
     from *FSS* 10–14 is more helpful.
7   Friedman 1999 and Richardson 1998 stress that the role of these is very much like
     that of Kant's principles of *a priori* synthesis: from the disconnected flux of direct
     sensory experience, they bring about a coherent and stable world of experience.

Chapter 3

1   Even here the matter is more complicated than one might expect. Cases of
     stimulus-synonymy are rarer than one might expect, and accord with the ordinary
     concept of synonymy less well than one might expect. See *WO* 49–51.
2   In the case of "No bachelor is married," it's rather the other way round. The felt
     synonymy of "bachelor" and "unmarried man" might be due simply to the fact
     that these bear so few theoretical connections to the rest of language; unlike, say,
     "force"—which is involved in a whole network of theoretically critical language—
     "bachelor" could be deleted from the language without incident. Cases like the
     analytic truths involving "bachelor" are really not very common and are felt to
     reveal uninteresting, unimportant and redundant bits of language—quite unlike the
     truths of physics or arithmetic. These points are made by Putnam 1962.
3   Do not worry that "same animal" occurs as part of "is part of the same animal as."
     "X is part of the same animal as Y" would be defined in terms of the existence of a
     spatio-temporally continuous sequence of animal-stages linking X with Y.
4   That this is the point of the story of the rabbit-stages is often missed, even by the
     sharpest minds; see for example Pinker 1994, pp. 153–7; Quine attempts to ward off
     this misunderstanding at *OR* 31.
5   For a comprehensive introduction to the field, see Pinker 1994 and Cook 1988.
6   The most visible example is Everett 2008.

Chapter 4

1   In later works, however, Russell would accept the idea that the physical world
     should be constructed from experience, not inferred from it.
2   Some may be naturally selected in obvious ways, if they directly increase the
     individual's chances of procreation; a disposition to growl menacingly at enemies
     might be an example. Others are naturally selected via complex variants of
     you-scratch-my-back-and-I'll-scratch-yours, played out over generations. The
     challenge for evolutionary biology is to explain how such seemingly altruistic yet
     innate behavior could be naturally selected, since it does not typically increase the
     individual's own prospects. See *TT* 55–66, Dawkins 1978.

3   See also Pinker 1998, Goodman 1979, p. 59ff.

4   The problem (at *RR* 76–8) concerns the case where the subject neither assents nor dissents, but "abstains." If the subject abstains from both apparent conjuncts, then still the subject might dissent from the conjunction ("It's a chipmunk and it's a mouse"), or it might be that the subject will abstain from the conjunction ("It's a mouse and it's in the kitchen"). So the ordinary particle "and" is not of itself a "verdict function" (the three verdicts being assent, dissent, abstain). Since abstain is a real feature of linguistic behavior, there is little choice but to accept that acquiring genuine truth-functions requires a modicum of theory.

5   What Quine calls *focal* observation categoricals, such as "When a dog growls, its hackles stand up," do involve reference (*PT* 10–11, *FSS* 27); but not just by virtue of being observation categoricals.

6   Though Quine was doubtful even in a 1931 graduate paper, age 22:

> But what are those "bare data" which such a process interprets? Certainly they are themselves a high refinement of abstraction. My experiment career is not simply a matter of consciously taking odds and ends and amorphous bits of unidentified data and fitting them into a system; what I see before me is a chair, not an array of varicolored quadrilaterals which I consciously assemble and classify as a chair. My immediate experience, rather than consisting of raw material to be interpreted, is already seething with interpretation; in peeling off the interpretation I am peeling off a goodly portion of the immediate datum ... my apprehension of the thing merely as a configuration of colors and shapes, far from being a naive datum, is itself the product of a conscious interpretative process not essentially different from that in which I classify the chair as to period or material ... In a word, my thesis is that no analysis of a given experience can yield another experience which is, in any full sense, the "bare datum" of the form of experience; any such analysis is, rather, merely a further interpretation (in Sinclair 2022; "Concepts and Working Hypotheses," March 10, 1931).

Chapter 5

1   The truth-value of a sentence whose main connective is a truth-functional sentence connective is determined by those of the immediately smaller sentences it connects. For example, if p is true, then "~p" is false, and if p is false, "~p" is true. If p is true but q is false, then "p→q" is false; otherwise "p→q" is true. Quine observes that just one truth-functional connective is necessary to define the others (Henry Sheffer, and perhaps Charles Sanders Peirce before him, made the discovery). Either joint denial (NOR or "neither-nor"—symbolized "↓"or "|", e.g., "p↓q" or "p|q"), or alternative denial (NAND, or "not both"—symbolized as "↑")—along with

parentheses, is sufficient to define the others. In his earlier *FLVP* 81, 83–4, Quine chooses the latter. In *ML* 46–9 Quine spells all this out.

2   With the resources of set theory in play, "x = y" can be defined as their belonging to all and only the same classes ("For every class S, x belongs to S if and only if y belongs to S"). See *PL* 61–4, *ML* 134f, *TT* 109, *WP* 180, *FLPV* 85.

3   See also *OR* 17. A kind of argument relevant to this goes back to Frege and Wittgenstein, even to Aristotle. Suppose we think of each predicate as naming an entity, a universal. Then in the sentence "Plato loves Socrates," "Socrates," and "Plato" name the philosophers, and "loves" names love. But if so, then what is the difference between asserting that sentence, and merely *mentioning*, in succession, Socrates, love, and Plato? A mere list of entities is not a sentence; "Socrates, love, Plato" is not a sentence.

4   Hacker 2005, for example, supposes that Quine must accept either the absurd idea that one "posits" one's *own* existence, or that there is at least one thing, namely the self, whose existence one accepts without positing. Obviously there is no such problem given what Quine means by "positing."

5   For differences between Quine's explication and Carnap's, see Gustaffson 2013.

6   "Nearly enough," writes Quine (*WO* 257); actually Weiner's definition is more complex, but the philosophical point is the same.

7   For further details on events see Davidson 1980.

8   The matter is more complicated than this, for at the time of the essay "Ontological Reduction and the Field of Numbers" (1964; *WP* 199–207) Quine positively denied this wholesale use of the Lowenstein-Skölem theorem, and one could be forgiven for not quite being able to tell by the time of "Ontological Relativity" (1968; *OR* 28–68) whether he had come to accept it. He is thinking that in order to make use of the theorem, one has explicitly to specify a "proxy-function"—one that delivers a unique number for each object of the original theory (and discussed immediately below)—not just declare that a suitable function exists, which is all that the theorem tells one. However, by time of "Whither Physical Objects" (1976b; *WPO?*) Quine had argued that one indeed could specify such functions. See my 2017a ("Is Everything a Set?") for more.

9   Every sentence of the first-order predicate calculus admits mechanically of transformation into a logically equivalent *prenex* formula: a formula with all its quantifiers coming first (provided we have both the existential and universal quantifier). Removing the initial string of quantifiers yields a *matrix*, an open sentence *all* of whose variables are free. Consider any matrix and any assignment of values to variables on which the matrix is true. By definition, the atomic open sentences in the matrix (ones not containing sentential connectives) retain their truth-values upon application of the proxy function and accompanying reinterpretation of predicates (call this the "proxy-transformation"). Since the

sentential connectives of the predicate calculus are truth-functional, the matrix as a whole retains its truth-value on the new assignment. But then the original sentence as a whole must retain its truth-value under the proxy-transformation. Since a universal quantification is true (for a given assignment of values to variables), just in case the open sentence it is attached to is true on that assignment on every reassignment of the variable governed by the quantifier, and an open sentence with a given truth-value on an assignment from the old domain retains that truth-value on that assignment under the proxy-transformation, the universal quantification retains its truth-value under the proxy-transformation. Similarly for existential quantifications, writing "some reassignment" for "every reassignment." So the truth-value (for each variable-assignment) of the formula obtained by restoring the right-most quantifier in the original string is unchanged under the proxy-transformation. Similarly for each quantifier, until we restore the whole sentence (or rather its prenex equivalent).

10   A problem is the inference from inscrutability of reference to ontological relativity, an inference which one might well agree with Quine is trivial; see my paper "In Favour of the Classical Quine on Ontology" 2020 for reasons to think it is not. Some have stressed the affinities between Quine's thesis and Putnam's "model-theoretic" argument for anti-realism (as in his 1981), but I have played down any such affinity because Quine is so evidently committed not only to realism—in an admittedly watered-down sense—but to immanentism, to the unintelligibility of a super-scientific point of view. See also this chapter, fn 8.

11   It is because of the artificial character of the metalanguage. Tarski's method ensures, without using the concept of empirical translation, that the sentence put for "p" must have the same truth-value as that put for "s" (some writers speak of "p" being a "copy" of s). What is true is that if we wished to discover whether or not a definition of truth for a natural language were correct, we would have to translate the language into our own language. See Davidson 1990, Kemp 2012.

12   Suppose the whiteboard has one sentence on it: "The sentence written on the white board is not true." The T-sentence is "'The sentence written on the white board is not true' is true iff the sentence written on the white board is not true." The rest is left as an exercise. See Quine's discussion in his "The Ways of Paradox," *WP* 1–18.

13   A central task of logical work on truth since Tarski has been to discover just how close it is possible to come to a theory or definition of truth for a language that is adequate to all mathematics (hence for whatever language we use to express our general theory of nature). Quine himself discusses the issue at *PT* 82–90; in more depth in *SLP* 242–50.

14   Again see Davidson 1990, 1999; for criticism of his view that truth is primitive, see my Kemp 2012.

15 This ignores a use-mention impropriety that can be rectified, but the needed
    explanation would be tedious here.
16 See Putnam 1981, Rorty 1979.

Chapter 6

1   The dominant idea (due to D. Lewis 1973) invokes possible worlds (or "situations"):
    a counterfactual is true iff its consequent is true at the closest possible world to the
    actual world at which its antecedent is true (where "closeness" is similarity of worlds).
    The price is too high, for Quine (see below). Quine also observed a certain vagueness
    in many counterfactual conditionals, as in the example-pair: "If Caesar were in
    command, he would use the atom bomb; If Caesar were in command, he would use
    catapults" (*WO* 222). It is only the particular speaker intention that can select which
    of these is appropriate. Lewis finds the supposition harmless; 1973, pp. 66–7.
2   This point together with the entanglement point of the last section may suggest
    the "Quine-Putnam Indispensability Argument" for mathematical ontology
    (see Putnam 1971). There are obvious parallels but the surrounding philosophies
    should make one cautious in speaking without further ado of an argument held in
    common.
3   Actually Frege did not regard "that" as part of the proposition-name; his idea was
    that in the "context" created by "believes-that," the sentence itself becomes a name
    of the proposition that normally it expresses. A further point is that propositions
    are what a sentence expresses at a context of utterance. Thus "Today is Monday"
    does not express a proposition, but it does so at a given context of utterance,
    yielding a proposition that is true or false depending on what day it is at the time of
    utterance.
4   Quine stresses repeatedly that if there were a scientifically satisfactory notion of
    synonymy, then there would be no problem accepting an ontology of propositions.
    For obviously sets of synonymous sentences would suffice as a criterion of their
    identity (and could serve as propositions).
5   One might wonder about sentences; aren't they abstract objects too? That is,
    sentences can't be classes of all inscriptions or vocal utterances of a certain form.
    For in that case any two sentences that have never been uttered or written down
    would be identical, since the relevant class in each case would be the empty set.
    One solution is to define sentences as sequences of letters: the sentence "Snow is
    white" for example is a sequence comprising the letter "S" followed by the letter
    "n," and so on. Sequences are readily definable as complicated kinds of sets. So as
    long as all the letters of the alphabet have been inscribed or uttered somewhere or
    sometime—which of course they have—then the principles of set theory guarantee
    the existence of all the relevant sequences. See *PL* 16–7, *WO* 194–5, *FSS* 95–6.

6   Quine wrote before the demotion of Pluto from planethood; I have changed his example from nine being the number of planets to eight.

7   Kit Fine 1994 argues that essential properties are different from necessary properties. For example, it is necessary of Kit Fine that he be a member of the set {Kit Fine}, but is not essential to him. Likewise it is necessary that he be such that 2+2=4, but is not essential to him.

8   Kripke 1963 showed how "Necessarily" and "Possibly" could be explained in a fully extensional metalanguage that quantifies over possible worlds. "Necessarily p" would be explained as the truth of p in all possible worlds. The worlds, in turn, could be taken as certain complicated set-theoretic objects. This makes possible soundness and completeness proofs of systems of modal logic, and so on. But this does not justify the idea that in fact, there are non-actual possible worlds—not just certain set-theoretic constructions out of the domain of the interpretation of some formal language—which encompass all that is really possible, and which we are really talking about when we use the adverbs "necessarily" and "possibly." Such entities might be accepted if we had independent reasons to believe in modal facts, but not otherwise.

Chapter 7

1   The analogy of the microscope implicitly refers to Frege's *Begriffsschrift* (1967), p. 6.

2   Note that ontological relativity, as explained with proxy-functions, is not underdetermination in the sense of interest here; since there is no syntactical difference between T and proxy-T, and nothing could be easier than translation from T to proxy-T and back. Quine: "Theories can differ utterly in their objects, over which their variables of quantification range, and still be empirically equivalent, as proxy functions show … We hardly seem warranted in calling them two theories; they are two ways of expressing one and the same theory" (*TT* 96).

3   See Moore 2011, 2015, and my responses, brief 2015 and extended 2016.

4   For a thorough introduction see Pinker 1994 and 1998.

5   An objection that drew an exasperated and I fear multiply mistaken response from Quine, is this. Quine thinks of one's language as a set of verbal dispositions. Chomsky points out that one's propensity to utter a given sentence in a given circumstance is vanishingly low, therefore of little theoretical value (it depends on the speaker's plans, intentions, memories, and so forth). The first mistake on Quine's part is his assumption that when Chomsky spoke of a "verbal disposition" he was referring to the absolute probability of utterance—"[s]olubility in water would be a pretty idle disposition," Quine says, "if defined in terms of the absolute probability of dissolving, without reference to the circumstance of being in water" (*CCE* 218). But although Chomsky did speak of the absolute probability of an utterance, his focus was on the probability of an utterance at a given circumstance

(Chomsky 1968, p. 58; 1975, pp. 190–1). This second mistake was that Quine thought the following response was sufficient to rebut Chomsky's complaint, that what he meant was "verbal dispositions in a *very specific* circumstance: a questionnaire circumstance, the circumstance of being offered a sentence for assent or dissent or indecision or bizarreness reaction" (*CCE* 218, emphasis added; so the conditional probability of one's saying "Yes" to a true observation sentence when asked is by comparison very high). But again Chomsky (1968, pp. 58–9, 1975, pp. 190–4) realizes this.

6   A recent comment on the problem by Berwick and Chomsky: "Our knowledge of how linguistic knowledge or 'grammars' might actually implemented in the brain is even sketchier" (than "any kind of cognitive computation"; 2016, p. 157).

7   An example is "Sailors sailors sailors fight fight fight." This is not a clause that generally is judged grammatical by ordinary speakers, yet not only is it entailed by standard models of relative clauses, one can see, with persistence, that in fact the construction does make sense (start with the simpler "Sailor sailors fight fight," i.e. "Sailors who sailors fight, fight"). For discussion see Collins 2008; see also Rey 2020, Chapter One. A related phenomenon is illustrated by Chomsky's example of the pair "I persuaded John to leave" and "I expected John to leave" (1965, p. 23). These require different structural analyses, showing that grammatical structure is not surface structure. It begins to emerge when one sees that among the pairs "I persuaded a specialist to examine John" and "I persuaded John to be examined by a specialist"; and "I expected a specialist to examine John" and "I expected John to be examined by a specialist," the latter pair, but not former, are cognitively equivalent (only in the first pair, the object of the verb "persuade" shifts from the specialist to John).

8   In *Pursuit of Truth* Quine has the translator as deploying a faculty of *empathy*:

> The observation sentence "Rabbit" has its stimulus meaning for the linguist and "Gavagai" has its for the native, but the affinity of the two sentences is to be sought in the externals of communication. The linguist notes the native's utterance of "Gavagai" where he, in the native's position, might have said "Rabbit."
>
> Empathy dominates the learning of language, both by child and by field linguist. In the child's case it is the parent's empathy. The parent assesses the appropriateness of the child's observation sentence by noting the child's orientation and how the scene would look from there (*PT* 42; see also *CCE* 112, *WO* 218–19).

Obviously this is no recipe for science. "A pioneer manual of translation," as Quine sums up the matter, "has its *utility as an aid to negotiation* with the native community" (*PT* 43; emphasis added). All this is true description, but for a more probing scientific account one must turn to the slightly later doctrine of Pre-established Harmony; see fn 2, this chapter.

References

Austin, J. L. 1962. *Sense and Sensibilia*. Oxford: Oxford University Press.

Ayer, A. J. 1959. *Logical Positivism*. New York, New York: The Free Press.

Barcan-Marcus, R. 1961. "Modalities and Intensional Languages." *Synthese* 13/4: 303–22.

Barrett, R. and R. Gibson. 1993. *Perspectives on Quine* (Philosophers and Their Critics). Oxford: Wiley-Blackwell.

Ben-Menahem, Yemima. 2006. *Conventionalism*. Cambridge: Cambridge University Press.

Bergström, L. 2000. "Quine, Empiricism and Truth." In *Knowledge, Language and Logic: Questions for Quine*. Boston Studies in the Philosophy and History of Science, ed. by A. Orenstein and P. Kotatko, 210, 63–79. Dordrecht: D. Reidel.

Bergström, L. 2004. "Underdetermination of Physical Theory." In Gibson 2004: 91–114.

Berwick, R. and N. Chomsky. 2016. *Why Only Us: Language and Evolution*. Cambridge, MA: MIT Press.

Carnap, R. 1937 [1934]. *The Logical Syntax of Language*, tr. by Amethe Smeaton. London: Routledge and Kegan Paul.

Carnap, R. 1942. *Introduction to Semantics*. Cambridge, Mass.: Harvard University Press.

Carnap, R. 1956 [1947]. *Meaning and Necessity*, second edition. Chicago, Ill.: University of Chicago Press.

Carnap, R. 1962. *Logical Foundations of Probability*, second edition. Chicago, Ill.: University of Chicago Press.

Carnap, R. 1967 [1928]. *The Logical Structure of the World* and *Pseudoproblems in Philosophy* (the *Aufbau*), tr. by R. George. Los Angeles: University of California Press.

Carus, A. W. 2007. *Carnap in Twentieth-Century Thought: Explication as Enlightenment*. Cambridge: Cambridge University Press.

Chomsky, N. 1959. "A Review of B. F. Skinner's *Verbal Behavior*." *Language* 35/1: 26–58.

Chomsky, N. 1965. *Aspects of the Theory of Syntax*. Cambridge, Mass.: MIT Press.

Chomsky, N. 1966. *Cartesian Linguistics*. Cambridge, Mass.: MIT Press.

Chomsky, N. 1968. "Quine's Empirical Assumptions." *Synthese* 19: 53–68. Reprinted in Davidson and Hintikka 1969.

Chomsky, N. 1972. *Language and Mind*, enlarged edition. New York, New York: Harcourt, Brace, Jovanivitch.

Chomsky, N. 1975. *Reflections on Language*. New York, New York: Fontana, Random House.

Chomsky, N. 1980. *Rules and Representations*. Oxford: Basil Blackwell.

Chomsky, N. 1986. *Knowledge of Language: Its Nature, Origin and Use*. New York, New York: Praeger.

Chomsky, N. 2000. *New Horizons in the Study of Language*. Cambridge: Cambridge University Press.

Coffa, J. A. 1991. *The Semantic Tradition from Carnap to Kant: To the Vienna Station*. Cambridge: Cambridge University Press.

Collins, J. 2008. *Chomsky: A Guide for the Perplexed*. London: Continuum.

Cook, V. J. 1988. *Chomsky's Universal Grammar*. Oxford: Basil Blackwell.

Creath, R. 1990. *Dear Carnap, Dear Van: The Quine-Carnap Correspondence and Related Work*. Berkeley, Cal.: University of California Press.

Davidson, D. 1980. *Essays on Actions and Events*. Oxford: Clarendon Press.

Davidson, D. 1984. *Inquiries into Truth and Interpretation*. Oxford: Clarendon Press.

Davidson, D. 1990. "The Structure and Content of Truth." *The Journal of Philosophy* 87: 279–328.

Davidson, D. 1999. "The Centrality of Truth." In *Truth and Its Nature (if any)*, ed. by J. Peregrin, 105–16. Dordrecht: Kluwer Academic Publishers.

Davidson, D. 2001. *Subjective, Intersubjective, Objective*. Oxford: Clarendon Press.

Davidson, D. and J. Hintikka. 1969. *Words and Objections: Essays on the Work of W. V. Quine*. Dordrecht: D. Reidel.

Dawkins, R. 1978. *The Selfish Gene*. London: Paladin.

Dreben, B. 2004. "Quine on Quine." In *The Cambridge Companion to Quine*, ed. by R. F. Gibson, Jr, 287–94. Cambridge: Cambridge University Press.

Duhem, P. 1954 [1906]. *Physical Theory: Its Objects and Structure*, tr. by P. Wiener. Princeton: Princeton University Press.

Ebbs, G. 2015. "Introduction to 'Preestablished Harmony' and 'Response to Gary Ebbs.'" In *Quine and His Place in History*, ed. by F.Janssen-Lauret and G. Kemp, 21–9. London: Palgrave.

Ebbs, G. 2017. *Carnap, Quine, and Putnam on Methods of Inquiry*. Cambridge: Cambridge University Press.

Everett, D. 2008. *Don't Sleep, There Are Snakes: Life and Language in the Amazonian Jungle*. New York: Pantheon Books.

Field, H. 1980. *Science without Numbers*. Princeton, NJ: Princeton University Press.

Fine, K. 1994. "Essence and Modality." *Philosophical Perspectives 8 (Logic and Language)*: 1–16.

Frege, G. 1953 [1884]. *The Foundations of Arithmetic*, tr. by J. Austin. London: Basil Blackwell.

Frege, G. 1967 [1879]. *Begriffsschrift*, in *From Frege to Gödel: A* Source Book *in Mathematical* Logic, *1879–1931*, ed. by J. van Heijenoort. Cambridge, Mass.: Harvard University Press.

Frege, G. 1979. *Posthumous Writings*, ed. by H. Hermes *et. al.*, tr. by P. Long and R. White. Oxford: Basil Blackwell.

Friedman, M. 1999. *Reconsidering Logical Positivism*. Cambridge: Cambridge University Press.

George, A. 1986. "Whence and Whither the Debate between Quine and Chomsky?" *The Journal of Philosophy* 83/9: 489–99.

Gibson, R., ed. 2004. *The Cambridge Collection to W.V. Quine*. Cambridge: Cambridge University Press.

Goodman, N. (with W.V. Quine). 1947. "Steps toward a Constructive Nominalism." *Journal of Symbolic Logic* 12: 105–22.

Goodman, N. 1979. *Fact, Fiction and Forecast*. Cambridge, Mass.: Harvard University Press.

Gustafsson, M. 2013. "Quine's Conception of Explication—and Why It Isn't Carnap's." In The *Blackwell Companion to Quine*, ed. by G. Harman and E. Lepore, 508–25. Oxford: Blackwell.

Hacker, P. 2005. "Passing by the Naturalistic Turn: On Quine's Cul-de-sac." *The Challenge of Philosophical Naturalism*, conference at the Rutgers University Institute for Law and Philosophy. www.lawandphil.rutgers.edu/hacker.pdf.

Hahn, P. and P. Schilpp. 1986. *The Philosophy of W V Quine*. La Salle, Ill.: Open Court.

Hertz, H. 1899. *The Principles of Mechanics Presented in New Form*. New York: Dover.

Hume, D. 2004 [1739]. *A Treatise of Human Nature*. London: Dover.

Hume, D. 2007 [1748]. *An Enquiry Concerning Human Understanding*. Cambridge: Cambridge University Press.

Hylton, P. 2007. *Quine*. London: Routledge.

Hylton, P. 2013. "Quine's Naturalism Revisited." In *A Companion to W. V. O. Quine*, ed. by G. Harman and E. Lepore, 148–60. London: Wiley-Blackwell.

Hylton, P. 2023. "Carnap and Quine on the Status of Ontology: The Role of the Principle of Tolerance." In *The Philosophical Project of Carnap and Quine*, ed. by S. Morris, 235–52. Cambridge: Cambridge University Press.

Janssen-Lauret, F. and G. Kemp. 2015. *Quine and His Place in History*. London: Palgrave Macmillan.

Kaplan, D. 1968. "Quantifying In." *Synthese* 19/1–2: 178–214.

Kemp, G. 2012. *Quine vs. Davidson: Truth, Reference and Meaning*. Oxford: Oxford University Press.

Kemp, G. 2015. "Quine: Underdetermination and Naturalistic Metaphysics." *Philosophical Topics, The Evolution of Modern Metaphysics: Responses to A.W. Moore with His Replies* 43/1–2: 179–88.

Kemp, G. 2016. "Underdetermination, Realism, and Transcendental Metaphysics in Quine." In *Quine and His Place in History*, ed. by F. Janssen-Lauret and G. Kemp, 2017, 168–88. London: Palgrave Macmillan.

Kemp, G. 2017a. "Is Everything a Set? Quine and (Hyper)Pythagoreanism." *The Monist* 2/100: 155–66.

Kemp, G. 2017b. "Quine, Publicity, and Pre-established Harmony." In R. Manning (special issue editor), *ProtoSociology* 34: 59–72.

Kemp, G. 2019. "Quine and the Kantian Problem of Objectivity." In *Science and Sensibilia by W. V. Quine the 1980 Immanuel Kant Lectures*, ed. by R. Sinclair, 91–114. London: Palgrave-Macmillan.

Kemp, G. 2020. "In Favour of the Classical Quine on Ontology." *Canadian Journal of Philosophy* 2/50: 223–37.

Kemp, G. 2022. "Observation Sentences Revisited." *Mind* 131/523: 805–25.

Kemp, G. forthcoming. "Naturalism: Chomsky vs. Quine." In *Naturalism and Its Challenges*, ed. by G. Kemp, A. Hossein-Khani, H. Sheykh-Rezaee, and H. Amiriara. London: Routledge.

Kim, J. 1988. "What Is 'Naturalized Epistemology?'" *Philosophical Perspectives* 2: 381–405.

Kripke, S. 1963. "Semantical Considerations on Modal Logic." *Acta Philosophica Fennica* 16: 83–94.

Kripke, S. 1980. *Naming and Necessity*. Cambridge, Mass.: Harvard University Press.

Leonardi P. and M. Santambrogio, eds. 1995. *On Quine: New Essays*. Cambridge: Cambridge University Press.

Lewis, C. I. 1929. *Mind and the World Order*. New York, New York: Charles Scribner and Sons.

Lewis, D. 1968. "Counterpart Theory and Quantified Modal Logic." *Journal of Philosophy* 65: 113–26.

Lewis, D. 1969. *Convention*. Cambridge: Harvard University Press.

Lewis, D. 1973. *Counterfactuals*. Oxford: Blackwell.

Lewis, D. 1986. *On the Plurality of Worlds*. Oxford: Blackwell.

Linsky, L. 1971. *Reference and Modality*. London: Oxford University Press.

Lugg, A. 2012. "W.V. Quine on Analyticity: 'Two Dogmas of Empiricism' in Context." *Dialogue* 51/2: 231–46.

Moore, A. 2011. *The Evolution of Modern Metaphysics*. Cambridge: Cambridge University Press.

Moore, A. 2015. "Replies." *Philosophical Topics, The Evolution of Modern Metaphysics: Responses to A.W. Moore with His Replies* 43/1–2: 329–83.

Morris, S. 2018. *Quine, New Foundations and the Philosophy of Set Theory*. Cambridge: Cambridge University Press.

Nado, J. 2021. "Conceptual Engineering, Truth, and Efficacy." *Synthese* 198: 1507–27.

Orenstein, A. and P. Kotatko. 2000. *Knowledge, Language, and Logic: Questions for Quine*. Boston, Mass. and London: Kluwer.

Pinker, S. 1994. *The Language Instinct*. London: Penguin Press.

Pinker, S. 1998. *How the Mind Works*. London: Penguin Press.

Putnam, H. 1962. "The Analytic and the Synthetic." In *Scientific Explanation, Space, and Time*. Minnesota studies in the philosophy of science 3, ed. by H. Feigl and G. Maxwell, 358–97. Minneapolis, Minn.: University of Minnesota Press.

Putnam, H. 1971. *Philosophy of Logic*. Abingdon: Routledge.

Putnam, H. 1981. *Reason, Truth and History*. Cambridge: Cambridge University Press.

Quine, W. V. 1943. "Notes on Existence and Necessity." *The Journal of Philosophy* 40: 113–27.

Quine, W. V. 1951. *Mathematical Logic*, revised edition. Cambridge, Mass.: Harvard University Press.

Quine, W. V. 1960. *Word and Object*. Cambridge, Mass.: MIT Press.

Quine, W. V. 1961. *From a Logical Point of View*, revised edition. Cambridge, Mass.: Harvard University Press.

Quine, W. V. 1968. "Replies." *Synthese* 19: 264–321, specifically 280.

Quine, W. V. 1969. *Ontological Relativity and Other Essays*. New York: Columbia University Press.

Quine, W. V. 1970. "On the Reasons for the Indeterminacy of Translation." *Journal of Philosophy* 67: 178–83.

Quine, W. V. 1974. *The Roots of Reference*. La Salle, Ill.: Open Court Press.

Quine, W. V. 1976a. *The Ways of Paradox*, revised edition. Cambridge, Mass.: Harvard University Press.

Quine, W. V. 1976b. "Whither Physical Objects?" In *Essays in Memory of Imre Lakatos*, Boston Studies in the Philosophy of Science, 39, ed. by R. S. Cohen, P. K. Feyerabend and M. W. Wartofsky, 497–504. Dordrecht: Springer.

Quine, W. V. 1981. *Theories and Things*. Cambridge, Mass.: Harvard University Press.

Quine, W. V. 1986. *Philosophy of Logic*, second edition. Cambridge, Mass.: Harvard University Press.

Quine, W. V. 1987. *Quiddities: An Intermittently Philosophical Dictionary*. Cambridge, Mass.: Harvard University Press.

Quine, W. V. 1990. *The Logic of Sequences. A Generalization of Principia Mathematica*. Harvard dissertations in philosophy. New York, New York: Garland.

Quine, W. V. 1992. *Pursuit of Truth*, revised edition. Cambridge, Mass.: Harvard University Press.

Quine, W. V. 1995a. *From Stimulus to Science*. Cambridge, Mass.: Harvard University Press.

Quine, W. V. 1995b. *Selected Logic Papers*, enlarged edition. Cambridge, Mass.: Harvard University Press.

Quine, W. V. 2008. *Confessions of a Confirmed Extensionalist*, ed. by D. Føllesdal and D. Quine. Cambridge, Mass.: Harvard University Press.

Quine, W. V. 2015a. "Response to Gary Ebbs." In *Quine and His Place in History*, ed. by F. Janssen-Lauret and G. Kemp, 29–32. London: Palgrave.

Quine, W. V. 2015b. "Pre-established Harmony." In *Quine and His Place in History*, ed. by F. Janssen-Lauret and G. Kemp, 33–5. London: Palgrave.

Quine, W. V. 2018. *The Significance of the New Logic*, ed. and tr. by W. Carnielli, F. Janssen-Lauret, and W. Pickering. Cambridge: Cambridge University Press.

Quine, W. V. 2019. "Prolegomena: Mind and Its Place in Nature." In *Science and Sensibilia by W. V. Quine The 1980 Immanuel Kant Lectures*, ed. by R. Sinclair, 19–36. London: Palgrave-Macmillan.

Quine, W. V. and J. Ullian. 1978. *The Web of Belief*, revised edition. New York: Random House.

Rosen, G. 2013. "Quine and the Revival of Metaphysics." In *A Companion to W. V. O. Quine*, ed. by G. Harman and E. Lepore, 552–70. London: Wiley-Blackwell.

Roth, P. 1999. "The Epistemology of 'Epistemology Naturalized.'" *Dialectica* 53/2: 87–109.

Rey, G. 2020. *Representation of Language*. Oxford: Oxford University Press.

Richardson, A. 1998. *Carnap's Construction of the World*. Cambridge: Cambridge University Press.

Rorty, R. 1979. *Philosophy and the Mirror of Nature*. Princeton, N.J.: Princeton University Press.

Russell, B. 1912. *The Problems of Philosophy*. London: Oxford University Press.

Ryle, G. 1949. *The Concept of Mind*. London: Hutchinson.

Scott-Arnold, G. 2013. *Carnap, Tarski, and Quine at Harvard: Conversations on Logic, Mathematics and Science*. La Salle, Ill.: Open Court.

Severo, R. P. 2008. "'Plausible Insofar as It Is Intelligible': Quine on Underdetermination." *Synthese* 161/1: 141–65.

Severo, R. P. 2022. "Quine's Argument 'from above.'" *European Journal of Philosophy* 30/2: 601–7.

Sinclair, R. 2002. "Stimulus Meaning Reconsidered." *The Southern Journal of Philosophy* LX: 395–409.

Sinclair, R. 2014. "Quine on Evidence." In *A Companion to W.V.O. Quine*, ed. by G. Harman and E. Lepore, 350–72. Oxford: Wiley-Blackwell.

Sinclair, R. 2022. *Quine, Conceptual Pragmatism and the Analytic-Synthetic Distinction*. American Philosophy Series. London: Lexington Books.

Skinner, B. F. *Verbal Behavior*. New York, N.Y.: Appleton-Century-Crofts.

Smith, B. 2014. "Quine and Chomsky on the Ins and Outs of Language." In *A Companion to W.V.O. Quine*, ed. by G. Harman and E. Lepore, 483–507. Oxford: Wiley-Blackwell.

Strawson, P. 1950. "On Referring." *Mind* 59: 320–44.

Stroud, B. 1981. "The Significance of Naturalized Epistemology." *Midwest Studies in Philosophy* 6, The Foundations of Analytic Philosophy: 455–71.

Tarski, A. 1983 [1936]. "The Concept of Truth in Formalized Languages." In A. Tarski, *Logic, Semantics, Meta-Mathematics*, tr. by J. Woodger, 152–278. London: Oxford University Press.

Tarski, A. 1983 [1955]. "The Establishment of Scientific Semantics." in Tarski: 401–8.

Uebel, Thomas. 2007. *Empiricism at the Crossroads: The Vienna Circle's Protocol-Sentence Debate*. La Salle, Penn.: Open Court.

Verhaegh, S. 2018. *Working from Within: The Nature and Development of Quine's Naturalism*. Oxford: Oxford University Press.

Verhaegh, S. 2023. "Carnap and Quine: First Encounters (1932–1936)." In *The Philosophical Project of Carnap and Quine*, ed. by S. Morris, 11–31. Cambridge: Cambridge University Press.

Williamson, T. 2007. *The Philosophy of Philosophy*. Oxford: Blackwell.

Wittgenstein, L. 1958. *Philosophical Investigations*, second edition, tr. by E. Anscombe and ed. by E. Anscombe and R. Rhees. London: Basil Blackwell.

Index